# MESSAGE IN THE BOTTLE

A Guide to Tasting Wine

TIM GAISER, MS

Copyright © 2022 by Tim Gaiser
All Rights Reserved
Deductive Tasting Method Format © 2017 Court of Master Sommeliers, Americas.
Used with permission.

*For Carla, Maria, and Patrick*

# Contents

| | |
|---|---|
| Introduction | vii |
| Foreword | ix |

## Part I
## The Basics

| | |
|---|---|
| 1. Setting the Stage: The Proper Setup for a Successful Tasting | 5 |
| 2. Glassware Stance: The Art of Smelling Wine | 8 |
| 3. The Deductive Tasting Grid Defined | 13 |
| 4. Assessing Structure | 32 |
| 5. Using a Decision Matrix For Deductive Tasting | 39 |
| 6. Markers for Classic White Wines | 50 |
| 7. Markers for Classic Red Wines | 63 |

## Part II
## Advanced Skills

| | |
|---|---|
| 8. Cause and Effect | 83 |
| 9. Fruit Groups and Fruit Quality | 92 |
| 10. Wine Faults and Context | 97 |
| 11. Impact Compounds | 102 |
| 12. Confronting the Evil Dwarves | 109 |
| 13. The Impact of Bottle Aging on Wine | 122 |
| 14. Judging Wine Quality | 132 |
| 15. Objective vs. Subjective in Tasting | 139 |
| 16. Using Pattern Recognition for Blind Tasting White Wines | 146 |
| 17. Using Pattern Recognition for Blind Tasting Red Wines | 154 |
| 18. On Tasting Notes | 163 |
| 19. A Tech Sheet Manifesto | 168 |
| 20. Suggested Producers for Tasting Practice | 173 |

Part III
# The Inner Game of Tasting

| | |
|---|---|
| 21. Clearing the Mechanism | 205 |
| 22. How to Use Overlapping to Find Your Zone | 209 |
| 23. "Front-Loading" and the "Basic Set" | 213 |
| 24. Using Submodalities in Tasting | 217 |
| 25. Using An Internal Visual Cue to Help Calibrate Structure | 224 |
| 26. Installing Olfactory Memories | 228 |
| 27. Label Check | 235 |
| 28. Associative Rehearsal, or Tasting Practice Without Wine | 243 |
| 29. Dealing With a Dominant Aroma In the Glass | 248 |
| 30. Using a Coravin For Tasting Practice | 251 |
| 31. Eating the Elephant: Advice for Beginning Tasters | 254 |
| 32. Tasting Exam Preparation Strategies | 257 |

Part IV
# Thoughts On Wine

| | |
|---|---|
| 33. C Is for Context | 265 |
| 34. For Love of a Rose | 270 |
| 35. Food and Wine Pairing in Less Than 500 Words | 274 |
| 36. It's Only Natural | 278 |
| 37. The Tao of Tasting | 286 |
| 38. The Dining Ritual | 291 |
| 39. Four Great Wine Experiences | 294 |
| 40. Taking Flight | 299 |
| Acknowledgments | 305 |
| About the Author | 309 |
| Notes | 311 |

# Introduction

My first wine epiphany occurred in Ann Arbor, Michigan on a cold Christmas night in 1982. I was in graduate school. My wife Carla and I opted not to go home to New Mexico for the holidays that second year of school. Armando Ghitalla, my trumpet professor, and his wife Pauline, kindly invited us to Christmas dinner. That night, the other guests included H. Robert Reynolds, director of bands at the music school, and his wife.

Some weeks before, good friend Bob Reyen, who would go on to be my daughter Maria's godfather, had given Carla and me a bottle of '76 Silver Oak Alexander Valley Cabernet. I had never heard of the winery, much less tasted the wine, but he assured me that it was outstanding. The bottle became our donation to Christmas dinner.

With the soup course cleared, Mundy — as we liked to call him — and Pauline disappeared into the kitchen to carve the roast beast. I opted to open and pour the bottle of Silver Oak. What happened next is not easy to describe. After serving the wine, I sat down and picked up my glass. Reynolds, who had just been extolling the virtues of the bottles of '61 Bordeaux in his collection (totally meaningless to me at the time), smelled the Cabernet in his glass and then immediately uttered a quiet

## Introduction

but very emphatic, "Wow!" Carla said that the room smelled like flowers.

I quickly put my nose in the glass only to be assaulted by a tsunami of blackberry jam and spice box. I had never experienced anything remotely like it before with any wine. It was the very first time wine didn't smell just like wine. It smelled like something — something I recognized. The bright lights shined and the angels sang — the whole enchilada. I finally got it. I finally knew what everyone was talking about. In short, I had my first wine epiphany. From then on whenever I put my nose in a glass, wine smelled like "things" instead of just wine. In that moment, everything changed and wine would never be the same. I would never be the same.

# Foreword

### Why another book on wine tasting?

Over the years, top wine industry people have written many books on tasting. Though most offer helpful information, not all deliver the necessary instruction and strategies to achieve professional level skills. *Message in the Bottle* is different. It's filled with insights and expertise accrued over more than three decades during my career as a sommelier and educator. And the information in the following chapters was gained teaching wine tasting at every level, from consumers to industry veterans.

*Message in the Bottle* balances basic how-to instructions with complete detail. Every chapter also is written with practicality and ease of use in mind. I offer in-depth information about every aspect of deductive tasting, including a detailed explanation of a tasting grid, markers for classic wines, strategies for structural assessment, methodologies used for developing conclusions in a blind tasting, and much more. I've also included strategies for students preparing for blind tasting examinations.

# Foreword

## Who is this book for?

The original target audiences for this book were students on a wine certification path preparing for exams and industry professionals wanting to improve their tasting skills: people with more than a fair amount of experience and familiarity with the basics of tasting. However, dear friend and fellow MS (Master Sommelier) Madeline Triffon offered some great insight. She pointed out that once released, there was no way to control who would read the book. It would also likely attract beginners whose interest in wine was just beginning to develop.

Madeline also noted that the book's readers would consist of consumers and wine enthusiasts who wanted to learn more to improve their tasting skills. She was, of course, right. That sent me back to the drawing board to rewrite various sections of the book and to also add a few chapters. However, I still consider the book primarily an academic text for those on a wine certification path. To that point, I've added author's notes at the beginning of each chapter describing what will be covered as well as author's suggestions at the end with hints on how to apply the material just presented.

Where I share an "important tip" you'll see the silhouette of a wine glass to the left of the tip. While that extra effort makes the book more user-friendly for those with minimal wine tasting experience, this isn't necessarily a book for the average novice — and it's not intended to simply address the basics. However, it will be helpful for anyone with a strong interest and passion for learning about tasting or polishing their skills.

## How to use this book

*Message in the Bottle* contains a lot of useful information — a serious understatement. I suggest taking the chapters one at a time and being patient with assimilating the information. Otherwise, the tasting process will not only seem confusing but impossible to master. It's also important to emphasize that becoming a skilled taster requires a lot of experience, repetition, and time. There are no shortcuts and no way to "hack" the process. I think that's a good thing. Experiencing and learning about wine is one of the most significant cultural gifts we can receive. There's no point in rushing the process.

## Why include memory strategies?

As a wine educator, I consider myself a strategist. Over the years, I've read many books on sports psychology, behavioral psychology, and energy psychology. All were studied to find new strategies I could share with students to make learning tasting easier.

Many of the strategies in Part III involve visualization. Visualization is simply is creating and using internal visual images. In regards to tasting, it's the process of internally representing aromas and flavors in visual terms. Visualization, like tasting, is an acquired skill for most of us. Some of us are better at it than others. But if you practice either, you'll get better at it with time. Otherwise, I felt compelled to include several different visualization strategies in the book because I've found them all to be useful, some profoundly so, in my own tasting practice. I've also used them in my teaching and coaching with considerable success. Some of the concepts may seem novel but can quickly be learned and used to great effect. I only ask that you try the strategies and find what works best for you.

It goes without saying that there are other tasting methods used by various wine certification organizations. This book does not ignore other opinions or tasting methods but instead focuses on the deductive tasting method that I've personally used and taught to thousands of students over the last 30-plus years.

Finally, a word to consumers and enthusiasts: Welcome. I appreciate your enthusiasm and interest in learning more about one of the most enjoyable pastimes and professions on earth. In the following pages, you'll find a lot of information, background, trivia, and tips to help you become a better taster, which will only add to your enjoyment of wine. With that, read on and enjoy the journey.

# PART I

# The Basics

### Introduction

Long before pursuing a career in wine, I spent many years studying music, including seven years in college and two degrees; a Bachelor of Arts in Music History ('79 University of New Mexico) and a Master of Music in classical trumpet performance ('83 University of Michigan). But my music training started in fourth grade when I joined the school band. I clearly remember those first few frustrating weeks when I was trying to get a clue as to how to make sounds on a piece of cold hard brass while also learning how to read music.

The entire prospect seemed overwhelming at times. It wasn't until many months later that I reached a comfort level of being able to play a tune on the trumpet while reading the music — without offending everyone in the vicinity. Then came the challenges of playing in tune and time, not to mention being in an ensemble where I had to blend in with the group.

The experience for someone just getting into wine tasting is similar. There's a lot to cover, including learning how to hold a wine glass properly, the proper smelling/tasting techniques, and how to look at, smell, and taste wine effectively. There's also having to learn a tasting grid in some form as well as dozens of wine terms to know. No doubt it can seem overwhelming.

Part I of the book has all the information you'll need to get started. As you go through the first seven chapters, you'll learn about what's required for setting up your wine tasting space and the best techniques for smelling wine. You'll also be introduced to the deductive tasting grid, the most detailed of all tasting grids used by industry professionals.

Other chapters in Part I cover how to assess the structure in a glass of wine (the levels of acidity, alcohol, phenolic bitterness, and tannin), how to make conclusions based on using the deductive grid, and critical common markers for aromas, flavors, and structural levels in classic grapes and wines. All the material is intended to help the student begin the process of learning to taste at a professional level, and be able to judge wine quality competently–the primary goal of any wine training.

I suggest taking your time going through the material. Chunk the information down into manageable bits. It will be far easier to manage and remember. For those just learning how to taste, I include suggestions at the end of every chapter with advice on learning and how to use and learn the preceding information. With that, here's a chapter guide for Part I. Let's get started.

## Part I Chapter Guide

*Chapter 1: Setting the stage*
Includes glassware basics and needs for setting up a tasting space.

*Chapter 2: Glassware stance*
Smelling techniques and much more.

*Chapter 3: The deductive tasting grid defined*
A breakdown of the deductive tasting grid with explanations for each aspect (Sight, Smell, Taste).

*Chapter 4: Assessing structure*
Structural elements are defined, and basic techniques for how to assess them.

*Chapter 5: Using a decision matrix for conclusions*
How to organize sensory information to make a good conclusion in the deductive tasting.

*Chapter 6: Markers for classic white wines*
Markers and common structural levels for classic white wines.

*Chapter 7: Markers for classic red wines*
Markers and common structural levels for classic red wines.

# 1

# Setting the Stage: The Proper Setup for a Successful Tasting

*Author's note: Following are some tips on setting up your tastings, including the tasting space, glassware, and more.*

Before getting down to actual tasting practice, ensuring your tasting environment is appropriately set up is essential. Consider the following.

**Tasting space:** Natural light is best for tasting, but a good source of incandescent light will work well. Avoid fluorescent lighting if you can, as it alters the color and renders everything in various shades of gray. Also, ensure that you have a piece of white paper or another white background to view the wines correctly. Finally, be sure your tasting space is quiet and free from noisy distractions that will make it difficult to focus on the wines.

**Extraneous odors:** Avoid any colognes, perfumes, garlicky foods, or other strong fragrances. All can overwhelm your sense of smell–and everyone else's in the vicinity. Likewise, *never* wear a strong scent to any professional tasting.

**Proper glassware:** An essential component. The glasses don't have to be outrageously expensive hand-blown crystal. However, any glass used for professional tasting must:

- Be clear without markings or etchings
- Be made from crystal
- Have a stem
- Be egg-shaped with a tapered bowl
- Have a capacity of at least 14 ounces
- Have a thin, cut lip

My favorite all-purpose tasting glass is the Riedel Vinum Zinfandel/Chianti Classico glass. It meets all the criteria above and more. It's also elegant, attractive, and doesn't cost a fortune. Other glasses I recommend for tasting include the Stölzel Exquisit Red Wine glass and the Schott Zwiesel Forte Red Wine glass.

**Tasting order:** Generally speaking, it's best to taste white wines before red wines. This is because the tannins in red wine (see Chapter 4) from grape skins and/or barrels red wines are often aged in, can alter one's perception of the texture and structure of a white wine. Otherwise, it's strongly recommended to taste dry wines before sweet wines. If tasted first, a wine with residual sugar can change one's impression of the structure, and even flavors, of a dry wine that follows.

**Number of wines:** A flight of 6-8 wines is the optimum number for tasting — and strongly recommended. Tasting more than eight wines in a single sitting can be challenging unless one has the required experience.

**Tasting and spitting:** In a professional tasting there's little, if any, drinking — at least until the task at hand is completed and everyone is enjoying a glass of their favorite wine while exchanging notes or pleasantries. As a professional, it's not uncommon to taste upwards of 75-100 wines in a day, so tasting and spitting is an absolute rule. In a more practical context, the difference between tasting and drinking is enormous. There are such strong associations to drinking that the brain has trouble separating the quenching thirst/survival mode from being able to analyze a wine properly.

Personally, when I taste, I learn as much, if not more, about a wine after spitting it out than when it's still in my mouth. I'm also very interested in observing how the wine changes as it travels across my palate — especially how it finishes. Both are challenging to do if one is simply drinking the wine.

*Author's suggestion: That covers all you need to know about setting up your tastings. Now on to the basics of how to best smell wine, the deductive tasting grid, and more.*

---
2
---

# Glassware Stance: The Art of Smelling Wine

---

*Author's note: Something often overlooked in most tasting books and classes is fundamental instruction on how best to pick up a glass of wine and, for lack of a better term, address it. An essential skill is discovering the best angle to hold a glass and smelling techniques to*

*get the most out of a wine's aroma. This chapter covers all that and more.*

*I also include the concept of finding one's starting eye position when smelling wine and how critical it is in becoming a consistent taster. While the subject of eye positions and movement may seem new, behavioral scientists have known about their importance vis-à-vis language patterns and sensory memory for some time.*

Smelling and tasting wine are a lot like hitting a golf shot. Both are very complex sequences using multiple senses to process a great deal of information in the moment to achieve a single goal. In golf, addressing the ball consistently before attempting a shot is probably the most crucial factor for success in the game. Likewise, consistency in technique when picking up a glass to smell wine is essential but something rarely, if ever, written about or discussed. I call this "glassware stance." Here's a breakdown of the important steps.

## The angle of the glass

Every wine glass has a "best angle" or sweet spot for smelling wine — the angle where the aromas can be most easily perceived and recognized. To find the best angle, start by placing the glass vertically underneath your nose and slowly tilt the glass up. Don't go too far! You'll inhale the wine. At some point, when the angle of the glass is between 45 and 50 degrees, the aromas of the glass will begin to "sing" and be easier to detect. It's important to note that different kinds/shapes of glasses (such as Bordeaux vs. Burgundy stems) have different best angles. Remember to check for this every time you pick up a new glass.

## Smelling techniques

Practically every source on tasting I've ever read suggests smelling wine using several short and gentle sniffs. I completely agree. The opposite — smelling wine with one prolonged hoover/ intense inhalation — is ineffective. That's because the alcohol in the wine can quickly overwhelm your sense of smell. I call that "carpal nasal."

## Passive vs. active inhalation

Most people smell wine by placing the lip of the glass directly on the upper lip just beneath the nose and then sniffing. I call this passive inhalation as it relies almost entirely on orthonasal smelling or, technically speaking, detecting the volatile compounds (aromatics) in wine by inhaling through the nasal passages. This doesn't work for me. It quickly overwhelms my sense of smell. Instead, I use a technique I learned in a Cognac master class several decades ago. I call it "active inhalation."

When smelling wine, I pull the glass away from my face by about a half-inch, open my mouth slightly (about ¼ - ½ an inch), and then breathe in (and out) gently through my mouth and nose at the same time. Why does active inhalation potentially work better? It's due to physiology. There are two methods of smelling: orthonasal, as mentioned above, and retro-nasal, which uses both nasal and oral cavities. What I call "active inhalation" uses ortho and retro-nasal smelling in tandem. It also more than doubles the physiological real estate used to smell. Will it work for you? No guarantees, but it's definitely worth checking out. Try it:

1. Start with the glass resting directly underneath your nose positioned at about a 45° angle.
2. Move the glass slowly out to at least half an inch away from your nose. Make sure the glass is also positioned near your mouth.
3. Open your mouth a quarter- to a half-an inch.
4. Smell the wine, breathing gently in and out through your mouth and nose at the same time.
5. Test the results: Are you able to smell better? Does the change make a difference at all? Try going back and forth between smelling with just your nose vs. nose and mouth together.

See what you think of the active inhalation technique. It may — *or may not* — work for you. But I think you'll find it especially effective when evaluating fortified wines like Port and Sherry as well as spirits because the high alcohol level in all of them can easily overwhelm one's sense of smell.

## Using a consistent starting eye position

The last aspect of glassware stance is perhaps the most important and, again, something rarely taught. As you put your nose in the glass to focus on all aromas, you might be aware that your head and torso tend to go slightly down. You might also notice that as you reach the spot where you can smell the best, your eyes probably end up looking down in front of you at around a 45-degree angle from the ground, either straight ahead, slightly to the left, or even slightly to the right. It's different for everyone. There is no right way to do it.

The position of your eyes may not seem important, but it's a vital part of being consistent with starting the complex internal sequence of smelling wine. The relationship between eye positions and various kinds of sense memory are called "vertical and lateral eye movements" or "eye accessing cues." I firmly believe that finding a consistent starting eye position is essential in becoming a professional taster. Most discover it unconsciously over time with a great deal of repetition. It would therefore seem preferable to find it sooner rather than later. Here are steps to find your starting eye position.

1. First, stand up so you have all the space you'll need to be able to do the exercise. You may also be able to focus better than when you're sitting down.
2. Pick up a glass with wine and start smelling it.
3. While smelling the wine, focus your eyes down straight ahead in front of you at a 40-45° angle above the floor. Also, use a soft focus with your eyes.
4. While continuing to smell the wine, take your free hand and point to the location where your eyes are looking.
5. Now move your eyes and free hand together, slowly, going from center to the left. Then move your eyes and hand back to the center and to the right — all the while continuing to smell the wine.

6. Gradually find the one place that feels the most comfortable and familiar — it shouldn't take long to locate it.
7. Once you find your "best" or starting place, be sure to mark it clearly in your memory.
8. This is your starting eye position. Be sure to use it whenever you begin to smell a wine.

Important: Remember that whatever position your eyes easily assume is just your starting place. After you begin to smell a wine, your eyes will quickly move to other various locations as different kinds of sensory memory (visual, auditory, etc.) are needed to process. That's because we're constantly asking questions internally as to what we're smelling, tasting, and remembering. However, what's important is that you remember to *start* in the same place every time. This will give you a "baseline" you can always return to. Being aware of your starting eye position is also priceless when taking a tasting exam. It gives you a "reset" place when a wine is proving difficult to process or identify.

*Author's suggestions: There are several concepts introduced above. For the sake of ease (and your sanity), I suggest taking them one at a time and working with them until they're second nature. If something doesn't seem easy at first, odds are you're doing it in a way that doesn't work for your brain. The moment you do find the right way your brain will let you know immediately. When that happens, make note of it and do it every time going forward. You'll be glad you did.*

# 3

# The Deductive Tasting Grid Defined

*Author's note: Every wine certification organization uses a tasting grid for classes and examinations. When placed side by side, the grids have more than a few similarities. After all, there are only so many ways to look at, smell, and taste wine. The grid we'll use in this book, and the subject of this chapter, is the deductive tasting grid.*

*The deductive tasting grid traces its roots back to 1977 when 17 Master Sommeliers formed the Court of Master Sommeliers to oversee and execute the organization's examinations. At the time, Brian Julyan, MS, and Barrie Larvin, MS, created a tasting grid for class and exam purposes. It gradually developed and was formalized with the help of the late John Brownsdon, MW. Improvement and changes to the grid have been ongoing since that time, and the grid will continue to change in the future as needed. The grid used in this book is an authorized derivate that differs slightly from the grid used by the CMS in its classes and exams, presented here with the permission of CMS.*

*Otherwise, following is the deductive tasting grid broken down into over 40 criteria with an explanation for each. It may seem overwhelming at first, but with practice and repetition you'll soon master it.*

Regardless of the specific certification or organization, one of the first things any wine student has to do is learn and memorize a tasting grid. Using a grid is mandatory not only for success in tasting exams, it's a vital key to learning a broad range of wine concepts as well as developing one's skill as a taster.

Tasting with a grid teaches us the discipline of visualizing, memorizing, and using a complex sequence for the sake of consistency. The deductive tasting grid has over 40 criteria that can be assessed in any given wine. Memorizing the grid can be a considerable challenge but is absolutely necessary for the student to have consistency in their tasting, much less success in classes and exams. Through repetition, they're also eventually able to take this very complex conscious process involving multiple senses to the unconscious level.

In essence, the grid is a checklist of sorts that requires one to pose a series of yes-no questions: Is the wine clear? Does it display aromas and flavors of oak? Is there minerality or earthiness in the wine? And so on. The challenge is if the answer to a question is "yes," then something must be described and the answer requires recognition and memory which in turn requires previous experience and practice.

We all have the same physiological hardware (nose, tongue, brain, and nervous system), but different sense memories, making it possible to recognize and remember how things smell and taste. While the grid is certainly about physically smelling and tasting, it's also a tool for organizing and retaining sensory information. I'll refer back to this grid throughout the book. As you become an experienced taster, this grid will make more sense and referring to it will become a natural part of your tasting process.

Message in the Bottle

# The deductive tasting grid

*Based on the Deductive Tasting Method developed by the Court of Master Sommeliers.*

| Sight | Notes |
|---|---|
| Clarity | Clear – Hazy – Cloudy |
| Brightness | Dull – Hazy – Bright – Day Bright – Star Bright – Brilliant |
| Intensity of color | Pale – Medium – Deep |
| Color - white wine | Water white – Straw – Yellow – Gold – Brown |
| Color - rosé | Pink – Salmon – Brown |
| Color - red wine | Purple – Ruby (red) – Garnet (reddish-brown) – Brown |
| Secondary colors - white | Silver – Green – Copper |
| Secondary colors - red | Black – Blue – Magenta/Pink – Ruby – Garnet – Orange – Yellow – Brown |
| Rim variation | |
| Gas | |
| Sediment | Tartrates vs. Sediment |
| Tears/legs | Light – Medium – Heavy |
| Staining | None – Light – Medium – Heavy |

| Nose | |
|---|---|
| Clean/faults | Clean vs. Brettanomyces, volatile acidity, TCA/corkiness, etc. |
| Intensity of aroma | Delicate – Moderate – Powerful |
| Age assessment | Youthful – Developing – Vinous |
| Fruit - white wine | Orchard – Citrus – Tropical – Stone Fruit – Melon |
| Fruit - red wine | Red – Black – Blue – dried |
| Fruit quality | Tart – Fresh – Ripe – Bruised – Dried – Candied – etc. |
| Non fruit | Floral – Herbal – Vegetal – Spice – Other |
| Earth | Forest floor – Compost – Mushroom – Truffle, Potting Soil – Clay |
| Mineral | None – Light – Medium – Heavy |
| Wood | Size of Barrel – Age of Barrel – French vs. American Oak – Other Origin |

| Palate | |
|---|---|
| Dry/sweetness | Bone Dry – Dry – Off Dry – Medium-Sweet – Sweet – Luscious |
| Body | Light – Medium-Minus – Medium – Medium-Plus – Full |
| Fruit | Confirm the nose |
| Fruit quality | Confirm the nose |
| Non fruit | Confirm the nose |
| Earth/mineral | Confirm the nose |
| Wood | Confirm the nose |
| Acidity | Low – Medium-Minus – Medium – Medium-Plus – High |
| Alcohol | Low – Medium-Minus – Medium – Medium-Plus – High |
| Phenolic bitterness | Low – Medium-Minus – Medium – Medium-Plus – High |
| Tannin | Low – Medium-Minus – Medium – Medium-Plus – High |
| Texture: White wine | Lean – Crisp – Austere – Linear – Soft – Creamy – Roundy – Waxy – Oily – etc. |
| Texture: Red wine | Round – Soft – Silky – Gritty – Grainy – Coarse – Hard – Rough |
| Balance | Balanced vs. Imbalanced – why? |
| Length/finish | Short – Medium-Minus – Medium – Medium-Plus – Long |
| Complexity | Low – Medium-Minus – Medium – Medium-Plus – High |

| Initial Conclusion | |
|---|---|
| Old World/New World | |
| Climate | Cool – Moderate – Warm |
| Grape variety/blend | |
| Age range | 1-3 years – 3-5 years – 5-10 years – 10+ years |

| Final Conclusion | |
|---|---|
| Grape variety/blend | |
| Country | |
| Region/appellation | |
| Quality level | |
| Vintage | |

## Sight: The most overlooked aspect of training

The title may be a dreadful pun, but no truer wine words were ever spoken. A quick look at a glass of wine can reveal a great deal of information concerning a wine's age, the climate of origin, cellaring conditions, winemaking techniques, and even a hint as to the specific grape variety.

Here is a list of all things visual to consider when looking at a glass of wine.

**Clarity:** When looking at a glass of wine, tilt it straight out in front of you at a 45° angle over a white background. From there, note if the wine is clear. Or is it hazy? The answer depends on the wine having been fined and filtered before bottling — or not. The clarity scale is as follows:

- Scale: Clear – Hazy – Cloudy

Is filtering wine a good thing? There are many who believe, some vehemently so, that filtering of any kind strips wine of volatile compounds responsible for the aromas and flavors. But filtering also helps to stabilize wine. If a winemaker intends to ship her or his wine internationally, then having a stabilized wine in the bottle is a must (regrettably, another pun). However, the debate rages on.

**Brightness:** Look at the wine again against a white background. Note the amount of light reflected in the glass and underneath on the tasting mat or table/countertop. White wines that are pale in color tend to reflect a good deal of light and can be described as brilliant. More deeply colored white wines display less brightness. Red wines from lighter-pigmented grapes such as Pinot Noir tend to reflect more light vs. those from more deeply pigmented grapes such as Syrah. The brightness scale is as follows:

- Scale: Dull – Hazy – Bright – Day Bright – Star Bright – Brilliant

**Intensity of color:** Once the clarity and brightness are assessed, describe the depth of color in the wine. To do so, use the following scale:

- Scale: Pale – Medium – Deep

**Color:** Speaks to the age and condition of a wine. The general rules of color for wine are as follows:

- White and rosé wines deepen in color as they age.
- Red wines get lighter in color as they age.

Here are the color scales for wines:

- White wines: Water white – Straw – Yellow – Gold – Brown
- Rosé wines: Pink – Salmon – Brown
- Red wines: Purple – Ruby (red) – Garnet (reddish-brown) – Brown

*Note: It's important for the student to recognize the difference between straw, yellow, and gold in white wines, and purple, ruby (red), and garnet (reddish-brown) in red wines.*

Secondary colors: There are secondary colors in practically every glass of wine. In white wine, hints of green, silver, or unpolished brass are commonly seen. These are usually signs that the wine is young and likely produced from grapes grown in a cooler climate. In red wines, secondary colors usually refer to rim variation or the difference in color between wine at the core/center of the glass and wine at the edge/rim of the glass (see below).

- White wine: Silver – Green – Copper

- Red wine: Black – Blue – Magenta/Pink – Ruby – Garnet - Orange – Yellow – Brown

A final thought about color in wine. It's important. Why? Because the color of any wine should tip you off as to its age, condition, or the possible winemaking techniques used. To this point, if someone at a gathering hands you a glass of white wine that's deep yellow-gold in color and says, "this is the latest vintage of Sonoma Coast Chardonnay from XYZ winery," you'll immediately know there's a problem. Likewise, the color of the newest release of a Cabernet Sauvignon should be a deep, vibrant ruby red, even purple, and not some shade of reddish-brown.

**Rim variation:** A phenomenon of color only important for red wine. Here it's important to note that the color of the wine at the center of the glass is usually deeper than the color of the wine at the rim or edge of the glass. This color gradation is called rim variation. It can be found in red wines of practically any age but the older the wine, the more variation in color and the more rim variation. Again, it rarely applies to white wines.

**Gas:** Trace amounts of CO2 (carbon dioxide) are sometimes present in wine from fermentation or malolactic fermentation/conversion. Small amounts of CO2 can also be added to the wine as a preservative at the time of bottling. If bubbles are present in the glass, be sure to note them.

**Sediment-tartrates:** Some white wines will display small, opaque white crystals resembling grains of sand. These crystals are tartaric acid or tartrates, and they are potentially present in all wine unless steps are taken to remove them. Most wineries choose to cold stabilize white wines by chilling them to right above freezing for several days before bottling to remove excess tartrates. However, other wineries choose not to cold stabilize and thus tartrates will inevitably form in the bottle if it is quickly chilled. If that's the case, the crystals will dissolve back into the wine once the temperature rises a few degrees.

Tartrates can also be found in minimally fined and filtered red wines in the form of deeply colored crystals on the bottom of the cork or in the neck of the bottle. These can be wiped away with a clean serviette (cloth napkin). They're tasteless and completely harmless.

**Sediment:** Older red wines often have sediment from pigments and tannins that precipitate over time. This sediment can either be fine as in an older red Burgundy or thick and chunky as seen in a bottle of old vintage Port. Sediment can also be found in young red wines that have undergone minimal or no filtration. Careful decanting of the wine will take care of the problem in any form.

**Tears/legs:** Swirl the glass and observe how the tears or legs of the wine set up and then make their way back down the sides of the glass. Two things to note: the size and width of the tears and how quickly or slowly they move down the sides of the glass. The legs or tears give us a first indication of the level of alcohol in the wine and/or the presence of residual sugar. Thin, quickly moving tears tend to indicate a wine that has lower alcohol and little, if any, residual sugar. On the flip side, if the tears are thick and slow to move, one can expect a full-bodied wine with relatively high alcohol or residual sugar — or both. A lack of tears, or sheeting, means the wine in question either has low alcohol or a lack of residual sugar–or the glass needs to be polished, if not cleaned. Finally, while tears can be an indicator of wine style, they are NOT an indicator of quality one way or another. The tears/legs scale is as follows:

- Scale: Light – Medium – Heavy

**Staining:** Again, a phenomenon for red wines only. As you swirl a glass of red wine, note if the wine stains the inside of the glass. If so, it's due to the wine's pigmentation (color) and concentration. A wine made from a more deeply pigmented grape such as Syrah will display considerable staining of the tears. The staining of tears scale is as follows:

- Scale: None – Light – Medium – Heavy

That's all the criteria relating to the appearance of a wine in the context of the grid. Next up it's the nose portion of the grid.

## Nose: The most important aspect of tasting

The sense of smell is the most important of the five senses when evaluating wine. While one can taste at least five things (sweet, sour, bitter, salty, and umami/savory from glutamic acid), scientists tell us that we can smell well over 100,000 different things. In the context of the deductive tasting grid, here are things to consider when evaluating the nose of the wine.

**Clean/faults:** When first smelling a wine, check it for faults. Is it corked? Does it smell like musty cardboard or old books and magazines? Does the wine smell like vinegar, which could be volatile acidity (aka VA)? Or does it smell like a barnyard, which could be Brettanomyces (aka Brett)? There are any number of things that can go wrong in the winery that will render a wine's quality less than pristine. Anything detected on the nose that might be considered a fault will be confirmed when you taste the wine. If the wine is clean and well-made, note that as well. More information about common wine faults can be found in Chapter 10.

**Intensity of aroma:** The intensity of aroma ranges from delicate to powerful and is derived from the specific grape variety, the climate where the grapes were grown, or winemaking techniques. In terms of powerful intensity, think of a young vintage Port with a great concentration of fruit and high alcohol. A delicate wine by contrast could be a young sparkling wine or Pinot Bianco from Alto Adige. Most table wines are somewhere in between. Use the following scale to describe it:

- Scale: Delicate – Moderate – Powerful

**Age assessment:** Does the fruit in the wine smell bright and youthful or dried and cooked? A young red wine will display vibrant fresh fruit while an older wine will reveal mature aromas such as dried fruits, leather, and spice box. This shouldn't come as a surprise if you've already noted either youthful or mature colors in the appearance of the wine. Think of it as building a case that will culminate with your conclusion of the wine's identity. Also, know that a red wine with age is often called "vinous" or the wine is referred to as having "vinosity." Here is the scale for age assessment:

- Scale: Youthful – Developing – Vinous

**Fruit:** Once past the fault check and age assessment, the next thing to consider in the wine is the kind of fruit. Here are the "fruit groups" for white and red wines.

**White wines:**

- Orchard fruit: Apple and pear (green apple, red apple, etc.)
- Citrus fruit: Lemon, lime, grapefruit, orange, tangerine, starfruit, and more

- Tropical fruit: Pineapple, mango, papaya, passion fruit, banana, and more
- Stone or pit fruit: Peach, apricot, and nectarine
- Melon: Green melon or cantaloupe

**Red wines:**

- Red fruit: Red cherry, red raspberry, cranberry, strawberry, red currant, red plum, pomegranate, and more
- Black fruit: Black cherry/berry, black currant, black raspberry, black plum, and more
- Blue fruit: Blueberry and boysenberry
- Dried fruit: Raisin, sultana, date, prune, and fig

**Fruit quality:** Is the fruit tart? Jammy? Cooked? Be sure to include your description of the fruit. Here's a list of possibilities:

- Tart – Fresh – Ripe – Bruised – Dried – Desiccated – Raisinated – Baked – Stewed – Jammy – Candied – Liqueured

**Non-fruit:** There are secondary aromas and flavors in practically every wine. These non-fruit aromas are derived from either the grapes or winemaking techniques. Some can be vitally important to the student for identifying the grape variety and origin of a wine. Here's a list of some of the most common and important non-fruit aromas.

**Floral:** Many wines offer floral aromas. In particular, wines made from the aromatic grape family (Viognier, Muscat, Gewürztraminer, and Torrontés) not only smell overtly floral, they taste floral as well. Red wines can also be floral too. Rose and violet aromas are often found in Cabernet Sauvignon family wines.

**Spices:** Can take the form of pepper spice (white pepper, black pepper, etc.) from the chemical compound called rotundone, or brown baking spices from oak aging.

**Grass/herb/vegetal:** Herbal and vegetal qualities are derived from a compound called pyrazines found in Cabernet Sauvignon family wines including Sauvignon Blanc.

**Other:** Includes fermentation aromas (yeast, toast, dough), butter (Diacetyl from malolactic fermentation), leather (age in red wines), honey (botrytis), animal (Brettanomyces), and more.

🍷 *Important note: Along with an accurate structural assessment, identifying non-fruit aromas and flavors is one of the most important keys in identifying a particular grape or wine. Many semi-aromatic white grapes and thinner-skinned red grapes have similar fruit profiles, but their non-fruit and structure levels are completely different.*

**Earth:** Generally speaking, wines from the Old World (Europe) tend to show a more pronounced mineral or earthy character. Wines from the New World (North America, South America, Australia, and New Zealand) tend to display more fruit and less mineral/earth qualities. Again, these are broad generalizations and exceptions can often be found. Regardless, after assessing the fruit and non-fruit, check the wine for minerality and earth. Here are some possibilities:

- Earth: forest floor – compost – mushroom - truffle - potting soil - clay

- Mineral: wet stone – limestone – chalk – slate – flint – dust – volcanic - granite

**Wood:** Oak-aging creates a subset of aromas and flavors in wine including vanilla, smoke, toast, baking spices, chocolate, coffee, tea, and more. The presence (or lack) of these aromas and flavors may be another clue as to a wine's identity. Certain white wines (Alsace, Germany, and others) rarely display the presence of oak while others such as White Burgundy and California Chardonnay often have considerable oak influence. The same goes for red wines. There are several factors that can affect the quality and degree of impact of oak influence in wine including the following.

**Size of barrel:** Smaller 55-60-gallon barrels, often called barriques, impart more oak influence in wine.

**Age of barrel:** Younger barrels impart more oak influence and older barrels less.

**French vs. American oak:** Twenty-five years ago the difference between French and American oak was striking and easy to discern. Now it's much more difficult to tell them apart for many reasons. Generally, American oak has pronounced vanilla, baking spice notes, dill, and coconut. French oak by contrast is not usually as spicy and has more smoke and toast elements.

**General oak descriptors:** None – Old vs. New – Large vs. Small – French vs. American vs. Other Origin

**Oak aroma descriptors:** Vanilla, cinnamon, nutmeg, star anise, cardamom, clove, caramel, coffee, cocoa powder, chocolate, black tea, toast, char, cedar, molasses, coconut, and dill.

🍷 *Important note: Don't get stuck on trying to identify French vs. American oak. It's far more useful to be able to recognize oak markers in a wine or the lack thereof.*

### Palate: Confirming the nose and calibrating the structure

In the context of the deductive tasting process and grid, tasting serves two purposes: to confirm what you've already smelled in the wine, and to calibrate the structural elements or levels of acid, alcohol, phenolic bitterness, and tannin. If you've done your work thoroughly on the nose, there will be few, if any, surprises when you taste the wine. Here are things to consider when evaluating the palate.

**Dry/sweetness:** How dry or sweet is the wine? Is it bone dry with a complete lack of residual sugar? Or off-dry with just a touch of sweetness? Is it a full-on dessert wine that's very sweet and hopefully balanced with enough acidity to keep it from being cloying? The level of sweetness or dryness can be a very important clue as to the variety, style, or origin of a wine. It's important not to confuse fruitiness with sweetness.

If in doubt, pay attention to how dry or sweet the wine is on the finish and not just the initial impression when you first taste it.

Here's a scale to use for assessing dryness/sweetness:

- Scale: Bone Dry – Dry – Off-Dry – Medium-Sweet – Sweet – Luscious

**Body:** In wine is determined by several factors including the level of alcohol, glycerin, residual sugar (if present), and dry extract (dissolved grape solids in the wine). Dairy products are often used to illustrate body in wine: a light-bodied wine can be compared to non-fat milk, a medium-bodied wine to half-and-half, and a full-bodied wine to heavy cream. The scale for body is as follows:

- Scale: Light – Medium-Minus – Medium – Medium-Plus – Full

**Confirming the nose**

Next, taste through the wine keeping in mind the information you've discovered on the nose.

**Fruit:** Taste the wine to confirm the primary and secondary fruit you've smelled in the glass. Are the same flavors on the palate? Are there different ones to note?

**Fruit quality:** Now that you've had a chance to taste the wine, is the fruit quality the same? More often than not, the fruit quality is tarter on the palate compared to the nose.

**Non-fruit:** Confirm the non-fruit characteristics. Are they the same? Different? If different, be sure to describe it.

**Earth/mineral:** Confirm both the mineral and earth qualities in the wine. Are they similar to those found on the nose? Different? If so, how are they different?

**Wood:** Confirm any oak flavors already smelled in the wine. When oak is used to excess, wine can taste overly tannic and astringent — which leads us to the structural elements.

### Calibrating structure

🍷 *Important note: Re-taste the wine again. After spitting, give yourself several seconds to get a good impression of the level of the structural elements in the wine (more on assessing structure can be found in Chapters 4 and 25).*

**Acidity:** There are four primary acids in wine: tartaric (the most important), malic (tart green apples), lactic acid (yogurt and other dairy products), and citric. Acidity creates balance in a wine and also the potential to age. When tasting for acidity, focus on your salivary glands. Medium acidity or lower will barely register any salivation while medium-plus and high acidity will cause them to work overtime. Use the following scale to assess the level of acidity:

- Scale: Low – Medium-Minus – Medium – Medium-Plus – High

**Alcohol:** Alcohol is sensed as heat in the nose, throat, or chest cavity. A low-alcohol wine like a Mosel Riesling at 8% ABV (alcohol by volume) will have a noticeable absence of this sensation of heat while a fortified wine like Port at 18% ABV will create considerable warmth in the mouth, throat, and chest. Be mindful of the alcohol level and connect it to the ripeness and quality of the fruit on the nose and palate. Otherwise, use the following scale to describe the alcohol:

- Scale: Low – Medium-Minus – Medium – Medium-Plus – High

🍷 *Important note: When checking the level of alcohol in a wine, say the letter "O" and inhale—AFTER you spit the wine out. You'll be able to get a quick read on the alcohol in the wine.*

**Phenolic bitterness (white wines only):** Phenols are a large family of chemical compounds found primarily in grape skins. Phenolic bitterness in white wine is caused by skin contact with the must either before or during fermentation or the wine after fermentation. Phenols taste bitter, are slightly astringent in feeling, and add structure to the wine. They can best be perceived on the finish. Use the following scale when describing phenolic bitterness:

- Scale: Low – Medium-Minus – Medium – Medium-Plus – High

**Tannin (red wines):** Tannin, or tannic acid, is derived from grape skins and barrels often used to age wine. Tannin is a preservative that gives red wine the potential to age. In moderation, tannin adds structure and complexity to wine. Excessive tannin can render a wine bitter and astringent (think overly-brewed tea). It should also be noted that tannin can sometimes be found in overly oaked white wines. The scale for tannin is as follows:

- Scale: Low – Medium-Minus – Medium – Medium-Plus – High

**Texture:** Also called *mouthfeel*. The texture in wine is generally determined by structural levels. Red wine with low tannin will feel silky on the palate while a high tannin red wine will feel gritty. Here are possible descriptors to use for the texture:

- White wine: Lean – Crisp – Austere – Linear – Soft – Creamy – Round – Waxy – Oily – Viscous

- Red wine: Round – Soft – Silky – Gritty – Grainy – Coarse – Hard – Rough

**Balance:** A useful definition for balance is harmony between all the various elements in a wine: fruit, acid, oak (if used), phenolic bitterness (white wine), or tannins (red wine). When tasting a wine, consider if there's harmony among all these elements. Or note if something is out of balance such as too much new oak.

**Length/finish:** Also known as the aftertaste of the wine. Is the finish short, long, or in between? If the finish lasts more than 20 seconds and is persistent, then it's a long finish. Odds are it's also a good quality wine. The general rule in tasting is the longer the finish, the better quality the wine. There are always exceptions. A deeply flawed wine might have a very long finish, just not one that's pleasant. Here's the scale for the finish:

- Scale: Short – Medium-Minus – Medium – Medium-Plus – Long

**Complexity:** There are many definitions for the term *complexity* in regards to wine. My definition is the number of aromas and flavors in the wine combined with how much it changes as it travels across your palate. For example, a simple wine will only display one or two aromas/flavors and change very little when you taste it. A more complex wine offers many different aromas/flavors and will change dramatically as it travels across your palate. Once poured, it will continue to change and develop in the glass over time revealing even more nuances. It's a "Mary Had a Little Lamb" versus a late Beethoven string quartet kind of a thing. Here's the scale for complexity:

- Scale: Low – Medium – Medium – Medium – High

That's the end of the sensory evaluation portion of the grid. Now it's time to formulate a well-reasoned conclusion using all the information seen, smelled, and tasted in the glass.

## Conclusions: Initial and final

**Initial conclusion**

Given all the previous information, it's time to start honing in on what the wine is and where it could be from. Don't get too picky about details — yet. Consider what drives the wine and the kind of climate where the grapes were grown.

**Old World/New World:** What dominates the wine? Fruit and winemaking? Or do other-than-fruit elements, especially mineral and earth qualities, dominate the wine? If so, the wine is probably from the Old World or at least made in an Old-World style. Conversely, if the wine is overtly fruity without earthiness and shows considerable new oak, chances are it's from the New World.

**Climate:** Does the wine have tart fruit, restrained alcohol, and higher acidity? If so, it's probably from a cool climate where the grapes didn't fully ripen. Or is the wine deeply colored with ripe fruit and higher alcohol? Then the wine is probably from a warmer growing region where the grapes were able to fully ripen. One can always make a call for "moderate climate" if the wine's fruit quality and structure fall in between.

- Scale: Cool – Moderate – Warm

**Grape variety/blend:** Assessing the grape variety or blend of grapes is arguably the most challenging aspect of the deductive tasting process. It requires knowing common markers for classic wines and a great deal of experience and tasting practice. Important non-fruit elements (impact compounds - see Chapter 11) and structural levels (acidity, alcohol, etc.) are the most important keys for calling the right grape or blend.

**Age range:** Given what you've seen, smelled, and tasted, is the wine young and vibrant with primary fruit? Or does the wine offer leathery, earthy, and secondary aromas and flavors from extended bottle aging? Or is the wine in between and evolving? Regardless, give the age range in the following increments:

- Scale: 1-3 years – 3-5 years – 5-10 years – 10+ years

**Final conclusion**

Now it's time to narrow down your focus and make a specific call on the wine. Given the previous, provide the following information.

**Grape Variety/blend:** Give the specific grape variety or blend using important markers and structural profile of the wine.

**Country:** State the country where you think the grapes were grown and the wine was made.

**Region/appellation:** Given the country, take the grape variety to the most appropriate region, i.e., "France, Merlot blend, Saint-Émilion," or "Germany, Riesling, Rheingau."

**Quality level:** Two possibilities: First, be aware that some countries and regions have specific legal hierarchies of quality. Think about Burgundy, Germany, Austria, and certain regions in Italy:

- Burgundy: AC – Premier Cru – Grand Cru
- German Prädikate: Kabinett – Spätlese – Auslese – Beerenauslese – Eiswein – Trockenbeerenauslese
- Germany VDP Grosse Lage: Gutswein – Ortswein – Erstes Gewächs – Grosses Gewächs
- Wachau: Steinfeder – Federspiel – Smaragd
- Chianti Classico: Normale – Riserva – Gran Selezione
- Rioja: Crianza – Reserva – Gran Reserva

Otherwise, make an informed assessment about the overall quality level of the wine. Is it a simple table wine? Or is it top-quality and ageable?

**Official style category:** For wines from a specific place or classification. Possible terms include Trocken (German and Austrian wines), Sec, Demi-Sec, and Moelleux (Vouvray), Aszú (Hungarian Tokaji), and Vendange Tardive and Sélection de Grains Nobles (Alsace).

**Vintage:** Give one year or two at the most. If you're calling a wine from the Old World, be mindful of giving two vintages as opposed to one. The quality of harvests/vintages can vary dramatically from year to year in Old World regions. Also, keep in mind the fact that Southern Hemisphere countries are always six months ahead in terms of harvest.

Now sit back, relax, and take a sip. You've earned it.

*Author's suggestion: Now that you have an explanation of the grid, the next thing you'll need to do is to memorize it. Perhaps the easiest way to do that would be to chunk it down into three-to-five bits of information at a time until the entire grid is memorized. From there, be able to explain the grid to someone who's not in the wine industry. Sit a friend or family member down and explain the entire grid to them. You don't need a glass of wine in hand to do this. To that point, Richard Feynman, the famous physicist, once said that if you can't explain something to an eight-year-old, you really don't understand it yourself. I completely agree.*

# 4

# Assessing Structure

*Author's note: Structure in wine is important — really important. By structure, I mean the levels of acidity, alcohol, and phenolic bitterness in white wine and tannin in red wine. Personally, I think a wine's structural elements are its very bones. They speak to the grape variety, place of origin, climate, timing of harvest, winemaking techniques, and so much more. Structure is by far one of the most important aspects of tasting and students must practice assessing it regularly to become consistent with it.*

Assessing the structure accurately and consistently in any wine is a necessity for any professional taster. It's also an important key to being able to judge wine quality at any level. Initially, it's important for the student to be able to separate the physical sensations of the different structural elements on the palate. Over time, students must then be able to quickly and consistently assess structural levels as well as connect the dots between structure and the overall character of the wine.

An example would be making the connection between high alcohol, restrained acidity (with possible acidulation), and ripe-raisinated fruit in a Barossa Shiraz, or the high acidity, restrained alcohol, and tart fruit in a Chianti Classico.

Everything I've just described requires practice, a duration of time, and experience. But to get started, here are the structural elements defined, as well as some basic strategies to practice tasting for them.

## Acidity

*Definition:*

There are four primary acids found in grapes: tartaric, malic, lactic, and citric. Tartaric acid is by far the most important, as it gives balance to both grapes and wine and creates the potential for aging. It also increases as grapes ripen. However, if lacking, it needs to be added to the must during fermentation or to the wine before bottling. Powdered tartaric acid derived from grapes is the most common acid additive.

*What does it smell like?*

Acidity doesn't smell like anything. However, smelling tart or under-ripe fruit can and should create expectations for a wine with elevated acidity.

*What does it taste like?*

Easily said: Acidity tastes sour.

*What does it feel like?*

On the palate, acidity is sensed by increased saliva production and activity in the salivary glands. High acidity is also often felt in the front of the mouth on the tongue, teeth, and gums.

*How do I check for it?*

Pay close attention to your salivary glands and saliva production after spitting out the wine. If in doubt, take a sip of water and note the complete lack of acidity as compared to the wine.

*Connecting the dots:*

It all goes back to place. Cooler climate places produce high acid-lower alcohol wines because the grapes don't completely ripen. Generally, cool climate wines also tend to have less depth of color and offer a more savory character when compared to wines made from grapes grown in warmer climates that have higher alcohol, riper fruit, and less natural acidity.

*Reference wines:*

Lower acid white wines: Gewürztraminer, Pinot Gris, Marsanne-Roussanne blends

Higher acid white wines: Riesling, Melon, Chenin Blanc

## Alcohol

*Definition*

Ethanol alcohol in wine is a by-product of fermentation. The alcohol level in table wine ranges from just over 5% up to 16%.

*What does it smell like?*

Alcohol in wine is odorless but perceived as heat on the nose. However, smelling jammy or raisinated fruit in a wine can and should create expectations for high alcohol on the palate.

*What does it taste like?*

Alcohol is tasteless. But as just mentioned, wines with high alcohol content have ripe, jammy fruit and lower natural acidity. Wines with less alcohol have higher natural acidity, less ripe fruit, and are tart on the palate.

*What does it feel like?*

Elevated alcohol can give wine a fuller body as well a richer texture on the palate. High alcohol can also give the illusion of sweetness even though the wine might actually be dry.

*How do I check for it?*

After spitting the wine out, say the letter "O" and inhale (remember, *AFTER* spitting out the wine). Note the sensation of warmth or heat perceived in the bridge of the nose, the mouth, throat, and even chest cavity if the alcohol is elevated.

*Connecting the dots:*

High alcohol means that the grapes used to produce the wine were ripe or even over-ripe. Thus, a high alcohol wine will show ripe, jammy, or even raisinated fruit as well as lower natural acidity. Also, a high-alcohol wine will often be acidulated with added tartaric acid.

*Reference wines:*

Lower alcohol white wines: Moscato di Asti (semi-sparkling), Riesling (Mosel)

Higher alcohol white wines: New World Chardonnay, New World Viognier, Southern Rhône Marsanne blends.

## Phenolic bitterness

*Definition:*

For white wines only. Phenols are a large family of compounds found in grape skins and seeds. Note that tannins in red wines are also part of the phenol family. In white wines, phenols are derived from the must being in contact with the skins before or during fermentation or the wine after fermentation. Phenolic bitterness is an important marker for many semi-aromatic and fully aromatic grapes.

*What does it smell like?*

Phenolic bitterness is odorless. However, smelling wines made from semi-aromatic and fully aromatic grapes with pronounced floral qualities can and should build expectations of phenolic bitterness on the palate.

*What does it taste like?*

As implied, phenolic bitterness tastes bitter. It's often described as "almond skin bitterness" on the finish of a wine.

*What does it feel like?*

In any quantity, phenolic bitterness feels astringent on the palate — especially on the finish of the wine.

*Note: It's important for the student to be able to separate phenolic bitterness from used oak in white wines. The latter is usually accompanied by other aromas and flavors pertaining to the oak itself.*

*How do I check for it?*

The best way to really experience phenolic bitterness is to taste a wine made from a fully-aromatic grape like Gewürztraminer. Take a sip and hold the wine on your palate for at least 10 seconds before spitting it out. Better yet, take a small sip and swallow while paying close attention to the bitter taste and touch of grittiness on the finish of the wine.

*Connecting the dots:*

Perceiving phenolic bitterness on the palate signals a semi-aromatic or fully aromatic white grape which can be connected to the overt floral qualities stemming from terpenes. The two are often found together.

*Reference wines:*

Lower phenolic bitterness white wines: Chardonnay, Melon

Higher phenolic bitterness white wines: Torrontés, Gewürztraminer, Viognier

## Tannin

*Definition:*

Generally, for red wines only. Tannin, or tannic acid, is derived from grape skins or oak barrels in which red wine is often aged. It should also be noted that white wine aged for an extended time in new oak can also display tannin.

*What does it smell like?*

Tannin is odorless. However, a deeply colored red wine with ripe fruit and aromas of oak aging should create an expectation of tannin.

*What does it taste like?*

In any quantity, tannin tastes bitter like overly brewed black tea.

*What does it feel like?*

Tannin feels astringent and even gritty on the palate. It's helpful to note the difference between grape and oak tannin in regards to their sensory "location" on the palate. It varies with the individual. For me, grape tannins are perceived in the front of the mouth and oak tannins in the back.

*Reference wines:*

Lower tannin wines: Gamay, Pinot Noir

Higher tannin wines: Cabernet Sauvignon, Nebbiolo

## Working with structure

Following are strategies for practicing tasting for structure. Gaining experience and accuracy in structural assessment again takes time and a lot of practice — just like everything else in tasting.

1. Get a Coravin: A Coravin is by far the most useful wine accessory there is for tasting practice. Using a Coravin will allow you to buy the best examples of wines and to taste them repeatedly over a period of time, thereby saving you thousands of dollars on wine purchases.

2. Taste wines in pairs: Our brains learn more easily with binary juxtaposition. Practice tasting wines in twos. Then do the following:

3. Calibrate structure using extremes: One of the easiest ways to learn consistent calibration of structural elements is by a comparative tasting of pairs of wines that show extremes in structure. Taste for one structural element at a time. And remember — only two wines at a time.

- Alcohol - lower vs. higher: Mosel Riesling vs. high alcohol Napa Valley Chardonnay
- Acidity - lower vs. higher: Alsace Gewürztraminer vs. Clare Valley Riesling
- Phenolic bitterness - lower vs. higher: Chablis AC vs. Alsace Gewürztraminer
- Tannin - lower vs. higher: Beaujolais-Villages vs. Barolo

4. Cause and Effect: Memorize the cause and effect (chapter 8) behind each criteria of the tasting grid, especially in regards to fruit quality and ripeness levels as they relate to structural levels. Connect the dots from color to fruit ripeness to the levels of acidity and alcohol.

5. Write personal grape variety descriptions: There are several sources of grape variety/wine descriptions including those listed in this book. However, I highly recommend writing your own descriptions as there will doubtless be markers for various wines that are unique to you. Make sure to include structural levels in your descriptions.

*Author's suggestions: Becoming proficient at assessing structure takes time and practice. Work on one of the structural elements at a time. I think it's useful to start by tasting wines in pairs that show extremes in a certain structural element. It's also important for each individual to become aware if they have a sensitivity to one of the structural elements. Some tasters are naturally sensitive to acidity while others aren't. If you discover a sensitivity to a certain aspect of structure, or lack thereof, seek the help of other experienced tasters to help calibrate your palate. Above all, be patient with your progress. Becoming a good taster is a process. As I've said before, it can't be rushed.*

5

# Using a Decision Matrix For Deductive Tasting

*Author's note: Several years ago I had a conversation with Adam Gazzaley, a neuroscientist based in San Francisco. During our chat, Adam said something along the lines of "all thinking is based on perception, recognition, and memory." One of the things I took from his comment was how much of tasting wine is based on memory. From there I quickly extrapolated that a good deal of the tasting process could — and should — be done without a glass of wine in hand. In particular, the deductive/thinking part of the tasting sequence is a candidate for internal rehearsal, so to speak. My term for this process is using a "Decision Matrix." This chapter outlines it in detail.*

"Baseball is 90% mental. The other half is physical."

Yogi Berra

In deductive tasting, the sensory evaluation sequence in which one gathers information about a wine's appearance, aroma, and palate is only part of the equation. What's equally important, arguably more so, is to be able to put all the information together in a meaningful way to come up with a logical conclusion. To this point, many times I've sat across a table from a student listening to them describe a wine in detail only to, in the words of the all-knowing Bugs Bunny, take a left turn at Albuquerque in the form of a conclusion that made absolutely no sense. It's as if the student either didn't listen to themselves while describing the wine or they couldn't connect the dots and come up with a conclusion that matched the information found in the glass.

Enter the Decision Matrix. The Matrix is a series of mini *if-then* evaluations that a taster can use when examining a wine to help them come up with a good conclusion. For example, looking at a glass of red wine that's lighter in color can quickly build expectations of a thinner-skinned, lighter pigmented grape variety grown in a cooler climate with red fruit dominating the nose and palate along with less alcohol, higher natural acidity, and moderate tannins. You get the idea.

While there are exceptions to all the so-called rules below, the Matrix will provide a foundation for you to build on. Remember that there is no replacement for knowing key markers for classic wines (Chapters VI and VII). Thorough knowledge of these is absolutely required to become an experienced taster. Finally, the Matrix is intended as a starting point for the student to use and then to go on and develop their own personal version.

## Sight

Color: White wines

Light or pale color:

- Youth
- Cooler climate
- Cooler vintage
- Lack of new oak aging

Deep yellow or gold color:

- Warmer climate
- Warmer vintage
- Overall age
- Extended new oak aging
- Botrytis-affected fruit (see Chapter 11)
- Extended skin contact

Green secondary color:

- Cooler climate
- Cooler vintage
- Youth

Color: Red wines

Lighter color

- Thinner-skinned, lighter-pigmented grape
- Cooler climate
- Cooler vintage
- Red fruit dominant wine
- Less overall ripeness of fruit
- Higher natural acidity
- Lower alcohol

Garnet color:

- Overall age and degree of oxidation
- Oxidative winemaking
- Extended oak aging

Deeper color:

- Thicker-skinned, deeper-pigmented grape
- Warmer climate
- Warmer vintage
- Dark fruit dominant wine
- Riper fruit qualities
- Lower natural acidity with possible acidulation (addition of tartaric acid to the wine)
- Higher alcohol
- Possible higher tannin

Rim variation:

Pink or purple color:

- Youth
- Lack of extended oak aging

Salmon – orange – yellow – brown:

- Overall age or level of oxidation
- Oxidative winemaking
- Extended oak aging
- Grape variety that shows oxidation in color even when young (i.e., Nebbiolo)

Legs/tearing

Quickly forming, thinner, and quickly moving tears/legs:

- Cooler climate
- Cooler vintage
- Lower alcohol
- Lower dry extract (see Chapter 8)
- Higher natural acidity
- Lack of residual sugar

Slower forming, thicker, and slower moving tears/legs:

- Warmer climate
- Warmer vintage
- Higher alcohol
- Lower acidity with possible acidulation
- Higher dry extract (see Chapter 8)
- Possible presence of residual sugar
- Possible fortification

Staining of the tears in red wine:

- Thicker-skinned, deeper-pigmented grape
- Concentrated wine from low-yielding vineyard
- Higher dry extract
- Possible warmer climate

## Nose

### Faults

Brettanomyces

- Possible Old World growing region
- Minimal intervention winemaking

Volatile acidity:

- Possible Old World growing region
- Minimal intervention winemaking

### Fruit

Fruit-dominant:

- New World region
- New World style

- Youth

Lack of overt fruit:

- Old World region
- Old World style
- Wine with age

Fresh, vibrant fruit:

- Youth
- Lack of oak aging

Dried or preserved fruit:

- Wine with age

Abundance of riper fruit:

- Warmer region
- Warmer vintage

Abundance of tart or otherwise unripe fruit:

- Cooler growing region
- Cooler vintage

Red wine

Abundance of tart or under ripe red fruit:

- Thinner-skinned, lighter-pigmented grape
- Cooler growing region
- Cooler vintage

Abundance of darker and/or riper fruit:

- Thicker-skinned, deeper-pigmented grape
- Warmer growing region
- Warmer vintage

Non-fruit characteristics

Dominant floral notes (terpenes - see Chapter 11):

- Aromatic grape (Gewürztraminer, Muscat, Viognier, etc.)

Herbal-vegetal notes (pyrazines - see Chapter 11):

- Cabernet Sauvignon family grape including Sauvignon Blanc

Pepper (rotundone - see Chapter 11):

- Rhône grape variety (Syrah, Grenache, Mourvèdre), Zinfandel, or other for red wines, and Grüner Veltliner for white wine

Earth-mineral qualities

Pronounced earth and mineral qualities:

- Old World region
- Old World style

Lack of overt earth and mineral qualities:

- New World region
- New World style

Oak

Dominant oak usage:

- New World region
- New World style

- Old World region/wine that traditionally uses new oak (Burgundy, etc.)

Used or neutral oak character:

- Old World region
- Old World style

## Palate: Structure

Acidity

Higher natural acidity:

- Cooler climate region
- Cooler vintage

Lower natural acidity:

- Warmer climate region
- Warmer vintage

Acidulation/acidification:

- Warmer climate
- Warmer vintage
- New World region
- New World style

## Alcohol

Lower alcohol:

- Cooler growing region
- Cooler vintage
- Possible Old World region or style

Higher alcohol:

- Warmer growing region
- Warmer vintage
- Possible New World region or style

**Phenolic bitterness (white wine)**

Little or no phenolic bitterness:

- Non-aromatic grape variety

Medium or higher phenolic bitterness:

- Semi-aromatic or fully aromatic grape variety

## Tannin (red wine*)

Lower tannin:

- Thinner-skinned grape variety
- Less new oak usage
- Possible cooler climate region
- *Also a white wine with extended oak aging

Higher tannin:

- Thicker-skinner grape variety
- More new oak usage
- Possible warmer climate region

## Finish

Shorter finish:

- Lesser quality wine
- Less complex wine

- Younger, less-developed wine

Longer finish:

- Better quality wine
- More complex wine

## Conclusion

Old World or Old World style wine:

- Less overt fruit qualities
- More non-fruit qualities
- More earth and mineral qualities
- High natural acidity from cooler growing region
- Lower alcohol from cooler growing region
- Less new oak usage
- Possible less winemaking influence

New World or New World style wine:

- More overt fruit qualities
- Possible less non-fruit qualities
- Less earth and mineral qualities
- Lower natural acidity from warmer growing region
- Possible acidulation because of warmer growing region
- Higher alcohol from warmer growing region
- More new oak usage
- More winemaking influence

*Author's suggestion: There's a lot of information above. I strongly recommend taking the information in small bits, and asking yourself simple questions such as the following:*

- *If a white wine has higher acidity, what could it mean?*
- *If a wine has higher alcohol, what could it mean?*

- *If a red wine is deeper in color, what could it mean?*

🍷 *Important note: I want to stress again that all this can easily be practiced without a glass of wine in hand. In fact, it should be done without wine because it's thinking work and not actual tasting. There are a lot of pieces to the puzzle listed above. Consistent practice over time will help put them all together.*

# 6

# Markers for Classic White Wines

*Author's note: The following is a list of important markers and common structural levels for classic white wines including important keys for identification. These descriptions will serve as a valuable tool for tasting study and practice.*

### Chardonnay: France - Chablis Premier Cru

**Sight:** Pale to medium straw with green.

**Nose:** Tart green apple, lemon-citrus, creamy mid-plate texture from lees contact, possible buttery notes from malolactic fermentation/conversion (ML), and chalky seashell minerality. Some producers use new oak imparting spice and wood aromas.

**Palate:** Medium-bodied with tart fruit and chalky mineral. The intensity of flavor and quality varies with the producer and the specific vineyard. Some producers also use oak, particularly with Premier Cru and Grand Cru wines.

**Structure:** Dry with medium to medium-plus alcohol and medium-plus to high acidity.

**ID keys:** Tart fruit, pronounced chalky-saline minerality, and elevated acidity are keys. Also, look for lees contact and notes of ML.

## Chardonnay: France - Côte de Beaune

**Sight:** Medium straw with green.

**Nose:** Apple-pear and citrus fruit with lees, ML notes, mushroom-earth, and vanilla and spice notes from oak.

**Palate:** Medium to full-bodied depending on the pedigree of the vineyard and the quality of the vintage.

**Structure:** Dry with medium to medium-plus alcohol and medium-plus acidity.

**ID keys:** The combination of tart ripe and apple/pear fruit with bright citrus, lees, ML notes, earth, and new oak flavors is key to recognition. Generally, the style of Chassagne-Montrachet tends to be somewhat richer, with Puligny-Montrachet known for elegance, and Meursault for pronounced earthiness. Keep in mind that these are broad generalizations and exceptions often occur.

## Chardonnay: California and Australia

**Sight:** Medium straw to medium yellow depending on the origin, producer, and vintage.

**Nose:** Cool climate wines: Tart green apple/pear, tropical fruit, and pronounced citrus notes with lees contact, ML, and oak commonly found. Lean and racy on the palate.

**Nose:** Warmer climate wines: ripe (even baked) apple/pear and peach fruit. Other flavors include floral, lemon/lime citrus, lees, ML notes, and oak spice.

**For both:** Barrel-fermentation and lees contact impart flavors of cream and yeast. Oak aging imparts flavors of vanilla, baking spices, and wood.

**Palate:** Ripe and/or tart orchard fruit with tart citrus, lees-contact, ML notes, and oak.

**Structure:** Dry to off-dry with medium-plus to high alcohol and medium to medium-plus acidity.

**ID keys:** The winemaking trio of lees contact, malolactic notes, and new oak usually make New World Chardonnay relatively easy to identify.

## Sauvignon Blanc: France - Loire Valley - Sancerre and Pouilly-Fumé

**Sight:** Pale to medium straw with green.

**Nose:** Green apple and tart citrus notes (grapefruit, lemon, and lime) with vegetal-herbal-grass notes (pyrazines) and chalky minerality.

**Palate:** Light to medium-bodied with little or no oak typical for Sancerre vs. used or new oak sometimes found in Pouilly-Fumé.

**Structure:** Dry with medium alcohol and medium-plus to high acidity.

**ID keys:** The combination of tart citrus, green pyrazine notes, and chalky minerality are keys to identification. Some wines from Pouilly-Fumé have oak.

## Sauvignon Blanc: New Zealand

**Sight:** Pale to medium straw with green.

**Nose:** Grapefruit and lime citrus, gooseberry, kiwi-passionfruit, and pronounced pyrazinic herbal-vegetal notes.

**Palate:** Medium-bodied with emphasis on ripe and tart fruit and herbal-vegetal notes. No oak.

**Structure:** Dry with medium-plus alcohol and medium-plus acidity.

**ID keys:** Vibrant citrus and tropical fruit combined with predominant green vegetal flavors are the keys to recognizing New Zealand Sauvignon Blanc. Some wines can also offer mineral notes.

## Chenin Blanc: Loire Valley - Vouvray and Savennières

**Sight:** Medium straw to medium yellow for wines with botrytis-affected fruit.

**Nose:** Ripe yellow apple, quince, lemon-lime citrus, floral, chamomile, green tea, spring greens, and pronounced mineral/wet stone. Botrytis notes (stone fruits, honey, and honeysuckle) and SO2 are also sometimes found. Some wines are barrel fermented and briefly aged in used wood.

**Palate:** Vouvray Sec and Savennières are intensely flavored wines that are dry to bone-dry with pronounced minerality. Vouvray Demi-Sec and Doux often have honey and botrytis notes (see Chapter 11) with tart citrus, minerality, and residual sugar.

**Structure:** Bone dry to medium sweet depending on the style with medium to medium-plus alcohol and medium-plus to high acidity.

**ID keys:** Ripe orchard fruit, elevated acidity, sulfur, and possible botrytis notes.

## Chenin Blanc: South Africa - Stellenbosch and Swartland

**Sight:** Deep straw to medium yellow.

**Nose:** Yellow apple and pear with ripe tropical fruit, and sweet and tart citrus. Also floral, lees, and mineral. Oak–used or new–is sometimes found.

**Palate:** Rich, focused, and layered palate with minerality and tart acidity.

**Structure:** Dry with medium-plus to high alcohol and medium-plus to high acidity.

**ID keys:** A richer, more concentrated style of Chenin with ripe and tart fruit, lees, minerality, and tart acidity.

## Chenin Blanc: U.S. - California - Washington State

**Sight:** Pale to medium straw.

**Nose:** A cornucopia of fruit: ripe melon, pear, and tropical with tart and sweet citrus notes. Little, if any, minerality. Oak is infrequently used.

**Palate:** Quality wines have a good balance of ripe fruit and tart acidity.

**Structure:** Off-dry to slightly sweet with medium alcohol and medium-plus acidity.

**ID keys:** A broad range of fruit with the presence of residual sugar and lack of oak influence.

## Albariño: Spain - Rías Baixas

**Sight:** Medium straw with green.

**Nose:** Fruit includes white peach, red apple, mandarin-orange, and lime-citrus with notes of citrus blossom, light herb, lees, and wet stone. Wood is infrequently used.

**Palate:** Medium-bodied with ripe-tart fruit, lees, and wet stone.

**Structure:** Dry with medium to medium-plus alcohol and medium-plus to high acidity.

**ID keys:** Combination of peach, sweet/tart citrus, and slight herbal character with aromas of flowers, beer/hops (lees), and mineral. A colleague once described Albariño as having a "Viognier nose with a Riesling palate."

## Grüner Veltliner: Austria

**Sight:** Pale to medium straw with green. Riper wines (Smaragd) can be deep yellow in color.

**Nose:** Cooler climate wines show tart green apple/pear and tart citrus with white pepper (rotundone) and herbal-vegetal notes (celery, caraway, radish, parsley, and lentils), and mineral. Warmer climate wines offer riper fruit (peach-nectarine and yellow apple) and both sweet and tart citrus as well as white pepper-vegetal and mushroom-earth notes.

**Palate:** Styles range from light and racy to rich, weighty, and grand depending on specific region and classification. Minerality/earth is usually present.

**Structure:** Dry to off-dry depending on the specific style or classification with medium to high alcohol and medium-plus to high acidity.

**ID keys:** The herbal-vegetal-white pepper combination makes Grüner Veltliner unique. In the Wachau classification, Steinfeder wines are lighter in style vs. richer Federspiel wines. Smaragd wines are full-bodied and often display botrytis notes as well as higher alcohol.

## Riesling: Germany

**Sight:** Pale straw to pale yellow with green depending on specific prädikat or vintage. Wines with botrytis are deeper in color.

**Nose:** A wide range of fruit aromas: light-bodied Kabinett wines offer green apple/pear, white peach, and tart citrus. Auslesen commonly display riper fruit including apple, peach, apricot, tropical and sweet citrus as well as botrytis notes of honey and honeysuckle. Slate/mineral is prominent in most of the wines and petrol/TDN notes are often found, especially in older wines (see Chapter 11). No wood is used.

**Palate:** Combination of ripe-tart fruit with elevated acidity, pronounced minerality, and possible TDN.

**Structure:** Dry (trocken) to very sweet depending on the classification with low to medium alcohol and medium-plus to high acidity.

**ID keys:** German Rieslings vary dramatically in style from light, delicate Kabinetts with just a touch of sweetness all the way to noble sweet wines such as Beerenauslesen with considerable botrytis character. Some wines have TDN (see Chapter 11).

## Riesling: France - Alsace

**Sight:** Medium straw with green. Wines with botrytis are deeper in color.

**Nose:** Ripe apple-pear and peach fruit with floral and earth-mineral notes. Wines with botrytis have honey-honeysuckle, saffron, and mushroom. Other wines offer TDN.

**Palate:** Full-bodied with tart acidity and considerable earth and mineral.

**Structure:** Dry to off-dry (some wines are slightly sweet) with medium-plus alcohol and medium-plus to high acidity.

**ID keys:** More ripeness and higher alcohol than most German Rieslings with some wines showing botrytis and TDN.

## Riesling: Australia - Clare Valley and Eden Valley

**Sight:** Pale to medium straw with green.

**Nose:** Tart green apple and lime fruit with floral and pronounced minerality. Many wines show TDN even when young.

**Palate:** Ripe-tart fruit, pronounced mineral, and high acidity.

**Structure:** Very dry with medium alcohol and medium-plus to high acidity.

**ID keys:** Laser-focused style with tart fruit, pronounced mineral, elevated acidity, and possible TDN.

## Pinot Gris: France - Alsace

**Sight:** Deep straw to medium yellow with possible rose/copper secondary color from possible skin contact.

**Nose:** Ripe, smoky yellow apple and melon with sweet-tart citrus, floral, and earth-mineral. Some wines show botrytis notes.

**Palate:** Medium-plus to full-bodied with ripe fruit and earthiness. Some wines have residual sugar.

**Structure:** Dry to off-dry with medium-plus to high alcohol, medium to medium-plus acidity, and phenolic bitterness on the finish.

**ID keys:** Full-bodied and off-dry with rich, smoky pear-melon fruit, earthiness, and phenolics.

## Pinot Grigio: Italy - Alto Adige

**Sight:** Pale to medium straw with green and a possible hint of rose-copper.

**Nose:** Tart apple, green pear, lemon-lime citrus, floral, lees, and mineral.

**Palate:** Medium-bodied with tart fruit, lees, and mineral.

**Structure:** Dry with medium alcohol and medium-plus acidity with a hint of phenolic bitterness on the finish.

**ID keys:** Tart fruit, delicate floral, lees, and mineral notes.

## Viognier: France - Northern Rhône

**Sight:** Medium straw to pale yellow with green.

**Nose:** Floral, stone fruit (apricot, peach, and nectarine), possible ML notes, lees, and mineral. Some wines are oak-aged.

**Palate:** Medium-to full-bodied with ripe and tart fruit, floral, and mineral.

**Structure:** Dry with medium to medium-plus alcohol, medium-plus acidity, and phenolic bitterness.

**ID keys:** Combination of floral, ripe stone fruit, lees, and minerality. Some wines display ML and new oak notes.

### Viognier: California - Australia

**Sight:** Medium straw to medium yellow.

**Nose:** Ripe stone fruit (apricot, peach, and nectarine), tropical fruit (pineapple and mango), and sweet-tart citrus with honey and pronounced floral notes. New oak is often used and lees and malolactic notes are often present.

**Palate:** Ripe fruit with lees, ML, and phenolic bitterness on the finish.

**Structure:** Dry to off-dry with medium-plus to high alcohol, medium-plus acidity, and phenolic bitterness.

**ID keys:** Some wines are Chardonnay-like with lees, ML notes, and the use of new oak. However, the floral-terpenic qualities and phenolic bitterness set Viognier apart from Chardonnay.

### Gewürztraminer: France - Alsace

**Sight:** Medium straw to medium yellow with green.

**Nose:** Exotic, highly perfumed nose of ripe stone fruit, lychee, sweet citrus, pronounced floral (rose petal and jasmine), and earth-mineral. Botrytis notes are common. Wood is rarely used.

**Palate:** Medium-plus to full-bodied with many of the wines having a texture that can be described as rich, viscous, and even oily.

**Structure:** Dry to off-dry (even slightly sweet) with medium-plus to high alcohol, medium-minus to medium acidity, and pronounced phenolic bitterness.

**ID keys:** Alsace Gewürztraminer is unmistakably flamboyant with its exotically perfumed floral nose, succulent off-dry fruit, and lower acidity. Some wines may also show botrytis notes.

## Muscat à Petits Grains: France - Alsace

**Sight:** Medium straw to medium yellow with green.

**Nose:** Pronounced floral with honeysuckle, rose, orange blossom, and elderflower. Fruit includes ripe citrus (orange and tangerine), ripe yellow apple, peach-apricot, and tropical fruit (pineapple and mango). Also, lychee, ginger, slight herbal-vegetal notes, and mushroom-earth.

**Palate:** Medium to full-bodied with ripe fruit, floral, and earth.

**Structure:** Dry with medium-plus to high alcohol, medium-plus acidity, and considerable phenolic bitterness.

**ID keys:** Similar to Alsace Gewürztraminer but often with higher acidity.

## Torrontés: Argentina - Salta

**Sight:** Medium to deep straw with green.

**Nose:** Ripe tropical fruit (pineapple, guava, papaya), sweet citrus (orange and Meyer lemon), and stone fruit (peach) with pronounced floral qualities (citrus blossoms, rose, jasmine, and geranium). Pine and cilantro notes are common and oak is rarely used.

**Palate:** Floral, almost soapy palate with forward fruit.

Structure: Dry with medium-plus alcohol, medium to medium-plus acidity, and phenolic bitterness.

**ID keys:** Torrontés is a fully aromatic grape that is intensely floral and even soapy on the palate. The abundance of fruit and lack of mineral qualities should take one to the New World.

### Marsanne-Roussanne Blend: France - Rhône Valley

**Sight:** Pale to medium yellow with green.

**Nose:** Ripe apricot and peach, yellow apple and quince, and citrus with lees, buttery ML notes, stony mineral, and possible nutty oxidative notes from oak-aging.

**Palate:** Full-bodied with ripe stone fruit and tree fruit, and pronounced mineral.

**Structure:** Dry with medium-plus to high alcohol, medium acidity, and phenolic bitterness.

**ID keys:** There are two general styles of Marsanne-Roussanne blends: one is fermented in stainless steel and fresher and lighter. The other style sees extended time in wood and tends to have a deeper color, riper fruit, and an oxidative character. Wood-aged wines also tend to have elevated alcohol.

### Sémillon Blend: France - Bordeaux - Pessac-Léognan Blanc

**Sight:** Medium straw to medium yellow with green.

**Nose:** Red and yellow apple, ripe pear, white fig, and tart citrus with notes of floral, wax-lanolin, and earth. Some wines are blended with a lesser percentage of Sauvignon Blanc and oak-aged. Other wines show a slight sulfur-like mercaptan note (see Chapter 10).

**Palate:** Medium-bodied with ripe-tart fruit, green herb, and waxy notes.

**Structure:** Dry with medium alcohol, medium-plus acidity, and phenolic bitterness.

**ID keys:** Waxy texture, mercaptan note, and herbal notes.

## Sémillon: France - Bordeaux - Sauternes and Barsac

**Sight:** Medium yellow to deep gold with green.

**Nose:** Botrytis notes (honey, ripe stone fruit, saffron, mushroom), earth-mineral, and oak spice notes.

**Palate:** Ripe and succulent fruit with botrytis character and oak influence.

**Structure:** Medium sweet to dessert sweet with medium-plus alcohol and medium-plus acidity.

**ID keys:** Sauternes and wines from satellite communes (Barsac, etc.) are one of the few classic botrytis dessert wines that commonly show oak influence.

## Semillon: Australia - Hunter Valley

**Sight:** Pale straw green or yellow gold depending on the style of the wine.

**Nose:** There are two distinct styles of Hunter Semillon: traditional wines that are oak-aged for long periods of time and show considerable oxidation. These wines offer baked fruits, butterscotch, sweet spices, vanilla custard, and oak. Lighter styled wines are produced from earlier-harvested fruit, stainless steel-fermented, and show bright lemon-lime citrus, tart apple, and floral notes.

**Palate:** Oak-aged wines are rich, full-bodied, and oxidative. Non-oaked wines are lighter-bodied and very tart.

**Structure:** Dry in style. Oak-aged wines are slightly fuller-bodied with medium-plus alcohol and medium-plus acidity. Stainless wines are medium-bodied with medium-minus alcohol and high acidity.

**ID keys:** Oak-aged wines show considerable oxidation and wood character. Stainless steel wines have lower alcohol, high acidity, and a narrower fruit profile.

## Melon de Bourgogne: France - Loire Valley - Muscadet

**Sight:** Pale straw with green.

**Nose:** Green apple and pear, white peach, and lemon-lime citrus with white floral, green botanical notes, lees, and saline-mineral.

**Palate:** Medium-bodied with tart fruit, lees, and mineral.

**Structure:** Dry with medium alcohol and medium-plus to high acidity.

**ID keys:** Lees contact and saline quality with elevated acidity.

## Assyrtiko: Greece - Santorini

**Sight:** Medium straw to medium yellow.

**Nose:** Yellow apple, peach, and lemon-lime with dried citrus blossoms, lees, and pronounced volcanic minerality. Wines with age can show TDN.

**Palate:** Ripe and tart fruit with pronounced mineral and tart acidity.

**Structure:** Dry with medium-plus to high alcohol and medium-plus to high acidity. The wines also tend to be phenolic.

**ID keys:** Combination of ripe fruit and tart acidity with pronounced minerality and phenolic bitterness.

*Author's suggestions: Having a list of markers for classic wines can be incredibly useful. However, I think that each grape variety/wine speaks a slightly different language to every individual. Thus, I strongly believe that everyone needs to create their own unique list of markers for the wines.*

# 7

# Markers for Classic Red Wines

*Author's note: The following is a list of important markers and common structural levels for classic red wines including important keys for identification. These descriptions will serve as a valuable tool for tasting study and practice.*

### Cabernet Sauvignon Blend: France - Left Bank Bordeaux

**Sight:** Deep ruby.

**Nose:** Black fruit (cherry, currant, and cassis) and red fruit (red currant, cranberry, and sour cherry) with violet, green olive, green herb (pyrazines), cedar, graphite, and earth. Oak aging adds smoke, toast, and baking spice notes.

**Palate:** Medium-to-full-bodied with ripe and tart fruit, green herbal notes, earth, and wood.

**Structure:** Dry with medium-plus alcohol (higher in warmer vintages), medium-plus acidity, and medium-plus to high tannin.

**ID keys:** Concentrated black fruit, pyrazinic notes, earthiness, and firm Cabernet Sauvignon tannins. Earthy, leathery, and Brettanomyces notes can also often be found (see Chapter 10).

### Cabernet Sauvignon: U.S. - California

**Sight:** Deep ruby.

**Nose:** Ripe black fruit (cherry, berry, and plum) with cedar, chocolate, and green herbal notes (pyrazines). Oak aging adds smoke, toast, and baking spices.

**Palate:** Full-bodied and ripe without the prominent earth-mineral component in Left Bank Bordeaux.

**Structure:** Dry with medium-plus to high alcohol, medium to medium-plus acidity, and medium-plus to high tannin.

**ID keys:** Ripe, intense black fruit with herbal notes, new oak, and considerable tannin.

### Cabernet Sauvignon: Australia - Coonawarra and Margaret River

**Sight:** Deep ruby.

**Nose:** Black fruit (berry, cherry, and currant) and tart red fruit (red currant, cranberry, and sour cherry) with possible mint/eucalyptus and pronounced green pyrazine notes. Oak aging adds vanilla, baking spices, and toast.

**Palate:** Full-bodied with ripe fruit and pronounced green qualities.

**Structure:** Medium-plus to high alcohol, medium to medium-plus acidity, and medium-plus to high tannin.

**ID keys:** Coonawarra Cabernet is very distinctive in style with classic Cabernet black fruit and a strong presence of pyrazines, mint, and eucalyptus.

## Merlot Blend: France - Right Bank Bordeaux

**Sight:** Deep ruby.

**Nose:** Ripe black fruit (cherry, berry, and plum) and tart red fruit (red currant, cranberry, and sour cherry) with considerable green herb (pyrazines), violet floral, and earth-mineral. Oak aging adds smoke, sweet spice, and toast notes.

**Palate:** Generally, softer tannins than Cabernet Sauvignon-based blends with more green herbal-vegetal qualities.

**Structure:** Dry with medium-plus alcohol, medium-plus acidity, and medium-plus tannin.

**ID keys:** Ripe and supple with dark fruit, earthy notes, tart acidity, and new oak.

## Merlot: California - Australia

**Sight:** Deep ruby.

**Nose:** Ripe black fruit (cherry, berry, and plum) and tart red fruit (red currant, cranberry, and sour cherry) with green herbs and oak. Mint and eucalyptus can be found in some Australian wines.

**Palate:** Lush and full-bodied with some wines riper than right bank Bordeaux wines.

**Structure:** Dry with medium-plus to high alcohol, medium-plus acidity, and medium-plus tannin.

**ID keys:** Ripe and supple with not as much tannin as Cabernet Sauvignon. Some wines are greener and more pyrazinic than others.

## Cabernet Franc: Loire Valley - Chinon and Bourgueil

**Sight:** Medium to deep ruby.

**Nose:** Tart black fruit (berry and cherry) and red fruit (sour cherry and cranberry) with pronounced herbal-vegetal notes (pyrazines) and chalky mineral-earth. Oak is generally used and sometimes new. Some wines display notes of whole cluster fermentation with forward fruit and stem tannins.

**Palate:** Medium-bodied with pronounced herbal quality and chalky minerality.

**Structure:** Dry with medium to medium-plus alcohol, medium-plus acidity, and medium to medium-plus tannin.

**ID keys:** Combination of tart fruit, pronounced pyrazines, and chalky minerality. Stem tannin may also be present.

## Malbec: Argentina - Mendoza

**Sight:** Deep purple.

**Nose:** Ripe black fruit (cherry, berry, and plum), blueberry, and secondary tart red fruit (sour cherry and cranberry) with violet-floral, green herb, and oak. Some wines display an earthy character and most offer notes of oak aging.

**Palate:** Medium-plus to full-bodied with ripe dark fruit and tart red fruit.

**Structure:** Dry with medium-plus to high alcohol, medium-plus acidity, medium-plus tannin.

**ID keys:** Opaque purple color with ripe blue, black, and tart red fruit with fewer secondary aromas and flavors. Some wines also display floral notes.

## Carménère: Chile

**Sight:** Deep ruby with purple.

**Nose:** Ripe black fruit (cassis, berry, cherry, and plum), violet floral, pronounced pyrazines (green bell pepper, green peppercorn, and herb), and oak.

**Palate:** Medium to full-bodied with concentrated dark fruit and pronounced green pyrazinic qualities.

**Structure:** Dry with medium-plus to high alcohol, medium-plus acidity, and medium to medium-plus tannin.

**ID keys:** Carménère is similar to Merlot with its supple fruit character but the vegetal-pyrazinic-green peppercorn qualities make it unique.

## Pinot Noir: France - Burgundy - Côte de Nuits

**Sight:** Medium ruby.

**Nose:** Red fruit (cherry, raspberry, and strawberry), with rose floral, tea-herb, and mushroom-earth. Oak aging adds smoke, sweet spice, and wood flavors. Wines take on gamy-earthy complexity with age.

**Palate:** Medium-bodied with ripe and tart red fruit.

**Structure:** Dry with medium alcohol, medium-plus acidity, and medium tannin.

**ID keys:** Pinot Noir is the most complex of the red-fruit dominant/lighter pigmented red wines, and red Burgundy can be the most complex of all. Stem inclusion sometimes used during winemaking adds green stem tannin.

## Pinot Noir: France – Burgundy - Côte de Beaune

**Sight:** Medium ruby.

**Nose:** Tart or ripe red fruit depending on the quality of the vintage. Cherry, raspberry, and cranberry are common. Non-fruit aromas include green herb, black tea, rose floral, and clay-earth-mineral notes. As with wines from the Côte de Nuits, age can add complex layers of gamey and savory-vegetal-earthy notes. Oak aging adds aromas of vanilla, baking spices, and toast.

**Palate:** Medium-bodied with red fruit and earthy complexity. Stem inclusion is sometimes used during winemaking adding green stem tannins.

**Structure:** Dry with medium to medium-plus alcohol, medium-plus acidity, and medium to medium-plus tannin.

**ID keys:** Generally, compared to the Côte de Nuits, wines from the Côte de Beaune can seem earthier with less firm tannins. There are always exceptions.

## Pinot Noir: U.S. - California

**Sight:** Medium to deep ruby.

**Nose:** Tart red fruit (ripe red and black fruits in warm vintages or regions) with herb, floral, tea, and more. Oak aging adds smoke, sweet spice, and wood flavors.

**Palate:** Medium to medium-plus bodied with ripe and tart fruit.

**Structure:** Dry with medium to medium-plus alcohol, medium-plus acidity, and medium to medium-plus tannin.

**ID keys:** The style of California Pinot Noir varies considerably with different climates. Wines from cool climate regions, such as West Sonoma Coast, show tart red fruit, herbal notes, restrained alcohol, and elevated acidity. Wines from warmer climates like the Santa Lucia Highlands offer riper red and dark fruit with higher alcohol. Regardless, stem tannins are sometimes present due to whole cluster fermentation.

### Pinot Noir: U.S. - Oregon - Willamette Valley

**Sight:** Medium to deep ruby.

**Nose:** Red fruit (with darker fruit in warmer vintages) with herbal, floral, tea, earth, and notes of oak aging.

**Palate:** Medium to medium-plus bodied and with ripe and tart fruit, herbs, earth, and wood.

**Structure:** Dry with medium to medium-plus alcohol, medium-plus acidity, and medium to medium-plus tannin.

**ID keys:** Vintage variation is an important factor with Oregon Pinot Noir as well as a broad range of micro-climates and soil types. Generally, the wines frequently display more herbal and earthy notes compared to their California counterparts.

### Pinot Noir: New Zealand

**Sight:** Medium ruby

**Nose:** Red fruit with herb, floral, tea, and mineral-earth. Oak aging adds smoke and sweet spice notes.

**Palate:** Medium to medium-plus bodied with ripe and tart fruit.

**Structure:** Dry with medium to medium-plus alcohol, medium to medium-plus acidity, and medium to medium-plus tannin.

**ID keys:** New Zealand Pinots are similar in style to California and Oregon with ripe and tart red fruit, spices, and new wood qualities. Some wines are distinctly herbal while others display minerality.

### Gamay: France – Beaujolais-Villages

**Sight:** Medium ruby with purple.

**Nose:** Notes of carbonic maceration (see Chapter 11) including candied fruit, banana, and fruit punch with green stem notes and stony mineral. No oak.

**Palate:** Tart candied fruit, green stemmy quality, and minerality.

**Structure:** Dry with medium alcohol, medium-plus acidity, and medium-minus to medium tannin.

**ID keys:** Carbonic maceration notes, mineral, and tart fruit qualities.

### Gamay: France – Beaujolais Cru

**Sight:** Medium to deep ruby.

**Nose:** Dark and red fruit with floral, green herb, and stone-mineral. Used oak is often found.

**Palate:** More depth and a broader range of fruit than Beaujolais-Villages with less carbonic notes–or none at all.

**Structure:** Dry with medium to medium-plus alcohol, medium-plus acidity, and medium to medium-plus tannin.

**ID keys:** Wines range in style from Fleurie, which tends to be more floral, fruit-forward, and softer, to wines from Moulin-a-Vent that tend to be more concentrated with darker fruit, savory, and earth notes with firmer tannin. Carbonic aromas and flavors are not always found.

### Sangiovese: Italy – Tuscany – Chianti Classico

**Sight:** Medium to deep ruby.

**Nose:** Tart red fruit (cherry, cranberry, and pomegranate) with anise, tomato leaf, green herb, sandalwood, chalky earth, and wood. Darker fruit can be found in warmer vintages.

**Palate:** Medium-plus to full-bodied with tart red fruit and herbal notes.

**Structure:** Dry with medium plus alcohol, medium-plus to high acidity, and medium-plus tannins.

**ID keys:** Tart red fruit, anise, tomato leaf-herb, chalky earth, and both grape and oak tannins.

## Sangiovese: Italy – Tuscany – Brunello di Montalcino

**Sight:** Deep ruby with garnet.

**Nose:** Ripe and tart dark (cherry and plum) and red fruit (cherry, cranberry, and pomegranate) with dried herb, sandalwood, leather, earth, and wood. Some wines display a chalky mineral quality. Others wines show considerable oak influence from barrique aging.

**Palate:** Full-bodied with ripe, tart, and dried fruit, dried herb, earth, and wood.

**ID keys:** By law, Brunello di Montalcino must be made from 100% Sangiovese Grosso. Generally, the wines tend to be more evolved on release than a typical Chianti Classico or Vino Nobile due to aging requirements. Some wines are aged in barrique and show more new oak character while other wines are aged in larger cooperage.

## Sangiovese: Italy – Tuscany – Vino Nobile di Montepulciano

**Sight:** Medium to deep ruby.

**Nose:** Ripe and tart dark (cherry and plum) and red fruit (cherry, cranberry, and pomegranate) with anise, tomato leaf, green herb, sandalwood, earth, and wood.

**Palate:** Medium-plus to full-bodied with ripe and tart black and red fruit, herbal notes, and earth.

**Structure:** Dry with medium to medium-plus alcohol, medium-plus to high acidity, and medium-plus tannin.

**ID keys:** Wines from Vino Nobile di Montepulciano can be made from up to 30% other grape varieties and thus often display more dark fruit characteristics as well as new oak influence.

## Nebbiolo: Italy - Piedmont - Barolo and Barbaresco

**Sight:** Medium ruby-garnet with considerable rim variation and evolved color at the rim even when the wines are young.

**Nose:** Tart and dried red fruit (cherry, cranberry), rose petal floral, tar, anise-herb-vegetal, earth-forest floor, and wood. Darker fruit can be found in warmer vintages.

**Palate:** Medium-plus body with a very dominant structure.

**Structure:** Dry to bone dry with medium-plus to high alcohol, high acidity, and high tannin.

**ID keys:** The combination of evolved color and secondary colors (orange at the rim), high acidity, and high tannin make Nebbiolo-based wines fairly easy to recognize. Also, look for the dried fruit and floral qualities. Some wines are bone dry, austere, and very tannic even when young.

## Barbera: Italy - Piedmont

**Sight:** Medium to deep ruby with purple.

**Nose:** Blackberry, sour red cherry, and red raspberry with floral, tea-herb, and earth. Oak aging is sometimes used.

**Palate:** Medium body with ripe and tart fruit, herbal notes, and earth character.

**Structure:** Dry with medium-plus alcohol, medium-plus acidity, and medium to medium-plus tannin.

**ID keys:** The style of Barbera ranges from old-school wines in a more oxidative style that are aged in large used barrels to a newer fruit-forward style fermented in stainless steel. Some wines are also aged in barrique and show more new oak influence.

## Corvina Blend: Italy - Veneto - Amarone

**Sight:** Deep ruby with garnet often found at the rim.

**Nose:** Ripe, jammy, and raisinated dark and red fruits (from passito or dried grapes) with possible botrytis notes (stone fruit), dried floral, chocolate, tar-resin, game, earth, and oak. Volatile acidity and Brettanomyces are sometimes found (see Chapter 11).

**Palate:** Full-bodied with raisinated character sometimes found.

**Structure:** Dry to off-dry with high alcohol, medium-plus acidity, and medium-plus to high tannin.

**ID keys:** Powerful and concentrated with raisinated character and earthy qualities. VA and botrytis notes are common markers.

## Aglianico: Italy - Campania

**Sight:** Deep ruby.

**Nose:** Ripe and baked black fruit (cherry, berry, and plum) with dried floral, dried herb, pronounced stone-mineral, and wood. Wines sometimes display volatile acidity.

**Palate:** Concentrated, powerful, mineral-driven, and tannic.

**Structure:** Dry with high alcohol, medium-plus acidity, and medium-plus to high tannin.

**ID keys:** Deep color and baked fruit quality with pronounced mineral notes and high tannin.

### Tempranillo: Spain - Rioja Reserva and Gran Reserva

**Sight:** Medium ruby to medium garnet depending on the style and age of the wine.

**Nose:** Traditional wines offer dried red fruit (cherry and cranberry), dried herb, dusty earth, and American oak (dill-dried herb, vanillin, sweet spice, sawdust).

**Palate:** Medium to full-bodied with oxidative character.

**Structure:** Dry with medium-plus alcohol, medium-plus acidity, and medium to medium-plus tannins.

**ID keys:** Traditional Rioja combines dried red fruit, leather, earth, and notes of American oak aging. Gran Reserva wines will show more oxidative character in every aspect of the wine, from the color to the fruit quality to the finish. It's important to note that more producers are now using French oak or a combination of French and American oak.

### Zinfandel: U.S. - California - Dry Creek Valley

**Sight:** Medium to deep ruby.

**Nose:** A range of tart to ripe and even raisinated fruit depending on the timing of the harvest and also due to the grape's tendency to ripen unevenly. Black and white pepper is commonly found along with bramble-briar-herb, sweet spice, and oak. Some wines offer peach, apricot, and yogurt notes.

**Palate:** Medium-plus to full-bodied and fruit dominant with spice character.

**Structure:** Dry with medium-plus to high alcohol, medium to medium-plus acidity, and medium to medium-plus tannins.

**ID keys:** The tendency for Zinfandel to sometimes ripen unevenly may be a key. Some wines will show both raisiny and under-ripe fruit. But generally Zinfandel tends to have ripe fruit and pepper-spice qualities.

## Syrah: France - Northern Rhône

**Sight:** Deep ruby with purple.

**Nose:** Ripe and tart black fruit (berry and cherry) and tart red fruit (sour cherry and cranberry) with white and/or black pepper, floral, savory herb, smoke, game-dried meat, stony mineral-earth, and wood.

**Palate:** Medium-plus to full-bodied with a broad range of fruit, savory herb, game, and spice notes.

**Structure:** Dry with medium to medium-plus alcohol, medium-plus acidity, and medium to high tannins depending on the specific appellation and wine.

**ID keys:** Range of fruit qualities, pepper, sanguine notes, and stony earthiness.

## Syrah: Australia - Barossa Shiraz

**Sight:** Opaque ruby with purple.

**Nose:** Combination of ripe black fruit, tart red fruit, and raisinated fruit with black pepper, herb, mint/eucalyptus, sweet spice, leather, and oak. American oak has been traditionally used offering pronounced vanilla, baking spices, and sawdust. More wineries are now using French oak.

**Palate:** Full-bodied and fruit-dominant with pepper-spice, mint/eucalyptus, and herbal notes.

**Structure:** Dry with high alcohol, medium to medium-plus acidity, and medium-plus tannin.

**ID keys:** Combination of ripe and raisinated fruit with pepper, herbs, mint, leather, and possible American oak notes.

## Grenache Blend: France - Southern Rhône

**Sight:** Medium to deep ruby.

**Nose:** Ripe (sometimes baked) red and black fruit with wild savory herbs (garrigue), black pepper, game notes, stony earth, and wood.

**Palate:** Full-bodied, concentrated, and sometimes powerful.

**Structure:** Dry with high alcohol, medium-plus acidity, and medium-plus to high tannin.

**ID keys:** Châteauneuf-du-Pape and Gigondas combine ripe-baked red and black fruit, pepper, garrigue, stony earth, high alcohol, and considerable tannin. Lighter wines such as Côte du Rhone are fruitier and sometimes made using carbonic maceration.

## Grenache: Australia - Barossa

**Sight:** Medium to deep ruby.

**Nose:** Ripe, jammy red and black fruit with pepper-spice, mint-eucalyptus, and oak.

**Palate:** Full-bodied, fruit-forward, and minty.

**Structure:** Dry with high alcohol, medium to medium-plus acidity, and medium-plus tannin.

**ID keys:** Jammy red fruit, pepper, mint-eucalyptus notes, and high alcohol.

## Mourvèdre: France - Provence - Bandol

**Sight:** Deep ruby.

**Nose:** Ripe black fruit, savory herb, pronounced earth, and wood.

**Palate:** Full-bodied and tannic.

**Structure:** Dry with medium-plus to high alcohol, medium-plus acidity, and medium-plus to high tannin.

**ID keys:** Concentrated dark fruit, savory herb, earthy-reductive notes, and high tannin.

## Monastrell (Mourvèdre): Spain – Jumilla

**Sight:** Opaque ruby purple.

**Nose:** Ripe even jammy black fruit (berry, cherry, and plum) and dried fruit (fig, date, and prune), with savory herbs, pepper-spice, dusty earth, and vanilla-oak notes.

**Palate:** Full-bodied with ripe-raisinated fruit and earth.

**Structure:** Dry with medium-plus to high alcohol, medium to medium-plus acidity, and medium-plus tannin.

**ID keys:** Monastrell from Jumilla combines jammy-raisinated fruits, savory herb, and mineral-earth, but the wines are generally not as tannic as those from Bandol.

## Carignan: Southern France

**Sight:** Medium to deep ruby.

**Nose:** Ripe and tart red fruit (cherry, raspberry, and cranberry) with green herb, black pepper, star anise, smoke, game/cured meat, and earth/mineral. Oak aging adds toast and spice notes.

**Palate:** Medium to full-bodied with a combination of ripe-tart fruit, smoked meat character, and earthiness.

**Structure:** Dry with medium-plus to high alcohol, medium-plus acidity, and medium-plus tannin.

**ID keys:** Ripe and tart red fruit with pronounced meaty/savory quality.

## Pinotage: South Africa

**Sight:** Medium to deep ruby.

**Nose:** Ripe blackberry, plum, and tart cranberry with green pepper, peppercorn, green herb, sanguine, and medicinal notes. Oak aging adds toast and spice notes. Some wines are earthy and reductive in character.

**Palate:** Medium to full-bodied with a combination of ripe-tart fruit, green character, sanguine notes, and earthiness.

**Structure:** Dry with medium to medium-plus alcohol, medium to medium-plus acidity, and medium to medium-plus tannin.

**ID keys:** Ripe and tart fruit with peppery, sanguine, reductive, and earthy notes.

*Author's suggestions: Once again, having a list of markers for classic wines can be incredibly useful. However, I think that every variety/wine speaks a slightly different language to each individual. Thus, I strongly believe that everyone needs to create their own unique list of markers for each grape and wine.*

# PART II

# Advanced Skills

## Introduction

*Welcome to Part II. In the previous chapters, I covered the basics any student needs to learn at the beginning of their wine education. In Part II, I introduce a number of advanced concepts that are required of any professional taster. In particular, the concepts of Cause and Effect, impact compounds, and fruit quality are "must haves" for anyone seeking a career in wine. As before, there is a great deal of information in the following chapters that will take time, practice, and repetition to learn. Remember to have patience with the process.*

## Part II Chapter Guide

*Chapter 8: Cause and Effect*
The concept of Cause and Effect and how it applies to all aspects of the deductive grid.

*Chapter 9: Fruit groups and fruit quality*
A breakdown of fruit groups for white and red wines as well as categories of fruit quality.

*Chapter 10: Wine faults and context*
A basic primer of common wine faults includes discussion of how context is important when assessing faults and wine quality.

*Chapter 11: Impact compounds*
A list and descriptions for the subset of the most important aromas and flavors with corresponding grape varieties.

*Chapter 12: Confronting the evil dwarves*
Easily confused white and red wines and how to tell them apart.

*Chapter 13: The impact of bottle aging on wine*
A primer of the effects of aging on wine including A/B comparisons of young vs. aged versions of classic wines.

*Chapter 14: On judging wine quality*
All the factors that go into judging wine quality as a professional.

*Chapter 15: Objective vs. subjective in tasting*
Noting which aspects of the deductive grid are objective, subjective, or a combination of the two.

*Chapter 16: Using pattern recognition for blind tasting white wines*
How to use a subset of the most essential markers and structural levels to help identify classic white wines when blind tasting.

*Chapter 17: Using pattern recognition for blind tasting red wines*
How to use a subset of the most critical markers and structural levels to help identify classic red wines when blind tasting.

*Chapter 18: On tasting notes*
A breakdown of what's needed for a tasting note template. Includes my personal tasting note template.

*Chapter 19: A tech sheet manifesto*
A breakdown of what's needed for a good industry tech/fact sheet.

*Chapter 20: Suggested producers for tasting practice*
A list of producers for classic white and red wines that can be used for tastings and exam practice.

8

# Cause and Effect

*Author's note: Cause and Effect is one of the most important concepts for any wine student to learn. In fact, I think it's an absolute prerequisite to becoming a competent professional taster. Knowing the "why" behind the way a wine looks, smells, and tastes is also a vital key to understanding typicity and quality.*

Anyone who's had the pleasure of entertaining a three-year-old for any length of time knows the exquisite torture that can be inflicted by even the sweetest toddler in the form of an endless series of "why" questions. One's patience can only be tested for so long before the inevitable and curt *"because I said so"* puts an end to it. Beyond random acts of parenting, why questions have always seemed problematic to me because they potentially create endless loop communication. Why? Because at some point there may not be a reason why.

"Why" questions, however, are valuable in the context of deductive tasting. They speak to the concept of Cause and Effect in regards to why a wine looks, smells, and tastes the way it does. Cause and Effect relationships are also useful for the student learning about classic wines in tasting practice, especially the deductive-thinking part. With that, here are potential Cause-Effect relationships for all the criteria in the deductive tasting grid.

## Sight

As stated before, sight is the most overlooked aspect of tasting. It's also true with Cause and Effect. With experience, a quick look at a glass of wine — especially red wine — can and should quickly build multiple expectations on the part of the taster when considering the general age of the wine, possible grape variety, fruit profile, structural levels, and the possible use of oak. Here is the sight portion of the grid broken down into Cause and Effect elements.

**Clarity:** Is the result of how much, if any, fining and filtration a wine undergoes before bottling, or the solids in the wine having settled to the bottom of the barrel/tank naturally over a period of time. The clarity scale ranges from a cloudy wine that's completely unfined and unfiltered to a pristinely clear wine that's put through considerable fining and filtration–and everything in between.

**Brightness:** Brightness in wine—especially noted in white wines—can be a function of clarity which again is a direct result of the degree of fining and filtering. Brightness in reds largely depends on the depth of pigmentation with various grape varieties as well as fining and filtration. Wines made from thinner-skinned, lighter-pigmented grapes such as Pinot Noir and Gamay will reflect more light in the glass than wines made from Syrah or Cabernet Sauvignon.

**Intensity of color:** In white wines, the depth and intensity of the color is usually the result of the age or level of oxidation in the wine due to time in barrel and/or bottle. Botrytis-affected fruit may also play a role in a more deeply colored white wine as will extended skin contact either prior to, during, or post-fermentation. With red wines, the intensity of the color is largely due to the depth of pigmentation in a specific grape variety and likewise the age and oxidation of the wine.

**Color:** The base color of a white wine — be it straw, yellow, gold, or brown — is largely determined by the age, degree of oxidation due to winemaking, or time spent in a barrel or bottle. Skin contact and the presence of botrytis can also contribute to a deeper color. In red wines, the primary color—purple, ruby (red), or garnet (reddish-brown) — is again determined by the depth of pigmentation found in the specific grape (Pinot Noir vs. Syrah) and the age and/or level of oxidation in the wine.

**Secondary colors:** In white wines, the color green can signify either youth and/or a wine produced from grapes grown in a cooler climate. Platinum, silver, and unpolished brass often accompany the color green in a young white wine. In red wines, secondary colors usually refer to rim variation or the difference in color between the core of the glass and the edge/rim of the glass (see below).

**Rim variation:** As just described, rim variation (not significant for white wines) is a term used to denote the color differentiation in red wine between wine in the center/core of the glass and wine at the edge/rim. The cause has to do with the amount of pigmentation in the specific grape, the climate of origin, the ripeness level of fruit at harvest, and the age/level of oxidation in the wine. Generally, the older the wine, the more rim variation and the more evolved the color at the edge or rim of the glass. Conversely, a young wine from a deeply pigmented grape might maintain a consistent color right up to the rim with the transition in color more abrupt.

**Gas:** $CO_2$ bubbles in a wine can be a by-product of primary fermentation, malolactic fermentation/conversion, or from $CO_2$ added as a preservative at the time of bottling.

**Sediment:** Sediment in a glass of red wine is due to either age (pigments and tannins precipitating out of solution) or non-filtration in the case of a younger red wine. Tartrates, or tartaric acid crystals, in either white or red wine, are the result of the wine not having been cold stabilized or having been minimally fined and filtered.

**Tears/legs:** Tears/legs in a glass of wine are a first indication of the possible levels of alcohol and/or the presence of residual sugar. Thin, quickly moving tears often point to a lower alcohol level and the lack of residual sugar in the wine. By contrast, thick and slowly moving tears are associated with higher levels of alcohol and possible residual sugar.

It's important to note that legs and tears in a glass of wine are an indication and not a rule. To begin, the glassware has to be clean and well-polished, or the assessment is inaccurate. However, there is science behind the phenomenon of tears/legs in a glass of wine. It's called the "Marangoni Effect" and is derived from temperature variation in the wine within different parts of the glass combined with surface tension.

**Staining:** In a red wine is the result of the depth of pigmentation in the specific variety as well as elevated levels of dry extract in the wine (dissolved solids in solution). Dry extract is further related to lower yields, the age of vines, and the degree of fining and filtration.

## Nose

The aromas in a wine are derived from a myriad of influences including the specific grape variety, the climate of origin, harvest timing, and winemaking practices. Here is the nose portion of the grid broken down into Cause and Effect elements.

**Clean/faults:** Does the wine smell clean and well-made or does it contain one or more common wine faults? These faults include TCA (from faulty corks or contaminated tanks or barrels), high VA or volatile acidity (fermentation issues); Brettanomyces or Brett (vineyard, barrel, or winery hygiene issues); sulfur compounds including H2S or mercaptan (fermentation issues), or excess SO2 added at the time of bottling (see Chapter 10 for more information on wine faults).

🍷 *It's important to note that with the exception of TCA, the context of practically every so-called fault has to be considered. For example, certain European wines such as a Northern Rhône Syrah often show noticeable levels of Brett-which is then not considered a fault. However, the same level of Brett in a Napa Valley Cabernet Sauvignon would be considered a fault. Context, as always, is important.*

**Intensity of aroma:** The overall intensity of aroma can be related to the specific grape variety, the climate of origin (ripeness level), structural elements (high alcohol), and winemaking influence in the form of ML, oak usage, and more.

**Age assessment:** In any wine, a youthful vs. evolving vs. vinous character is due to the age of the wine, oxidative winemaking, or extended wood or bottle aging.

**Fruit:** Specific kinds of fruit in wine are derived from aromatic compounds naturally found in specific grapes as well as the result of fermentation. The degree of ripeness or condition of the grape at harvest (botrytis) can also play a part.

**Fruit quality:** The quality of the fruit (i.e., tart, ripe, or jammy) is the result of the climate of origin, specific vintage (warm year, etc.), harvest timing (late harvest, passito, etc.), and the overall age and level of oxidation in the wine.

**Non-fruit:** Is derived from aromatic compounds found in the specific grape, the condition of the grape at harvest (botrytis), and the winemaking process. Common non-fruit aromas include floral, herbal, and spice notes. It's important to note that many so-called impact compounds (see Chapter 11), which are important markers for classic wines, are found in the non-fruit category.

**Earth:** The presence of inorganic and organic earth notes in wine is thought to be from the microbiome in a given vineyard soil, and how specific strains of bacteria and ambient yeast populations influence fermentation. The role that micro-flora/fauna and yeast populations found in vineyard soil play in fermentation is still being researched.

**Mineral:** Same as above with the origin, specific soil type, and micro-organic life found in the vineyard where the grapes were grown. The presence of Brettanomyces and/or Dekkora from the vineyard or the winery environment should also be considered as a possible cause of earthiness.

**Wood:** The use of oak during the winemaking process for fermentation and aging lends a wide range of aromas from vanilla (vanillin) to brown spices, coffee, tea, chocolate, toast, smoke, dill, and more. The age, size, and type of barrel all play an important role in the intensity of wood influence in the finished wine.

## Palate

As previously stated, tasting in the context of using the deductive grid has two purposes: To confirm what has already been smelled and to determine the level of structural elements in wine including acidity, alcohol, phenolic bitterness, and tannin (if a red wine). Here is the palate portion of the grid broken down into the elements of Cause and Effect.

**Dry/sweetness:** Wine is either fermented dry or contains varying amounts of residual sugar due to the fermentation being stopped by sterile filtration, the addition of SO2 (sulfur dioxide), or fortification.

**Body:** Is determined by a number of factors including the level of alcohol, presence of residual sugar, or level of dry extract (particulate matter in solution). The latter is further determined by the quality of fruit and the degree of fining and filtration used during the winemaking process.

**Fruit:** Specific kinds of fruit tasted in a wine are derived from esters and other aromatic compounds naturally found in the grape(s) or from fermentation. The condition of the grape at harvest (botrytis) can also play a part.

**Fruit quality:** Often changes from nose to palate and is again determined by the ripeness level of fruit at harvest, the specific vintage (warm year, etc.), harvest timing (late harvest, passito, etc.), and the overall age or level of oxidation in the wine.

**Non-fruit:** From compounds found in the grapes as well as winemaking techniques.

**Earth/mineral:** The origin, specific soil type, and micro-organic life found in the vineyard where the grapes were grown all contribute to mineral and earth qualities on the palate of a wine. The possibility of Brett as a factor for earthiness should also be considered.

**Wood:** Due to the use of oak during fermentation and aging.

**Acidity:** Ripeness of fruit/level of acidity at harvest or the addition of tartaric acid to the fermenting must or the finished wine.

**Alcohol:** Is determined by the ripeness of the fruit at harvest or other means. The alcohol level in a wine can be increased by chaptalization, or adding sugar to the must prior to fermentation. It can also be decreased through various forms of filtration including cross-flow and reverse osmosis.

**Phenolic bitterness:** In white wines is due to the must (or wine) being in contact with the skins before, during, or after fermentation.

**Tannin:** In red wine is derived from grape skins as a result of pre- and post-fermentation maceration as well as the addition of press wine. Oak aging also plays an important role in the tannin level in regards to the duration of time wine is kept in the barrel, the size and type of cask, and the percentage of new vs. used oak. Powdered tannin may also be added at several different points during the fermentation and aging of the wine.

**Texture:** Can be influenced by any number of different factors including the ripeness of the grapes at harvest, the use of oak, and the degree of fining and filtration.

**Length/finish:** The length and quality of the finish are determined by the quality of the fruit combined with the intensity of certain structural components (alcohol, acidity, and tannin) and winemaking practices such as ML, lees contact, and the use of oak.

**Balance:** Is largely a result of harmony among the structural components as well as fruit ripeness.

**Complexity:** Although arguably one of the more subjective aspects of the deductive grid, the degree of complexity in a wine is influenced by the vineyard origin, quality of the fruit, timing of the harvest, and winemaker's skill–or lack thereof.

## Conclusion

After collecting all the evidence seen, smelled, and tasted in the wine, the conclusion is still based on previous memory and experience using if-then logic. Here Cause and Effect still plays a vital role in the deductive thinking required to determine style (Old World vs. New World), grape variety or blend of grapes, the origin of the wine, level of quality, and the specific vintage. Following is the conclusion portion of the grid — both initial and final — broken down into Cause and Effect elements.

**Initial Conclusion**

**Old World/New World:** Is primarily influenced by the specific location of the vineyard. Winemaking techniques such as blending different appellations and/or varieties, high alcohol, excessive oak, and considerable filtration can also play a part in influencing–or obscuring–typical style.

**Climate:** The specific location of the vineyard and given conditions of a specific growing year (cool vs. warm vintage) as they are reflected in the structural levels in the wine.

**Grape variety/blend:** Classic markers for specific grapes/wines with an emphasis on impact compounds such as pyrazines (Cabernet family grapes including Sauvignon Blanc), rotundone (Syrah and Grüner Veltliner), and others.

**Age range:** Determined by the overall degree of oxidation (or lack thereof) perceived in the wine.

**Final Conclusion**

**Grape variety/blend:** From classic markers and other factors perceived in the wine.

**Country, region, appellation (as applicable):** From the specific origin of the wine.

**Quality level:** The balance and typicity of the wine as well as the origin and respective laws if applicable.

**Vintage:** The quality of the wine as related to a vintage character as far as specific attributes (ripeness and structural elements).

*Author's suggestions: Now that you have an explanation of Cause and Effect as it applies to the deductive tasting grid, the next thing you need to do is to memorize the information. As with learning the deductive grid itself, perhaps the easiest way to do that would be to chunk it down into three-to-five bits of information at a time until the entire concept is memorized.*

*From there, I suggest that you be able to explain it to someone who's not in the industry. Sit a friend or family member down and explain the Cause and Effect to them. You don't need a glass of wine in hand to do this- although it might help things. I have to again mention the famous physicist, Richard Feynman, who said that if you can't explain something to an eight year-old you really don't understand it yourself. I completely agree.*

# 9

# Fruit Groups and Fruit Quality

*Author's note: This chapter deals with assessing fruit and fruit quality when smelling and tasting wine. To me, assessing the specific kinds of fruit in a glass of wine are important only in passing as they can be so subjective. However, assessing the quality of the fruit — be it tart, ripe, or whatever — is important because it is directly related to the concept of Cause and Effect (see the previous chapter) and connected to criteria like harvest timing, the climate of origin for the grapes, and the structural elements of the wine.*

Assessing fruit in wine could be the single most subjective aspect there is to tasting. That's because fruit aromas/flavors anyone recognizes in wine are based on their unique life memories. This means that in a given wine my lemon could easily be your lime, and my grapefruit your kumquat. So it's not the individual fruits per se that are important, but the categories of fruit that can and should be linked to other factors that help make up the quality and style of the wine. When assessing fruit, this should be the focus. More on that in a moment. For now, here is a breakdown of the categories of fruit that can be found in white and red wines.

## White wines

*In white wines, specific groups or families of fruit are named.*

**Orchard fruit:** Some form of apple or pear that can be found in practically every white wine. However, more specificity is needed here in the form of calling green vs. red apple, etc.

**Citrus fruit:** Broken down further into tart citrus (lemon, lime, grapefruit, etc.) and sweet citrus (orange, tangerine, Mandarin).

**Tropical fruit:** Pineapple, mango, passion fruit, papaya, etc.

**Stone fruit:** Peach, apricot, and nectarine.

**Melon:** Green, white, and orange.

## Red wines

*In red wines, colors or qualities of the fruit are used. However, once a color/quality is identified, the taster/student needs to be more specific in describing the fruit.*

**Red fruit:** Fruits that are sour (think cool climate and less ripening) including red cherry, red raspberry, red currant, strawberry, cranberry, plum, and pomegranate.

**Black fruit:** Fruits that are riper (think warmer climate and more ripening) including black cherry, blackberry, black raspberry, black currant, and black plum.

**Blue fruit:** Blueberry and boysenberry and could include other more esoteric berries such as olallieberry, huckleberry, and schnozzberry (just kidding on that last one).

**Dried fruit:** Raisin, prune, sultana, fig, and date.

## Fruit quality

Once specific kinds of fruit have been identified, the quality of the fruit needs to be assessed. The quality of fruit in a wine is important. In fact, I think it's one of the three most critical aspects of tasting. For the record, the other two are impact compounds (Chapter 11) and accurately assessing structure (Chapter 4).

Here's a list of commonly found descriptors regarding fruit quality. Note that there are more descriptors than listed here:

- Fresh
- Tart
- Sweet
- Ripe
- Candied
- Dried
- Jammy
- Cooked
- Stewed

**Some examples:** In a young Riesling from Germany's Mosel Valley, one might find green apple, mango, white peach, and lime, and describe them as fresh and tart in quality. The fruit and qualities are connected to the grape itself as well as the cool continental climate found in the Mosel.

Likewise, the fruit in a Zinfandel from Paso Robles might be described as ripe, jammy, and even raisinated. The range of different fruit qualities here is linked to Zinfandel and its tendency to sometimes ripen unevenly, the very warm climate of Paso Robles, and the possibility of the fruit having been harvested late in the season when it is fully ripe and beyond.

## Fruit quality as it relates to Cause and Effect

The takeaway from fruit quality? It should always be linked to the climate of the growing region, the timing of the harvest, and more. All of which lead directly to the concept of Cause and Effect (covered in Chapter 8). The concept of Cause and Effect poses the question of "why" — why a wine looks, smells, and tastes the way it does. The answers have to do with climate once again, the timing of the harvest, the quality of the vintage, and a myriad of decisions made in the vineyard and the winery. Consider the following fruit categories commonly found in red wines and how they equate to Cause and Effect.

A red fruit-dominant wine like Pinot Noir: Lighter pigmented grape, cooler climate, less overall ripening, lower alcohol, and higher natural acidity.

A dark fruit-dominant wine like a Cabernet Sauvignon: More deeply pigmented grape, warmer climate, riper fruit, higher alcohol, and lower natural acidity with possible acidulation.

Dried fruit-dominant wine like a Gran Reserva Rioja: Oxidative character due to the actual age of the wine including an extended time aging in barrel and bottle as required by law.

Two further thoughts on assessing fruit when smelling and tasting wine:

First, note the fruit you smell and taste in a given wine but pay more attention to the fruit quality, important non-fruit impact compounds, and the structure. These are the keys to identifying a wine.

Second, work with your memory of fruits commonly found in wine without physically tasting them. That also goes for non-fruit and any other aromatic/flavor. A good first step in working with your memory is what I call the "Basic Set" — the smaller subset of aromas and flavors that appear in over 80% of all wines. Chapter 22 is about the "Basic Set" and how to practice and improve your smell and taste memory using it.

*Author's suggestions: First, memorize the categories of fruit listed above for white and red wines. Next, memorize the range of fruit qualities and connect the dots between tart fruit and the structure in cool-climate wines in the form of lower alcohol and higher acidity. Do the same for ripe/jammy fruit as it relates to the structure in warmer climate wines with elevated alcohol and less natural acidity.*

*Remember that warmer climate red wines are often acidulated (addition of tartaric acid). Finally, if you need some work with memory and kinds of fruits, you might jump ahead to Part III of the book and the chapters on the Basic Set (Chapter 23) and Submodalities (Chapter 24). Both offer suggestions and strategies for how to work with and improve your memory for various aromas and flavors.*

# 10

# Wine Faults and Context

*Author's note: Knowledge of common wine faults is mandatory for any professional taster. It's also a critical asset for any wine buyer to be able to consistently and accurately judge quality. Like any aroma or flavor, one needs to work on recognition and memory of the common faults. Remember, however, that individual tasters may differ widely in their sensitivity to various wine faults.*

*As with many things in the wine world, context is important when evaluating wine faults. That's because some of them can be found in small and even trace amounts in many classic wines. Thus experience is required for one to be able to assess the quality in a wine displaying volatile acidity or Brettanomyces. Chapter 36: "It's Only Natural," goes into more detail about context and faults. For now, here is basic information on the most commonly found wine faults.*

## TCA (2,4,6-trichloroanisole)

TCA, or corkiness, is the most common wine fault. TCA is a chemical compound (haloanisole) created from the interaction between microbial metabolites (mold) and chlorine. It is formed during cork bark harvest, storage, and the production of cork stoppers.

**Cause:** Created during cork bark harvest, storage, and production.

**Smells like:** Wet, moldy cardboard, old books and magazines, and wet concrete floor. The human threshold for detecting TCA is thought to be as low as six parts per trillion.

**Context:** TCA is universally considered a fault. Although natural corks are often the culprit, TCA can also form in the winery environment as well as in fermentation or storage vessels such as tanks or barrels.

## Oxidation

A wine that smells oxidized shows dried or developed fruit and non-fruit qualities that are incongruous with the wine's age. For example, a three-year-old New World Chardonnay showing a stewed fruit character and a deep golden color.

**Cause:** An excess of oxygen during the winemaking process, at the time of bottling, or a faulty cork.

**Smells like:** Secondary and tertiary aromas in a young wine.

**Context:** There are a number of classic wines in which oxidation plays a major role in style and character. For example, Gran Reserva Rioja and solera-aged Sherry both traditionally show considerable oxidation.

## Maderization

One of the most common wine faults due to poor storage conditions. When exposed to heat for any period of time, wine thermally expands inside the bottle pushing the cork up and even out. Oxidation is also common with maderized wines.

**Cause:** Wine being exposed to excessive heat over a duration of time.

**Smells like:** Cooked or burned (like Madeira).

**Context:** Unless the wine is an actual Madeira or other solera-aged fortified wine, Maderization is usually considered a fault.

## Acetaldehyde

Acetaldehyde is a Sherry-like compound and aroma from oxidation of ethanol alcohol.

**Cause:** Forms with the oxidation of ethanol. Also occurs with the presence of the surface film on wine in a tank or barrel, which then forms yeasts and bacteria.

**Smells like:** Sherry, roasted nuts, or dried straw.

**Context:** Acetaldehyde is an important marker for Fino and Manzanilla Sherry.

## Volatile Acidity - Acetic acid (VA)

VA is a by-product of fermentation and is therefore present in trace amounts in most wines.

**Cause:** Created by many different wine spoilage yeasts and bacteria.

**Smells like:** Acetic acid smells like vinegar.

**Context:** VA is often found in several classic wines including Amarone, Barolo, and certain Syrahs from the Northern Rhône.

## Volatile Acidity - Ethyl acetate (EA)

EA is another form of volatile acidity.

**Cause:** EA is produced by wine spoilage yeasts and the chemical reaction of ethanol and acetic acid.

**Smells like:** Nail polish remover, glue, or varnish.

**Context:** Ethyl acetate is sometimes found in detectable amounts in high-alcohol red wines as well as botrytis dessert wines.

## Brettanomyces (or Dekkera)

Brettanomyces is a yeast or unicellular type of fungus.

**Cause:** Brett, as it's often called, or Dekerra, originates in vineyard soil and finds its way into the winery environment including barrels, tanks, and other equipment.

**Smells like:** Earth, leather, barnyard, horse stable, antiseptic, medicinal, sweaty, cheesy, and rancid. Sensitivity — and tolerance — to Brett varies widely. Some tasters are ultra-sensitive to it while others can tolerate — even prefer — it in high concentrations.

**Context:** More than any other so-called fault, Brett is accepted, even anticipated, in any number of classic Old World red wines including certain styles of Bordeaux, Burgundy, and more.

## Sulfur Dioxide (SO2)

SO2 is a valuable antimicrobial and antioxidant that has been used for over two thousand years. Today it is used judiciously in beverage and food production.

**Cause:** When too much SO2 is added before bottling.

**Smells like:** Excessive amounts of SO2 smell like a lit wooden matchstick, burnt rubber, or mothballs.

**Context:** High levels of SO2 are traditionally used in wines with residual sugar capable of long-term aging such as German Rieslings, Loire Valley Chenin Blancs, and various botrytis dessert wines.

## Hydrogen Sulfide (H2S)

H2S is the most intense smelling sulfur compound. Wines displaying H2S are sometimes called "reduced."

**Cause:** When yeast draws on sulfur compounds for a nitrogen source during fermentation.

**Smells like:** Sewer gas or rotten eggs.

**Context**: H2S is universally considered a fault.

## Mercaptan

Mercaptan is another sulfur compound often referred to as reduction in wine–or reduced.

**Cause:** When H2S is not removed quickly from the must, it can further react with other compounds to form mercaptan and other disulfides. Mercaptan can also be formed in a wine that is allowed prolonged lees contact.

**Smells like:** Natural gas, onions, or garlic.

**Context:** Though usually considered a fault, a whiff of mercaptan can sometimes be found in Graves Blanc as well as White Burgundy.

*Author's suggestion: I highly recommend reading Jamie Goode's book, "Flawless: Understanding Wine Faults." Goode offers in-depth information in his book on all the above faults and more. He also presents a different view on faults such as Brett and excessive VA in regards to how context, place, and the specific wine are all part of the wine hygiene equation. There's more than a bit of hard science in Goode's book but it is well worth reading.*

11

# Impact Compounds

*Author's note: Impact compounds are a subset of a dozen or so aromas and flavors that a student absolutely must learn and even own, so to speak. These compounds are derived from several sources including grape chemistry, vineyard environment, and winemaking techniques. Needless to say, the compounds are key markers for identifying classic wines. I can't emphasize enough how important they are to the learning curve of becoming a professional taster as well as a necessity for success in tasting exams.*

If I had to prepare for the MS tasting exam all over again, I would make the process as streamlined as possible. The aspects of tasting I would spend the most time on are the concepts of Cause and Effect (see Chapter 8), impact compounds, and accurate structural assessment. While other sections of the book dwell on Cause and Effect and structural assessment, this chapter focuses on important impact compounds found in white and red wines.

A disclaimer: I am *not* a chemist. In fact, I've never even impersonated a chemist, much less taken chemistry in high school or college. I am a product/victim of a '60s Catholic school education. By the time I arrived at a public high school, my math and science skills were beyond woefully inadequate. But I could diagram a sentence with the best of them. In all seriousness, the focus on chemical compounds here is all about sharpening the Occam's Razor of deductive tasting. Onward.

## Botrytis

The botrytis mold is responsible for many of the world's great non-fortified dessert wines including Sauternes, Hungarian Tokaji, and Trockenbeerenauslese from Germany and Austria. Botrytis influence in wine smells and tastes like honey/honeysuckle, ripe/overripe stone fruits, marmalade, toffee, saffron, ginger, and button mushroom. It's important to note that botrytis character can also often be found in non-dessert dry table wines, including Alsace Pinot Gris and Riesling, Loire Valley Chenin Blanc (Vouvray), and German Grosses Gewächs Riesling.

## Brettanomyces

A yeast whose origins have been traced to the Senne Valley in Belgium. Brett, as it is often called, originates in vineyard soils and can also find its way into winery environments. It smells like leather, barnyard, animal, fecal, and medicinal/Band-Aid. The threshold for detecting Brett as well as tolerance—even preference—varies dramatically with the individual, ranging from zero-tolerance to actual preference. As noted in Chapter 10, the presence of Brett is *highly* contextual in wine. The presence of higher levels of Brett in certain classic Old World wines is far from unusual. Old school Bordeaux, Burgundy, Rhône wines (both North and South), and other traditional Old World reds fall into this category. For the student, it's important to be able to detect Brett-related aromas and connect them to these wines and places of origin.

## Carbonic maceration

A winemaking technique often associated with wines from Beaujolais. The intent of carbonic maceration is to extract maximum color and fruit from the grapes without excessive tannin. Wines made with carbonic maceration display overtly fruity aromas and flavors that are often described as candied or artificial. Jolly Rancher candy, banana, and Hawaiian Punch are also common descriptors.

Carbonic wines also tend to display green woody notes as stems are naturally included during fermentation. Aside from Beaujolais, carbonic maceration is often used for some Côtes du Rhône red wines, mass-market commercial Zinfandel, Shiraz blends, and others.

## Diacetyl

A by-product of malo-lactic fermentation/conversion responsible for the butter/cream/dairy notes in Chardonnay. Recognizing diacetyl is important not only for Chardonnay-based wines but other white wines that undergo Chardonnay "treatment," such as Viognier.

## Lees contact

Aromas and flavors resulting from wine in contact with fine lees after primary or secondary fermentation. The term "autolysis" describes the gradual breakdown of lees over time. Lees contact in white wine smells and tastes like yeast, brioche, bread dough, and toast. Lees contact also adds a richer, creamier texture to the finished wine. Lees aging (contact) is an important method used in making Chardonnay as well as Muscadet, Pinot Grigio, Grüner Veltliner, Albariño, and certain dry Rieslings. Finally, it must be mentioned that lees contact is a vital part of the process used to make classic method sparkling wines.

## New oak

The use of new oak imparts a wide range of aromas and flavors to a wine including vanilla, baking spices, chocolate, coconut, dill, smoke, toast, coffee, tea, and more. It's important for the student to be able to identify the markers of new oak vs. a wine without oak-aging— and to be able to describe them.

## Phenolic bitterness

Phenolic bitterness in certain white wines is derived from the must being in contact with either the grape skins before or during fermentation or the wine after fermentation. Grapes/wines displaying phenolic bitterness include the following:

- Albariño and Grüner Veltliner: Medium alcohol with phenolic bitterness
- Alto Adige Pinot Grigio: Medium aromatic intensity with phenolic bitterness
- Alsace Pinot Gris: Medium-plus phenolic bitterness on the finish along with riper fruit, elevated alcohol, possible botrytis, and possible residual sugar
- Viognier and Gewürztraminer: Highly aromatic grapes/wines with elevated alcohol and pronounced phenolic bitterness

🍷 *It's important not to confuse phenolic bitterness with used oak on the palate. The latter will always be accompanied by aromas and flavors from oak aging. Phenolic bitterness is just that — bitter.*

## Pyrazines

A chemical compound that smells and tastes like green bell pepper, asparagus, and cut grass. Grapes/wines displaying that display pyrazines include the following:

- White grapes: Sauvignon Blanc
- Red grapes: Cabernet Sauvignon family grapes including Cabernet Sauvignon, Merlot, Cabernet Franc, Petite Verdot, and Carménère

## Raisination

Wines displaying raisinated fruit characteristics can be caused by several different factors: grape varieties that ripen unevenly, making wine from overripe grapes, or making wine from dried grapes.

## Rotundone

A chemical compound called a *sesquiterpene* that accumulates in grape skins, increasing in concentration between véraison and harvest. Rotundone accounts for the peppery aroma found in certain white and red wines.

- White wines: Grüner Veltliner from Austria
- Red wines: Syrah/Shiraz
- Old World: Wines from Northern Rhône Valley appellations of Côte-Rotie, St.-Joseph, Crozes-Hermitage, Hermitage, and Cornas
- New World: Syrah/Shiraz wines from Australia, California, Washington, and others

Other red wines with rotundone: Grenache and Mourvèdre as well as the Italian red varieties such as Schioppettino and Vespolina. Zinfandel from California also contains this compound.

## Stem inclusion

The use of stems during fermentation is commonly practiced in red winemaking in Burgundy as well as Beaujolais. In the latter, the practice of stem inclusion is the result of fermenting whole clusters of grapes via carbonic and semi-carbonic maceration. Aromas and flavors from stem inclusion can best be described as green and woody.

## TDN

TDN is the source of the petrol or kerosene character most commonly associated with Riesling. Technically, TDN is a chemical compound called 1,1,6-trimethyl-1,2-dihydronaphthalene. It was first isolated by German scientists in 2006. A more recent study by the Australian Wine Research Institute found that high concentrations of TDN could be the result of wines made from fruit grown in a region with a shorter, warmer ripening cycle. It's also thought that the combination of water stress, soil nitrogen deficiency, specific yeast strains, and clonal selection can all potentially affect the development of TDN in wine.

## Terpenes

Terpenes are intensely aromatic compounds with pronounced floral and sweet citrus notes. Common terpenic compounds include:

- Rose oxide: Found in roses and rose oil; responsible for Gewürztraminer's rose and litchi notes
- Linalool: Highly floral and ginger-spice notes in Muscat Grapes
- Geraniol: The scent of geraniums and lemon
- Nerol: The scent of roses and orange
- Alpha-terpineol: Grapey, pine-like aromas found in Torrontés

Grapes/wines displaying terpenic qualities include the following:

- Medium terpenes: Albariño (with lees contact and phenolic bitterness) and Riesling (with TDN and possible botrytis)
- Medium terpenes and elevated alcohol: Viognier (with possible diacetyl from malo-lactic fermentation and oak usage) and Torrontés
- High terpenes: Gewürztraminer (lower acidity and elevated alcohol) and Muscat (slightly higher acidity and less alcohol)

## Thiols

Thiols are sulfur-containing compounds that are present as odorless precursors in ripe grapes. During fermentation, yeasts can cause thiols to become volatile. These compounds are known as mercaptans that can smell and taste like rubber, garlic, or onions. Thiols can be incredibly pungent but can also provide certain varietal aromas such as grapefruit, blackcurrant, passion fruit, and lemongrass.

## Volatile acidity

Volatile acidity, or VA, is a by-product of fermentation and therefore present in all wines in trace amounts. Detectable acetic acid is usually considered a fault. However, like Brettanomyces, VA is highly contextual. In wines such as Amarone and Gran Reserva Rioja, higher levels of VA are acceptable and viewed as an aspect of wine style.

*Author's suggestion: I recommend chunking down impact compounds into groups of two or three at a time to learn them. From there, it's important to connect the compounds to their respective grapes and wines.*

# 12

# Confronting the Evil Dwarves

*Author's note: One of the major challenges for students in tasting practice or exams is confusing similar wines. The keys to identification have to do with certain impact compounds — important aromatics and flavors — and differences in structural levels. This chapter focuses on easily confused white and red wines and lists important criteria for being able to identify them and tell them apart.*

In blind tasting practice and exams, there are two sets of wines that consistently cause students anxiety. I call these the "Evil Dwarves." Each set is populated by wines easily confused for one another. The first set is made up of wines made from semi-aromatic white grapes including Albariño, Grüner Veltliner, Loire Valley Chenin Blanc, Alsace Pinot Gris, Northern Italian Pinot Grigio, and dry Riesling from Alsace (also Austria and Germany). The other set comprises wines made from lighter pigmented red grapes such as Pinot Noir, Gamay, Sangiovese, Tempranillo, and Grenache.

One would think that it wouldn't be that difficult to tell the various wines apart. But stop for a moment and think about how similar the fruit and fruit quality can be for wines within each set. Add to that the fact that within each group the color of all the wines can be remarkably similar. Thus, if a student is keying off color or fruit trying to tell the grapes apart, identifying the wines will be an endless nightmare.

There is good news in that practically all the wines have a strong signature in terms of impact compounds such as botrytis, TDN, and phenolic bitterness. Combine these compounds with the unique structural profiles of the wines (levels of acidity, alcohol, phenolic bitterness, and tannins) and you have a blueprint to be able to tell classic examples of the wines apart. And that's a very good thing. So, without further ado, here's a road map to help identify the Evil Dwarves and tell them apart from their brethren.

For our purposes, we'll use the following white wines as models for their respective grapes:

- Albariño: Spain – Rías Baixas
- Grüner Veltliner: Austria
- Chenin Blanc: Loire Valley - Vouvray and Savennières
- Pinot Gris: France - Alsace
- Pinot Grigio: Italy - Alto Adige
- Riesling: France – Alsace

## PART I: SEMI-AROMATIC WHITE GRAPES/WINES

### Albariño: Spain – Rías Baixas

**Look for:** Floral (terpenes), ripe-tart fruit, lees contact (hops/beer notes), stony mineral, and no oak.

**Structure:** Medium to medium-plus alcohol, medium-plus to high acidity, and phenolic bitterness.

**How it's different from:**

**Grüner Veltliner:** Albariño lacks the white pepper and botanical/vegetal qualities found in Grüner Veltliner. Smaragd Grüner will also be a much richer wine than Albariño with its pepper/vegetal qualities and possible botrytis notes.

**Loire Valley Chenin Blanc:** Chenin Blanc, even when dry, often shows botrytis notes and green olive/green herb character as well as pronounced chalky minerality. Structurally, Chenin has medium-plus alcohol and high acidity. It also usually lacks the overt terpenic qualities of Albariño.

**Alsace Pinot Gris:** Albariño lacks botrytis notes sometimes found in Pinot Gris. Structurally, Pinot Gris also has higher alcohol, lower acidity, and sometimes displays residual sugar.

**Northern Italian Pinot Grigio:** Albariño and Alto Adige Pinot Grigio can be similar in weight and structure but Pinot Grigio is less terpenic, less fruity, with only slight phenolic bitterness on the finish.

**Riesling:** The presence of TDN (petrol/fusel/kerosene notes - see Chapter 11) in Riesling sets it apart from Albariño. Alsace Riesling—especially Grand Cru quality—and German Grosses Gewächs Riesling also tend to be richer wines with slightly higher alcohol and higher acidity. Finally, the fruit profile in Riesling is also much broader than Albariño with botrytis notes sometimes found even in dry wines.

## Grüner Veltliner: Austria

**Look for:** Pepper (rotundone), herbal-vegetal notes (radish, daikon, celery, parsley, etc.), stony mineral, and used or no oak.

**Structure:** Medium to high alcohol, medium-plus to high acidity, and phenolic bitterness.

**Considerations:** Ripeness levels as applied to the Wachau classification (Steinfeder, Federspiel, and Smaragd) or reserve wines from other regions.

**How it's different from:**

**Albariño:** Pepper/vegetal notes and fewer terpenes.

**Loire Valley Chenin Blanc:** Chenin will often be a richer wine with lighter floral notes, chalky minerality, and possible sulfur notes.

**Alsace Pinot Gris:** No rotundone in Pinot Gris. It will also usually be a richer wine with slightly lower acidity, phenolic bitterness, and possible residual sugar as well as botrytis character.

**Northern Italian Pinot Grigio:** Can be similar in weight and structure to some lighter Grüner Veltliners but again lacks the pepper/vegetal qualities. Pinot Grigio will also tend to have less phenolic bitterness on the finish.

**Riesling:** Pepper/vegetal qualities of Grüner Veltliner vs. the TDN and possible botrytis notes of Riesling.

## Chenin Blanc: Loire Valley - Vouvray and Savennières

**Look for:** Floral (terpenes), possible botrytis character including honey (even in dry wines), chamomile-botanical-herb, chalky minerality, and used or no oak. Wet wool and lanolin are also common descriptors.

**Structure:** Medium-to-medium-plus alcohol, medium-plus to high acidity, and phenolic bitterness.

**Considerations:** Appellation in the form of Vouvray Sec and Demi-Sec vs. Savennières.

**How it's different from:**

**Albariño:** More pronounced terpenes in Albariño set it apart from Chenin Blanc.

**Grüner Veltliner:** Chenin completely lacks the rotundone character found in Grüner Veltliner.

**Alsace Pinot Gris:** Both can show botrytis notes but Pinot Gris will offer a richer texture, more phenolic bitterness, and will usually have lower acidity.

**Northern Italian Pinot Grigio:** Loire Chenin will be a richer wine showing chalky minerality, possible sulfur notes, and higher acidity.

**Riesling:** Both can show botrytis character and have high acidity but Chenin lacks the TDN of Riesling.

## Pinot Gris: France - Alsace

**Look for:** Floral (terpenes), possible botrytis character, mushroom-earth-mineral notes, used or no oak, and phenolic bitterness. In style, the wines are often off-dry to slightly sweet.

**Structure:** Medium-plus to high alcohol, medium to medium-plus acidity, and medium phenolic bitterness.

**Considerations:** AC vs. grand cru wines in terms of quality, concentration, and complexity.

**How it's different from:**

**Albariño:** Albariño generally is a lighter wine than Pinot Gris with higher acidity, lack of botrytis notes, and lack of residual sugar on the finish.

**Grüner Veltliner:** While it can match the weight and richness of a Smaragd Grüner Veltliner, Pinot Gris will lack rotundone pepper and herbal-vegetal qualities.

**Loire Valley Chenin Blanc:** Both grapes can show botrytis character but Chenin has chamomile-herbal notes, chalky minerality, SO2, and higher acidity.

**Northern Italian Pinot Grigio:** Will be a lighter wine than Pinot Gris from Alsace. Pinot Grigio will also lack any botrytis notes and will be a dry wine.

**Riesling:** Alsace Pinot Gris can easily match the weight and richness of Riesling from the same region not to mention Riesling from Germany or Austria. However, Pinot Gris lacks the acidity and TDN qualities of Riesling, and it also shows phenolic bitterness on the finish.

## Pinot Grigio: Italy - Alto Adige

**Look for:** Delicate floral (terpenes), lees contact, stony mineral, slight phenolic bitterness, and no oak.

**Structure:** Medium alcohol, medium-plus acidity, and slight phenolic bitterness.

**How it's different from:**

**Albariño:** Both grapes can be similar in weight and texture but Pinot Grigio is a more narrowly defined — almost neutral — grape/wine by comparison. Pinot Grigio is also not as floral/terpenic as Albariño.

**Grüner Veltliner:** Pinot Grigio lacks the pepper and herbal/vegetal qualities of Grüner.

**Loire Valley Chenin Blanc:** Pinot Grigio is generally a lighter-bodied wine compared to Loire Chenin. A typical Pinot Grigio will also not show botrytis character and has less acidity.

**Alsace Pinot Gris:** Alto Adige Pinot Grigio is a scaled-down version compared to wines from Alsace but with higher acidity, more restrained alcohol, no botrytis character, and no residual sugar.

**Riesling:** Pinot Grigio lacks any TDN qualities and botrytis character, and also has less acidity.

## Riesling: France - Alsace

**Look for:** Floral (terpenes), fusel-petrol (TDN), possible lees contact, earth/mineral qualities, and no oak.

**Structure:** Low to medium-plus alcohol, medium-plus to high acidity, and possible phenolic bitterness in dry wines.

**How it's different from:**

**Albariño:** TDN, possible broader fruit profile, and higher acidity set Riesling apart from Albariño.

**Grüner Veltliner:** The rotundone pepper, herbal/vegetal in Grüner vs. the TDN in Riesling.

**Loire Chenin Blanc:** Although both can show botrytis notes, the chalky minerality and lack of TDN set Chenin apart from Riesling.

**Alsace Pinot Gris:** Both wines can show botrytis character but Riesling will often display TDN and have higher acidity.

**Northern Italian Pinot Grigio:** TDN, more complexity, and higher acidity will set Riesling apart from Pinot Grigio.

## PART II: LIGHTER PIGMENTED RED GRAPES/WINES

As with the white wines, the color and fruit qualities of red wines produced from lighter pigmented grapes can be similar making them challenging to tell apart. Again, practically all display unique signatures from impact compounds that can be an important aid in identifying each grape/wine. Add the unique set of structural qualities (levels of acid, alcohol, and tannin) found in each wine and you have a blueprint to be able to tell classic examples of any of the wines apart. For our purposes, we'll use the following red wines as models for their respective grapes:

- Pinot Noir: France - Côte de Nuits/Beaune or U.S. - California/Oregon
- Gamay: France – Beaujolais-Villages
- Sangiovese: Italy - Tuscany - Chianti Classico
- Tempranillo: Spain - Rioja Reserva and Gran Reserva
- Grenache Blend: France - Southern Rhône
- Nebbiolo: Piedmont - Barolo and Barbaresco

## Pinot Noir: France - Côte de Nuits/Beaune or U.S. - California/Oregon

**Old World – Burgundy:** Red fruits, rose-floral, tea-herb, possible green stem quality (stem inclusion), possible Brettanomyces, soil-mineral-game, and oak usage.

**Structure:** Medium to medium-plus alcohol, medium-plus acidity, and medium to medium-plus tannin.

**Considerations:** Quality level in the form of AC vs. Premier Cru vs. Grand Cru wines in regards to oak usage, concentration, complexity, and price.

**New World:** Fruit-dominant (primarily red), floral-herbal notes, possible earth-mineral, and oak usage.

**Structure:** Medium to medium-plus alcohol, medium-plus acidity, and medium to medium-plus tannin.

**How it's different from:**

**Gamay:** Pinot Noir usually lacks the candied/artificial fruit character from carbonic maceration as well as stem inclusion and granite/stony minerality. Pinot Noir also frequently offers more oak influence.

**Sangiovese:** Pinot Noir lacks the tannin of Sangiovese—specifically grape tannin often perceived in the front of the mouth on teeth and gums. Sangiovese also has higher acidity as well as anise-herbal flavors.

**Tempranillo:** Extended aging in American Oak (coconut, dill, herb, pronounced vanilla, and baking spices) sets traditional Tempranillo-based Rioja apart from Pinot Noir.

**Grenache:** Though both wines can be lighter in color, Southern Rhône Grenache blends have riper fruit, higher alcohol, and higher tannin. Pinot Noir also lacks the peppery-rotundone and savory herb/garrigue qualities of Grenache. Larger cooperage is also traditionally used for a Grenache/blend vs. a smaller barrique in Pinot Noir.

**Nebbiolo:** The alcohol, acid, and tannin levels in Nebbiolo are higher than Pinot Noir.

## Gamay: France – Beaujolais-Villages

**Look for:** Candied and confected red fruits from carbonic maceration, green stemmy quality from stem inclusion, stony-earth, and little or no oak.

**Structure:** Medium alcohol, medium-plus acidity, and medium-minus to medium tannin.

**Considerations:** Villages vs. cru wines with less carbonic character in the latter.

**How it's different from:**

**Pinot Noir:** The carbonic character in Beaujolais-Villages sets it apart from Pinot, whether from Burgundy or the New World. Beaujolais-Villages will also lack the overt oak character often found in Pinot Noir.

**Sangiovese:** Carbonic notes again differentiate Gamay from Sangiovese with the latter also having more tannin. Stem inclusion is not a common practice for quality Sangiovese wines.

**Tempranillo:** Carbonic notes and lack of overt oak influence—specifically American Oak influence.

**Grenache:** Lack of carbonic notes in classic Grenache blends with the latter also having more non-fruit complexity (pepper, dried floral, garrigue/herbs, and savory qualities). Structurally, Grenache has higher alcohol and more tannin with little, if any, stem inclusion.

**Nebbiolo:** Has higher levels of alcohol, tannin, and acidity compared to Gamay as well as an oxidative character and a completely different fruit/non-fruit set. No carbonic character and stem inclusion in Nebbiolo wines.

## Sangiovese: Tuscany - Chianti Classico

**Look for:** Ripe and tart red fruit with darker fruits in wines from warmer vintages or those containing Cabernet family grapes; also tomato-green herb, anise, sandalwood, chalk-mineral-earth, and oak usage – large cooperage or barrique.

**Structure:** Medium to medium-plus alcohol, medium-plus to high acidity, and medium-plus to high tannin.

**Considerations:** Degree of oak influence in regards to the use of barriques vs. larger barrels.

**How it's different from:**

**Pinot Noir:** More grape tannin in Sangiovese as well as higher acidity and more anise/herbal character.

**Gamay:** Lack of carbonic fruit character in Sangiovese as well as a higher level of tannin.

**Tempranillo:** The oxidative style and American Oak set Tempranillo apart from any form of Sangiovese. The latter is usually more tannic as well.

**Grenache:** Lack of pepper/rotundone character in Sangiovese. Grenache blends also offer a higher level of alcohol with somewhat less acidity.

**Nebbiolo:** Sangiovese vs. Nebbiolo is one of the more challenging side-by-side comparisons. There are many similarities between the two, but in the end, Nebbiolo in the form of Barolo and/or Barbaresco is usually more tannic and acidic as well as offering more floral and high-toned aromatics including floral.

## Tempranillo: Spain - Rioja Reserva and Gran Reserva

**Look for:** Dark, red, and dried fruits, dried floral-potpourri, dried herb, dust-soil-terra cotta, American oak notes, and oxidative character.

**Structure:** Medium to medium-plus alcohol, medium-plus acidity, and medium to medium-plus tannin.

**How it's different from:**

**Pinot Noir:** Oxidative winemaking-aging and American Oak set Tempranillo apart from Pinot Noir regardless of origin.

**Gamay:** No carbonic character or stem inclusion in Tempranillo. Oxidative style and American Oak in the Rioja.

**Sangiovese:** Oxidative style and American Oak. Sangiovese is generally more tannic as well.

**Grenache:** Although some styles of Grenache blends may show oxidation similar to Tempranillo with age, the wines won't display American Oak notes. Grenache blends will also offer more alcohol as well as pepper and Mediterranean herb (garrigue) notes.

**Nebbiolo:** American Oak is rarely, if ever, found in Barolo and Barbaresco. The latter two will also be far more tannic and acidic than Tempranillo.

## Grenache Blend: France - Southern Rhône

**Look for:** A broad range of dark, red, and dried fruit; pepper (rotundone), savory herb (garrigue), sanguine notes (roasted meat, blood, iodine), pronounced earth-mineral (possible Brett), and oak usage (usually large cooperage).

**Structure:** high alcohol, medium-plus acidity, and medium-plus to high tannin.

**How it's different from:**

**Pinot Noir:** Too much richness, alcohol, and tannin on the part of Grenache. The peppery and herbal qualities in Grenache/blends also set the wines apart from Pinot Noir.

**Gamay:** Unless it's a basic Côtes du Rhône, use of carbonic is infrequent for Grenache blends. Thus, the artificial fruit qualities of Gamay set it apart from the latter. Grenache will also offer more richness, higher alcohol, and pepper/herb notes.

**Sangiovese:** Grenache is richer with higher alcohol and peppery qualities compared to Sangiovese. Sangiovese will usually offer more grape tannin as well.

**Tempranillo:** Grenache/blends lack the American Oak character of traditionally made Tempranillo-based wines.

**Nebbiolo:** more acid and tannin (most notably grape tannin) in the Nebbiolo.

## Nebbiolo: Italy - Piedmont - Barolo and Barbaresco

**Look for:** Ripe-dried red and dark fruits, pronounced rose-floral, dried herb, black tea, mushroom-earth-tar, and oak usage, both barrique, and large cooperage.

**Structure:** Medium-plus to high alcohol, medium-plus to high acidity, and high tannin.

**How it's different from:**

**Pinot Noir:** Nebbiolo is far too tannic and acidic to be Pinot Noir.

**Gamay:** Same as above concerning tannin and acidity. Note that Nebbiolo rarely, if ever, displays carbonic notes and often shows the new oak influence.

**Sangiovese:** As mentioned above, Sangiovese — especially Brunello — can often be confused with Nebbiolo. Generally, the latter will have higher levels of acidity, tannin, and alcohol. Nebbiolo also tends to display more floral and high-toned aromatics than Sangiovese.

**Tempranillo:** There's too much tannin and acidity in Nebbiolo to be confused for Tempranillo. American Oak in the former also makes it easy to differentiate from Nebbiolo.

**Grenache:** Nebbiolo offers higher levels of acidity and tannin than Grenache as well as more floral and high-toned aromatics.

*Author's suggestion: There's a lot of information here. I recommend starting with the most easily identifiable grape/wine in a group of white or red wines and using it as a "control" to compare the others against. From there, I strongly recommend that you only taste two wines at a time. Our brains learn easily in binary or two's. Finally, use a Coravin for your tasting practice so you can buy top examples of the wines and taste them repeatedly over a period of time.*

# 13

# The Impact of Bottle Aging on Wine

*Author's note: Although scientists still don't know the entirety of what happens in a bottle of wine chemically as it ages, we as professional tasters can do a thorough job of explaining the changes we perceive in the glass.*

*This chapter is about wine and aging, specifically how the appearance, nose, and palate of certain wines tend to change over time. Also, the general tendencies of wine aging are discussed and examples of specific classic wines are listed, comparing notes between young and aged versions.*

Perhaps the most often asked question is about the meaning of life. The answer is, of course, 42. Sorry, inside joke. The second most often asked question is, "what happens to wine as it ages?" That question has a far more problematic answer because scientists don't completely know what happens to wine as it ages in the bottle. And what they do know they can't even agree on. Exhibit "A," a quote from the chapter on "Oxidation" from Jamie Goode's book *Flawless: Understanding Common Wine Faults:*[1]

*"I would add that the exact mechanisms of chemical oxidation of wine are still not completely understood, and there are multiple theories to explain the chemistry at this point. This is a somewhat controversial field."*

Wine as a living thing is never static in the bottle. The alcohol and acids react together constantly to form new compounds while other compounds dissolve. These changes happen over time and at different rates. No surprise that every time a bottle is opened the wine inside is at a different stage in its evolution. Thus there are no hard or fast answers to the wine aging question.

However, we in the industry need to be able to understand the general changes that *tend* to take place in wine as it ages in regards to the way it looks, smells, tastes, and even feels on the palate. Further, we need to be able to communicate these changes to our customers/clients/guests in such a way as to be easily understandable.

This chapter is an attempt to do just that with information about what tends to happen in wine as it ages. Notice again my emphasis on the word *tends*. That's because the aging process for any wine always has the potential to delight, surprise, and disappoint.

## How wine tends to change with age

**Color**

Most reading this chapter will already know that white and blush wines grow darker in color as they age, while red wines do the opposite — they get lighter in color because the pigments and tannin precipitate out of solution over time forming sediment. Over time the color in wine will change showing oxidation in various ways. The color intensity will either increase if a white wine or blush wine, or diminish in the case of a red wine. Otherwise, the following changes in color generally apply:

**White wines:** Straw and pale-yellow color in a young wine vs. deeper yellow, gold, and even amber in an older wine.

**Pink wines:** Various shades of pink in a young rosé vs. salmon and orange in an older wine.

**Red wines:** Vibrant ruby or purple in a young wine vs. various shades of garnet or garnet-brown in an older wine.

## Aromas and flavors

**Fruit:** Generally, young wine offers more overt primary fruit aromas and flavors vs. an aged wine. After a time, a wine will also show less primary fruit with secondary (even tertiary) non-fruit and earth-mineral aromas tending to dominate.

It's also fairly easy to recognize two or more distinct kinds of fruit in a young wine but difficult in an older wine where the fruit has melded together.

**Fruit quality:** Fresh, vibrant fruit in a young wine vs. dried, stewed, compoted, or raisinated fruit in an older wine.

**Non-fruit floral:** Fresh flowers and blossoms in a young wine vs. dried flowers, pressed flowers, or potpourri in an older wine.

**Non-fruit herbal:** Fresh green herbs in a young wine vs. dried herbs in an older wine.

**Non-fruit spice (either pepper-spice or oak spice):** Fresh spices in a young wine vs. dried spices in an older wine.

**Earth-mineral:** Wines with age show more pronounced earth and mineral character simply because of the decreased intensity of fruit and non-fruit elements.

**Oak:** Pronounced vanilla and spice character in a young wine with new oak vs. dried, less distinct spice in an older wine. Also, less overall overt oak presence.

🍷 Important: Note the pattern here. Over time practically everything in a wine regarding aroma and flavor goes from fresh to dry. Thus it probably wouldn't make sense to describe a wine as having dried fruit and fresh herb notes. An aged wine will show dried fruit, dried herb notes, and less overt oak if any was used in the winemaking process.

**Structure**

How does our perception of the structural element in wine change as it ages? What are the reasons for the change vs. the wine simply smelling and tasting differently? The answer involves a myriad of factors.

**Residual sugar:** The level of measurable residual sugar in wine does not change with age. However, over time certain molecules and aldehydes form new combinations that can change our perception of sweetness making an older wine seem like it tastes drier.

**Acidity:** Once bottled, the level of acidity in wine remains almost constant with age. However, our perception of the acidity can change because as wine ages the tartaric acid may bond with potassium ions to form potassium bitartrate, which is responsible for the crystals often found in the wine as well as the neck of the bottle and on the bottom of the cork. This also results in a slight, but measurable decline in acidity as well as a softening of the palate.

**Alcohol:** After fermentation, the alcohol level in wine remains the same. However, as phenolic compounds link together and the wine's primary flavors fade with age, there *may* be times during a wine's development when the alcohol will seem more or less pronounced.

**Tannin:** Tannins found in grape skins and seeds taste bitter and feel astringent on the palate. Over time, tannins soften because they polymerize, or form long chains with each other. The tannin polymer molecules taste less bitter and feel less harsh. Also, some of the tannins will precipitate out of the wine as sediment with age making it, for lack of a better word, smoother on the palate.

Given all the above, here are examples of certain classic wines and how they tend to change over time. As previously noted, all are *general* tendencies.

## Sparkling and white wines

Vintage Champagne

**Young wine:**

**Sight:** Pale straw color with hints of green and a persistent bead (bubbles).

**Nose and palate:** Tart vibrant apple-pear and citrus fruit, floral, autolytic notes (from the breakdown of yeast left from secondary fermentation) of yeast, toast, brioche, and possible earth-mineral notes.

**Aged wine:**

**Sight:** deeper straw in color with brassy highlights and less persistent bead.

**Nose and palate:** Dried orchard and citrus fruit, dried floral, more toasty autolytic notes, and more mushroom-earth-mineral character.

Riesling - Mosel Spätlese

**Young wine:**

**Sight:** Pale straw color with green.

**Nose and palate:** A myriad of fresh vibrant fruit including green apple, stone fruit, tropical fruit, and sweet/tart citrus fruit. Also, fresh citrus blossom, possible lees character (yeast); slate-mineral, and little, if any, TDN/petrol character.

**Aged wine:**

**Sight:** Yellow gold in color with hints of green.

Nose and Palate: less fruit overall and the fruit quality is dried/preserved. Also, dried floral, crystalized honey, more pronounced slate-mineral quality, and more TDN/petrol character.

Chardonnay - California

**Young wine:**

**Sight:** Light yellow in color with a hint of green.

**Nose and palate:** Fresh and ripe apple-pear, tropical, and citrus fruit with lees notes (yeast, bread dough, etc.), butter from malolactic fermentation/conversion, and pronounced vanilla-spice notes from new oak usage.

**Aged wine:**

**Sight:** Yellow-gold in color.

**Nose and palate:** Dried, stewed, or compoted fruit including apple-pear and citrus with less distinct lees, butterscotch, and spice character from the oak influence. Also, oxidative notes such as honey and roasted nuts.

Chardonnay – Côte de Beaune

**Young wine:**

**Sight:** Straw-yellow in color with green.

**Nose and palate:** Fresh and ripe apple-pear and citrus fruit with lees (yeast, bread dough, etc.), butter from malolactic fermentation/conversion, possible matchstick-SO2 notes, mineral-earth notes, and vanilla spice from oak.

**Aged wine:**

**Sight:** Yellow-gold in color.

**Nose and palate:** Dried, stewed, or compoted fruit including apple and preserved citrus with less distinct lees, butterscotch, more pronounced mineral-mushroom-earth notes, and any matchstick-SO2 integrated into the wine. Also, less overt oak influence but with honey and roasted nut oxidative notes.

## Red wines

Pinot Noir – New World

**Young wine:**

**Sight:** Medium ruby color with a pink hue.

**Nose and palate:** Vibrant, fresh red fruit (red cherry, cranberry, and strawberry) with fresh rose floral, green herb, and oak spices.

**Aged wine:**

**Sight:** Garnet-ruby in color with secondary lighter garnet hue.

**Nose and palate:** Dried-compoted red fruit, dried floral and herb, possible tertiary mineral and earth notes, and less spice from oak.

Pinot Noir – Red Burgundy

**Young wine:**

**Sight:** Medium ruby color with a pink hue.

**Nose and palate:** bright, fresh red fruit (red cherry, cranberry, and strawberry) with rose floral, green herb/tea, possible green stemmy notes, mineral-earth, and vanilla-spice from oak.

**Aged wine:**

**Sight:** Garnet-ruby in color with secondary lighter garnet hue.

**Nose and palate:** Dried red fruit with dried floral, herb, tea, stems, and pronounced mineral-earth notes including game, truffle, and mushroom. Also, less spice and overt oak influence. Note that an older bottle of quality red Burgundy often displays complexities on the nose and palate that are almost impossible to describe.

Syrah – Barossa Shiraz

**Young wine:**

**Sight:** Opaque ruby purple in color.

**Nose and palate:** Ripe, jammy black fruit (blackberry, cherry, and plum), tart red fruit (cherry and cranberry), and dried fruit (raisin, prune, date, and fig). Also, black pepper spice, savory herb, mint and eucalyptus, savory notes (soy and beef jerky), and pronounced vanilla-spice from new oak.

**Aged wine:**

**Sight:** Deep purple with garnet hue.

**Nose and palate:** Dried raisinated character overall including riper and tarter elements. Also, dried pepper, leather, mint, herbs, dried savory spice and meat, and less pronounced oak.

Syrah – Northern Rhône

**Young wine:**

**Sight:** Deep purple in color.

**Nose and palate:** ripe and tart black fruit (blackberry, cherry, and plum), tart red fruit (cherry and cranberry), and dried fruit (date and fig). Also black and/or white pepper spice, fresh floral, green herb, savory notes (smoked meat, soy, jerky, iodine, and blood), mineral-earth, and oak notes including smoke, toast, and spice.

**Aged wine:**

**Sight:** Deep purple with garnet hue.

**Nose and palate:** Dried raisinated fruit character overall with riper and tarter notes. Also, dried pepper, dried floral and herbs, dried savory spice, savory meaty character, pronounced mineral-earth-mushroom, and less overt oak notes. Like aged red Burgundy, a top-quality wine from Cornas, Hermitage, or Côte Rotie can show remarkable complexity over time that defies description.

Cabernet Sauvignon – California

**Young wine:**

**Sight:** Opaque ruby purple in color.

**Nose and palate:** Ripe, jammy, and concentrated black fruit and raisinated fruit with violet floral, green herb, and pronounced new oak notes including vanilla, spices, toast, and more.

**Aged wine:**

**Sight:** Deep ruby garnet in color.

**Nose and palate:** Dried black and raisinated fruit with dried floral, dried herb, cedar, and less oak influence.

Cabernet Sauvignon Blend - Bordeaux

**Young wine:**

**Sight:** Opaque ruby in color.

**Nose and palate:** Concentrated, vibrant black fruit (cherry, berry, currant, and plum) and tart red fruit (cherry and currant) with violet floral, green herb-vegetal, mineral-earth notes, and vanilla-spice from oak.

**Aged wine:**

**Sight:** deep ruby garnet in color.

**Nose and palate:** Dried, stewed, and compoted black and red fruit with dried floral, dried herb-vegetal, more pronounced mushroom-earth-mineral, and less spice and oak influence.

## Dessert wines

Botrytis Sweet Sémillon Blend - Bordeaux

**Young wine:**

**Sight:** Deep straw-yellow in color.

**Nose and palate:** Candied ripe stone fruit (peach, apricot, and nectarine), sweet citrus (orange, Mandarin, and tangerine) with honeysuckle floral, honey, mineral-earth, and pronounced new oak character with vanilla and spice.

**Aged wine:**

**Sight:** Deep burnished gold in color.

**Nose and palate:** Dried, crystallized stone fruit and preserved sweet citrus fruit and citrus peel with dried floral and pronounced botrytis notes including dried honey, saffron, and marmalade. Also, pronounced mushroom and dark earth character with less overt oak spice notes.

*Author's suggestions: Building a personal database of memories for young and older versions of classic wines takes time and experience. Try to attend as many trade tastings as you can because an older vintage is often included to compare against the younger wines. From there, keep detailed notes of the older bottles you get to taste for future reference. Finally, do some work with your memory in regards to younger vs. older wines, even down to individual aromas and flavors. Submodalities (Chapter 24) can be a useful strategy for memory practice.*

# 14

# Judging Wine Quality

*Author's note: The ability to accurately judge wine quality is one of the ultimate goals of any wine training and a necessary tool for any professional. This chapter is an outline of all the aspects that make up wine quality — and how to judge it.*

There is no faking it. As professionals, we are judged by how well we do it. It separates the novice from the professional, and it's the unwritten — even unspoken — goal of any wine training. What is this mysterious coin of the realm? Simple: judging wine quality.

When hired for most jobs in the industry, this is what we are being employed to do. Whether it's buying for a three-star Michelin restaurant wine list or choosing the best currently available sub ten-dollar Merlots for a supermarket, we as professionals are being paid to taste wine and judge quality.

What determines quality in wine? What are the criteria for judging it? How does one develop the experience necessary to be able to competently judge wine quality? Following are some answers to all the previous.

## Wine quality defined

Judging wine quality comprises several basic but important criteria: balance, typicity, context, and previous experience. Here's how they break down.

## Balance

If the wine displays harmony among all its elements, it's said to be balanced. Most of these elements have to do with a wine's structure, as in the levels of alcohol, acid, phenolic bitterness, and tannin. If one or more sticks out like the proverbial sore thumb, the wine isn't balanced and is probably lacking in quality. For example, if a wine is overripe and lacks acidity, it's poorly balanced and lacks quality. Likewise, if a wine is too tannic or oaky, it's also not well-balanced and probably, but not always, of lesser quality. More about that in a moment.

Fruit plays an important role in balance as far as matching the level of acidity. For practically any white or pink wine (and for many minimally oaked or unoaked red wines), the fruit and acid must be balanced for the wine to be of any quality.

A good example of fruit-acid balance in white wine comes from a memory of a tasting some years ago. I was in Germany at the time with a group of MS colleagues. On the last morning of the trip, we met at Weingut Franz Künstler in the Rheingau. If not familiar, winemaker Günter Künstler is one of the best in the Rheingau — and in Germany for that matter. He's one of the few that makes both brilliant dry wines and fruity-styled wines with residual sugar. His noble sweet wines are also off the chart. Günter's winery and vineyards lie at the eastern edge of the Rheingau in the village of Hochheim.

The tasting was amazing. Günter opened over 40 bottles for us in the form of five-year verticals of some of his best wines both dry and sweet. The wine of the visit for me was the 2001 Hochheimer Kirchenstück Spätlese Riesling. The wine had extraordinary intensity and depth, and the balance between the succulent sweet-tart fruit and high acidity was like a razor's edge. It was just about perfect. The wine is still etched in my memory. I have since judged every non-Mosel Spätlese Riesling against it either consciously or unconsciously.

One last note about balance. Context, which is discussed below, comes into play in that some wines of high quality aren't balanced when young. For example, a recent vintage of Nebbiolo-based Barolo can have high tannin and high acidity compared to many other red wines but can also be outstanding — even world-class — in quality.

## Typicity

**Typicity:** a deceptively simple concept. That wine should look, smell, and taste like a good example of others from the same grape and origin. There are many factors that make a wine typical.

**Color:** Is the wine too light in color? Too deep in color? A young, unoaked white wine should be a pale straw in color vs. an older or oaked wine that's yellow or even gold.

**Aromatics:** Lots of factors here including the ripeness and quality of the fruit, the presence or lack of important non-fruit markers (many of which are impact compounds or important varietal aromas and flavors), the presence of earth/mineral, and the use of oak. As I said, there are lots of factors.

**Purity of fruit:** Regardless of price point, grape, or origin, a quality wine to me has a purity of fruit that is easy to recognize. Be it apple, lime, or whatever, the fruit in a wine of any quality always sings through the other aromatics and is easily identifiable.

**Palate:** Does the wine show appropriate fruit ripeness and structure levels? Or is it underripe, possibly meaning early harvesting or a cooler than usual vintage? A ripe or overripe wine signifies the opposite: late harvesting or a warmer than usual vintage. Connecting the dots between fruit quality/character and structure is also important. Finally, the length of the finish speaks to quality. The phrase "the longer the finish the better quality the wine" may be trite but there is something to a wine having length and persistence that is directly related to quality.

**Complexity:** Quality wines will often, but not always, show a good deal of complexity on nose and palate. Here I'm defining complexity in regards to the number of aromas and flavors in a wine combined with how much it evolves on the palate. However, complexity is not always so straightforward. Some wines don't show complexity when young and only develop it over time with age. Other commercially-produced wines won't ever show a good deal of complexity, but still show balance and typicity which can account for quality.

In thinking about typicity, not long ago I tasted a Pouilly Fumé from a warmer vintage. The first impression on the nose was of ripe, almost exotic fruit and a complete lack of the green quality (pyrazines) that's an important marker for any Sauvignon Blanc-based wine. On the palate, the wine lacked acidity and was clumsy. It could have been a lesser quality Central Coast Chardonnay.

Why was the wine so different? Simple answer: the vintage. The year 2018 was a warmer than average year for the Central Vineyards in the Loire, hence the wine was far riper than usual with higher alcohol and markedly less acidity. However, was the wine still of quality? The answer was yes, but with a caveat: it was a well-made wine from a warm year but lacked important varietal markers and therefore was atypical.

The opposite could also be true. Imagine a Cabernet Sauvignon from a well-known region from a cooler vintage. The wine could be lighter in color, red-fruit dominant, and have a pronounced green pyrazinic character. Not exactly typical, but the wine could still be balanced and the quality good.

## Context

As with everything in wine, context is an important factor when judging quality. It comes into play in any tasting experience in the form of the tasting environment, the taster, and the wine itself. Here are a few examples of how context can potentially impact judging quality when tasting.

**The tasting environment:** Includes appropriate lighting, a good ambient temperature, a lack of extraneous noise and odors, and good glassware.

**The wine:** Appropriate tasting temperature and free from faults. Also, the proper tasting order of wines i.e., tasting whites before reds, dry wines before sweet wines, and less tannic reds before tannic reds.

**The taster:** Taster, know thyself! Here I'm referring to the individual knowing their personal sensitivities to structural elements (i.e., avoiding wines with high tannin) as well as being aware of personal likes, dislikes, and even biases. For example, someone may have a strong dislike for new oak in white wine. When asked to select high-end California Chardonnays for a restaurant list, they must be able to set personal bias aside and judge the wines in front of them for quality regardless of oak usage.

Another example would be someone who considers the presence of Brettanomyces in any amount to be a fault. If they're asked to taste through a flight of high-end Northern Rhône Syrah, they would need to be able to put aside their Brett aversion to be able to do a credible job of selecting the best wines.

Finally, the wine price tier also figures into context. Is the wine an inexpensive mass-produced commercial Chardonnay or a pricey domain-bottled White Burgundy? Ultimately, it shouldn't matter. A professional needs to have a frame of reference for both and to be able to judge quality without bias.

## Previous experience

This is the one piece of the quality-judging equation that cannot be replaced or faked. Previous experience is absolutely required to be able to judge quality. Knowing how typical examples of classic grapes and wines are supposed to look, smell, and taste can only be gained through a great deal of tasting experience. Add to that knowledge of vintage variations and specific producers whose wines are atypical but still of high quality.

Yes, it's complicated. But who said tasting was easy? To be any good at it one has to taste a lot of wine over a duration of time. That brings up the question of how one can get the needed experience in order to be able to judge wine quality — regardless of type — at a professional level. Here are some suggestions:

- Taste with a group of other professionals regularly. Other palates and opinions can only expand your tasting universe.
- This may seem obvious, but taste good examples of classic grapes and wines regularly. Initially, don't spend a lot of time tasting atypical wines.
- Mix blind tasting with non-blind tasting. Looking at labels when tasting helps make important memory connections.
- Go to as many trade events as you can — especially those that focus on top producers from a classic region or a consortium of top producers. Taste carefully, listen and take copious notes. Then read your notes later and try to remember the best wines from that particular tasting in as much detail as possible. Do this a couple of times in the following 24-48 hours after the tasting.
- Take a class on wine faults. It will prove invaluable. Also, read up on wine faults and be able to explain why so many of them are contextual.
- Periodically taste lower-tier mass-produced commercial wines so you have a clue about them. This includes White Zinfandel and box wines. Don't lose touch with these wines because at some point in your career you'll have to deal with them. Tasting these wines on a semi-regular basis will help you establish — and maintain — a frame of reference of how good examples in the category should taste. I also recommend tasting commercial and domain wines next to each from time to time. Carefully analyze what defines quality in each category.

*Author's suggestion: Ultimately, your goal is to be able to pick up a glass of wine regardless of the environment or distractions (as in, all hell breaking loose around you) and be able to quickly and completely assess it, provide an opinion about the wine's quality, and be able to explain why. The total analysis may only take 30-plus seconds, but years of previous experience are required to be able to make the right call. This doesn't happen overnight. It happens one glass at a time.*

15

# Objective vs. Subjective in Tasting

*Author's note: The terms objective and subjective are used almost at random when it comes to describing wine. This chapter breaks down most of the criteria on a deductive grid in the context of objective vs. subjective.*

It's a common scenario: An industry person is leading a consumer tasting. During the tasting, two people in the crowd have completely different responses when asked about one of the wines. And their descriptions are wildly different compared to that of said industry person — the one who theoretically should have a clue. The crowd then turns to the industry person who says, "It's OK. Everybody's different. Besides, wine is all subjective."

I'm calling foul here. Saying wine is "all subjective" is not only a monumental cop-out, it's simply wrong. It also reinforces one of the widely held urban myths that wine is impossible to understand and that industry pros like us are making it all up. While one could argue that the entire wine experience is subjective because it's based on one's personal response and interpretation, there is a great deal of it that can actually be quantified.

Before going further, it might be useful to examine the terms *objective* and *subjective* as they apply to the tasting experience. To do so I'll use the deductive tasting grid without the conclusion segments as a guideline to determine which criteria fall under the objective category vs. subjective. There may also be a third category. More on that in a moment.

To begin, working definitions for the terms "objective" and "subjective" are needed. For the purposes of this chapter, I'll use the following:

*"Objective experience: Of, relating to, or being an object, phenomenon, or condition in the realm of sensible experience independent of individual thought and perceptible by any observer."*

*"Subjective experience: Refers to the emotional and cognitive impact of a human experience as opposed to an objective experience which are the actual events of the experience. ... For instance, we are all having a subjective experience whenever we experience pain."*

Now let's map these definitions over to the tasting experience. In wine, certain criteria can be isolated, identified, and quantified through lab analysis. We'll call these elements "objective." Other criteria are described by a taster using their personal and unique life memories. These are subjective as they are based on individual interpretations and are different for everyone.

I want to introduce a third category at this point that combines both objective and subjective experience in regards to tasting. These particular criteria display extremes (little or none vs. a lot) that can easily be identified and are clearly objective. However, the degrees between the two extremes are more open to interpretation and therefore subjective. Hence, objective-subjective.

## The grid

Following are criteria taken from the Deductive Tasting Grid broken down into objective elements that can be quantified, subjective elements that are always shaped by personal interpretation, and finally those that fall into the third objective-subjective category.

## Sight

**Clarity:** In wine is the result of filtration and fining—or the lack thereof. The difference between a clear wine placed next to a cloudy or hazy wine is easy to discern and agree on, as is that in between. Objective.

**Brightness:** The brightness scale in the deductive grid goes from dull to brilliant with several stages in between. While the extremes are easy to identify if placed next to each other, the degrees in between are definitely not. Subjective - Objective.

**Intensity of color:** Extremes in color depth–pale and deep–can easily be seen. Not so true concerning everything in between. Subjective - Objective.

**Color:** Color scales for all major styles of wine have long been established. The actual names for colors may vary, depending on the source. However, anyone in the industry can connect the dots between the color of a wine and a commonly used name. Objective.

**Secondary colors:** Observing the presence of green or silver in a young white wine or garnet highlights in an older red wine is straightforward. Objective.

**Rim variation:** There is always a difference between the color at the core of a glass of red wine and that at the rim or edge. Objective.

**Gas:** The bubbles are either there–or not. Objective.

**Sediment:** Regardless of tartaric acid crystals or actual sediment from non-filtration or age, sediment can easily be seen and identified. Objective.

**Tears/legs:** Here for the first time we're in the subjective universe. The intent of observing the legs/tears/Marangoni effect in a glass of wine is to gain a first impression of the body and/or weight of the wine, which is further related to the level of alcohol, glycerin, or the presence of residual sugar. However, observing legs-tears generates a general impression at best and presupposes multiple things including the use of quality glassware that is cleaned and polished. Subjective.

## Nose

**Clean/faults:** While the degree of sensitivity to common wine faults is unique to the individual and varies, the presence of TCA (trichloranisole), high levels of VA (volatile acidity), Brettanomyces, or other compounds can be isolated and measured in the lab. Objective.

**Intensity of aroma:** Intensity of aroma is directly related to fruit ripeness, certain impact compounds, and structural levels, especially alcohol. Given that, one could place a Pinot Grigio from Alto Adige next to a Gewürztraminer from Alsace and the difference in aromatic intensity would be obvious. However, tasting experience would be needed to calibrate the degrees of aromatic intensity between the two extremes. Objective – Subjective.

**Age assessment:** Oxidative character in wine is due to time spent in barrel or bottle. Again, the two extremes are useful in determining age in the context of this discussion: a young, vibrant, and fresh white wine vs. the same wine, which has been in a bottle for a decade or longer, showing dried fruit character as well as secondary and tertiary aromas and flavors. Hence, old vs. young vs. degrees of development. Objective – Subjective.

**Fruit:** At heart, describing fruit in wine is really the source of the entire objective-subjective debate. Our response to fruit qualities in wine is always dependent on our unique life memories of said aromas and flavors. Hence, my "kiwi" call on a particular white wine could be your Bartlett pear, which might be someone else's Fuji apple. In this case, we are all equally correct in our calls. Subjective. *And thus, it will always be...*

**Fruit quality:** Back to the objective universe. Tart fruit due to lack of ripeness results in less alcohol and higher natural acidity. Ripe, even raisinated fruit qualities are due to ripe and raisinated fruit, which means higher alcohol and less natural acidity in the wine. Fruit quality can easily be linked to structural elements that can easily be quantified in a lab. I'm calling objective here.

**Non-fruit:** Here a mix of objective-subjective with a strong nod to objective. With subjective, one's life memories come into play in calling various flowers, herbs, and spices in a wine. Beyond that, the non-fruit category lands squarely in the objective camp in the form of important impact compounds in wine, many of which are chemical in nature. Objective - Subjective.

**Earth:** While the debate over earth-mineral has long raged in the industry and beyond, recent use of DNA sequencing technology shows that bacteria and yeasts in vineyard soil play an important role during fermentation as well as the chemical compounds in the finished wine. However, it's worth noting that smelling and tasting minerals and earth in wine is something that usually requires experience on the part of the taster. Objective - Subjective.

**Wood:** Beyond the obvious aromas and flavors from oak aging, putting wine in a barrel adds chemical compounds from the actual wood as well as properties from tasting/caramelizing the inside of the cask. Objective.

## Palate

**Dry/sweetness:** Due to the presence of (or lack of) residual sugar. Easy call: Objective.

**Body:** Due to the levels of alcohol, glycerin, and dry extract. All are easily measurable and therefore Objective.

**Fruit:** Confirm what was smelled in the wine. Again, the fruit falls squarely into the Subjective camp.

**Fruit quality:** Confirming that fruit quality is the result of structural levels as they relate to harvest timing and regional climate. Objective.

**Non-fruit:** As with the nose, bits of subjectivity are overshadowed by impact compounds and other elements which can be cultured out in a lab. Objective-Subjective.

**Earth-mineral:** Ditto the nose. Objective - Subjective.

**Wood:** As above: Objective.

**Acidity:** While every individual has unique tolerances to each of the structural elements (levels of acidity, alcohol, phenolic bitterness, and tannin), all can easily be quantified in a lab. Objective.

**Alcohol:** Ditto above. Objective.

**Phenolic bitterness:** Ditto above. Objective.

**Tannin:** Same. Objective.

**Texture:** This is one of the more challenging aspects of the palate to quantify. Subjective.

**Balance:** Regardless of definition, defining balance in a wine tends to be a moving target, and finding universal agreement is far from easy. Subjective.

**Length/finish:** The length of the finish of any wine is not always agreed on — even by seasoned pros. Subjective.

**Complexity:** There are many definitions of the term complexity. We'll go with the one that says complexity in wine is determined by the number of aromas and flavors combined with how much the wine changes on your palate. If it's a matter of counting, then an objective vote makes sense. However, how a wine evolves on the palate does not make for universal agreement. Objective-subjective.

## Scorecard

I used 32 of the 40-plus total criteria on the deductive grid. My scorecard breaks down as follows:

**Objective:** 17 criteria or 53%

**Objective-subjective:** 9 criteria or 28%

**Subjective:** 6 criteria or 19%

## Coda

What can we take away from this less-than-official survey? That tasting is a blend of objective and subjective experiences with a fair amount of the two combined. Perhaps the most important takeaway is that one cannot generalize tasting as "all subjective" because it's not true. Further, the more experienced one is as a taster, the more objective wine becomes. The less experienced, the more subjective. To that point, Michael Meagher, MS, once told me, "Once I viewed deductive tasting as not something that I subjectively did, but rather as something that was purely objective and driven by unadulterated data, it became a lot easier to connect the dots." I couldn't agree more.

Ultimately, it's our job as professionals and educators to make absolutely clear to consumers and students alike that tasting is a combination of subjective and objective experience. If we do our job, everyone will avoid massive confusion, especially those just getting into wine. And that's a very good thing indeed.

*Author's suggestion: Objective vs. subjective is a good topic to revisit every now and again. Over time, the wine tasting experience will become more objective for you. If it seems frustrating now, stay with it. In time, you'll be delighted to discover how much you know and remember — and how objective tasting has become.*

# 16

# Using Pattern Recognition for Blind Tasting White Wines

*Author's note: Every second of the day we're bombarded with over a billion bits of sensory information. If our brain didn't filter out 99.9% of it, our motherboards would constantly freeze. What's interesting is how we're able to constantly categorize all the information and look for patterns we recognize so the world makes "sense" to us. This allows us to find a friend in a sea of faces or remember how to get dressed in the dark (or not). Pattern recognition is also an important strategy for identifying grapes and wines when blind tasting, not to mention judging quality and assessing typicity.*

The following is a guide of sorts to classic white wines, each with a subset of the most important impact compounds, fruit qualities, and structural levels. Memorizing these subsets will help to form unique internal "patterns" for recognizing grapes and wines during an exam. It goes without saying that these patterns are my own. I strongly recommend that students use them as a point of departure and create their own list.

### Chardonnay: France - Chablis Premier Cru

**Fruit quality:** Tart.

**Impact compounds:** Lees contact - possible malolactic (ML) - pronounced chalky minerality - possible use of oak.

**Structure:** Dry - medium to medium-plus alcohol - medium-plus to high acidity.

### Chardonnay: France - Côte de Beaune

**Fruit quality:** Tart - ripe.

**Impact compounds:** Lees – ML – mushroom/earth/mineral – oak usage (often new).

**Structure:** Dry - medium to medium-plus alcohol - medium-plus to high acidity.

### Chardonnay: U.S. - California

**Fruit quality:** Tart – ripe - overripe.

**Impact compounds:** Lees contact – ML – oak usage (often new).

**Structure:** Dry to off dry - medium-plus to high alcohol - medium to medium-plus acidity.

### Sauvignon Blanc: France - Loire Valley - Sancerre and Pouilly-Fumé

**Fruit quality:** Tart.

**Impact compounds:** Green herbal/vegetal (pyrazines) - pronounced chalky minerality - possible oak in Pouilly-Fumé.

**Structure:** Dry - medium alcohol - medium-plus to high acidity.

### Sauvignon Blanc: New Zealand

**Fruit quality:** Tart - ripe.

**Impact compounds:** Green herbal/vegetal (pyrazines) – possible mineral.

**Structure:** Dry - medium-plus alcohol - medium-plus acidity.

### Chenin Blanc: Loire Valley - Vouvray and Savennières

**Fruit quality:** Tart - ripe – possible botrytis influence.

**Impact compounds:** SO2 - possible botrytis – chalky minerality.

**Structure:** Bone dry to medium sweet depending on style - medium to medium-plus alcohol - medium-plus to high acidity.

### Chenin Blanc: U.S. - California and Washington State

**Fruit quality:** Tart - ripe.

**Impact compounds:** Overt fruity quality - possible residual sugar.

**Structure:** Off-dry to slightly sweet - medium alcohol - medium-plus acidity.

### Albariño: Spain – Rías Baixas

**Fruit quality:** Tart - ripe.

**Impact compounds:** Floral (terpenes) - pilsner-lees contact – mineral.

**Structure:** Dry - medium to medium-plus alcohol - medium-plus to high acidity - phenolic bitterness.

### Grüner Veltliner: Austria

**Fruit quality:** Tart – ripe - possible botrytis influence.

**Impact compounds:** White pepper (rotundone) - herbal-vegetal-botanical notes – lees contact - earth/mineral - botrytis influence depending on style.

**Structure:** Dry to off dry - medium to high alcohol - medium-plus to high acidity – phenolic bitterness.

### Riesling: Germany

**Fruit quality:** Tart – ripe - possible botrytis influence.

**Impact compounds:** Possible SO2 – TDN - possible botrytis influence - slate/mineral.

**Structure:** Dry (trocken) to very sweet depending on classification - low to medium alcohol - medium-plus to high acidity.

### Riesling: France - Alsace

**Fruit quality:** Tart - ripe - possible botrytis influence.

**Impact compounds:** TDN - possible botrytis - earth/mineral.

**Structure:** Dry to off-dry - medium-plus alcohol - medium-plus to high acidity.

### Riesling: Australia - Clare Valley and Eden Valley

**Fruit quality:** Tart - ripe.

**Impact compounds:** Considerable TDN - pronounced mineral.

**Structure:** Dry - medium alcohol - medium-plus to high acidity.

### Pinot Gris: France - Alsace

**Fruit quality:** Ripe – possible botrytis influence.

**Impact compounds:** Ripe fruit quality - possible botrytis.

**Structure:** Dry to off-dry - medium-plus to high alcohol - medium to medium-plus acidity - phenolic bitterness.

### Pinot Grigio: Italy - Alto Adige

**Fruit quality:** Tart.

**Impact compounds:** Floral (terpenes) – lees contact – mineral.

**Structure:** Dry - medium alcohol - medium-plus acidity – slight phenolic bitterness.

### Viognier: France - Northern Rhône

**Fruit quality:** Tart - ripe.

**Impact compounds:** Floral (terpenes) – less contact – ML – mineral – oak usage.

**Structure:** Dry - medium to medium-plus alcohol - medium-plus acidity - phenolic bitterness.

### Viognier: New World - California and Australia

**Fruit quality:** Ripe – overripe.

**Impact compounds:** Considerable floral (terpenes) – lees contact – ML – oak usage.

**Structure:** Dry - medium-plus to high alcohol - medium to medium-plus acidity - phenolic bitterness.

### Gewürztraminer: France - Alsace

**Fruit quality:** Ripe – overripe – possible botrytis influence.

**Impact compounds:** Pronounced floral (terpenes) – possible botrytis – earth/mineral.

**Structure:** Dry to slightly sweet - medium-plus to high alcohol - medium-minus to medium acidity - pronounced phenolic bitterness.

### Muscat à Petits Grains: France - Alsace

**Fruit quality:** Tart – ripe – overripe.

**Impact compounds:** Pronounced floral (terpenes) – possible botrytis influence – earth/mineral.

**Structure:** Dry - medium-plus to high alcohol - medium-plus acidity - considerable phenolic bitterness.

### Torrontés: Argentina - Salta

**Fruit quality:** Tart - ripe.

**Impact compounds:** Overt fruit quality - considerable floral (terpenes) – common lack of earth/mineral.

**Structure:** Dry - medium-plus alcohol - medium to medium-plus acidity – considerable phenolic bitterness.

### Marsanne-Roussanne Blend: France - Rhône Valley

**Fruit quality:** Tart - ripe.

**Impact compounds:** Floral/terpenes in lighter style – oxidative character in oak-aged wines – earth/mineral – possible oak usage.

**Structure:** Dry - medium-plus to high alcohol – medium to medium-plus acidity - phenolic bitterness.

### Sémillon: France - Bordeaux - Graves Sec - Pessac-Léognan

**Fruit quality:** Tart and ripe.

**Impact compounds:** Possible SO2/mercaptan note – mineral – phenolic bitterness – possible oak usage.

**Structure:** Dry - medium alcohol - medium-plus acidity – slight phenolic bitterness.

### Sémillon: Bordeaux: France - Sauternes and Barsac

**Fruit quality:** Ripe – overripe - preserved - botrytis influence.

**Impact compounds:** Botrytis – residual sugar – pronounced earth – oak usage.

**Structure:** Medium sweet to dessert sweet - medium-plus alcohol - medium-plus acidity.

### Semillon: Australia - Hunter Valley

**Fruit quality:** Tart – under ripe - ripe.

**Impact compounds:** Two styles: stainless steel wines with floral/terpenes – mineral – phenolic bitterness; oak-aged wines - oxidative character – mineral – oak usage.

**Structure:** Dry - medium-minus to medium-plus alcohol – medium-plus to high acidity.

### Melon de Bourgogne: France - Loire Valley - Muscadet

**Fruit quality:** Tart.

**ID keys:** Lees contact – pronounced mineral.

**Structure:** Dry - medium alcohol - high acidity.

## Assyrtiko: Greece - Santorini

**Fruit quality:** Tart – ripe.

**ID keys:** Tart-ripe fruit quality - pronounced minerality – possible oak usage.

**Structure:** Dry - medium-plus to high alcohol - medium-plus to high acidity –phenolic bitterness.

*Author's note: Here are some suggestions on how to use the information in this chapter:*

- *There is a great deal of information above. Break it down into three-to-five wines at a time to make it manageable.*
- *Once again, remember to use this list as a point of departure. I recommend that students use it to help create their own list.*
- *I also recommend using a laptop, iPad, or other tablet for writing tasting notes so one can easily organize them and access them in the future.*
- *Remember to have fun with the process.*

# 17

# Using Pattern Recognition for Blind Tasting Red Wines

*Author's note: This chapter also deals with pattern recognition, specifically for blind tasting practice with classic red wines.*

In keeping with the last chapter, the following is a guide to classic red wines, each with a subset of the most important impact compounds, fruit qualities, and structural levels. Memorizing these subsets will help to form unique internal "patterns" for recognizing grapes and wines during an exam. Again, I strongly recommend that students use this list as a point of departure and a vehicle to help create their own list.

### Cabernet Sauvignon Blend: France - Left Bank Bordeaux

**Fruit quality:** Tart - ripe.

**Impact compounds:** Green herbal/vegetal (pyrazines) – considerable earth/mineral – oak usage.

**Structure:** Dry - medium-plus alcohol - medium-plus acidity - medium-plus to high tannin.

### Cabernet Sauvignon: U.S. - California

**Fruit quality:** Ripe – overripe – raisinated.

**ID keys:** Possible raisination – possible green herbal/vegetal (pyrazines) - new oak usage.

**Structure:** Dry - medium-plus to high alcohol - medium to medium-plus acidity - medium-plus to high tannin.

### Cabernet Sauvignon: Australia - Coonawarra and Margaret River

**Fruit quality:** Tart – ripe.

**ID keys:** Pronounced green herbal/vegetal notes (pyrazines) – possible mint/eucalyptus – oak usage.

**Structure:** Dry - medium-plus to high alcohol - medium to medium-plus acidity - medium-plus to high tannin.

### Merlot Blend: France - Right Bank Bordeaux

**Fruit quality:** Tart – ripe.

**Impact compounds:** Green herbal/vegetal (pyrazines) – considerable earth/mineral – oak usage.

**Structure:** Dry - medium-plus alcohol - medium-plus acidity - medium-plus tannin (softer tannin than Left Bank wines).

### Merlot: New World - California

**Fruit quality:** Ripe – overripe.

**Impact compounds:** Possible green herbal/vegetal (pyrazines) – oak usage.

**Structure:** Dry - medium-plus to high alcohol - medium-plus acidity - medium-plus tannin (softer tannin than Cabernet Sauvignon).

### Cabernet Franc: Loire Valley - Chinon and Bourgueil

**Fruit quality:** Tart – ripe.

**Impact compounds:** Pronounced green herbal/vegetal (pyrazines) – possible stem inclusion - considerable chalky mineral – oak usage (used).

**Structure:** Dry - medium alcohol - medium-plus acidity - medium to medium-plus tannin.

### Malbec: Argentina - Mendoza

**Fruit quality:** Tart – ripe.

**Impact compounds:** Opaque purple color – possible green herbal/vegetal (pyrazines) – oak usage.

**Structure:** Dry - medium-plus to high alcohol - medium-plus acidity - medium-plus tannin.

### Carménère: Chile - Central Valley

**Fruit quality:** Tart - ripe.

**Impact compounds:** Pronounced vegetal/green peppercorn (pyrazines) - possible earth – oak usage.

**Structure:** Dry - medium-plus to high alcohol - medium-plus acidity - medium to medium-plus tannin.

### Pinot Noir: France – Burgundy - Côte de Nuits

**Fruit quality:** Tart - ripe.

**Impact compounds:** Lighter color - possible stem inclusion – considerable earth/mineral – oak usage.

**Structure:** Dry - medium to medium-plus alcohol - medium-plus acidity - medium to medium-plus tannin.

### Pinot Noir: France – Burgundy – Côte de Beaune

**Fruit quality:** Tart - ripe.

**Impact compounds:** Lighter color - possible stem inclusion – considerable earth/mineral – oak usage.

**Impact compounds:** Lighter color – possible stem inclusion – potentially earthier than Côte de Nuits – oak usage.

**Structure:** Dry - medium to medium-plus alcohol - medium-plus acidity - medium to medium-plus tannin.

### Pinot Noir: U.S. - California and Oregon

**Fruit quality:** Tart – ripe.

**Impact compounds:** Possible stem inclusion – possible earth/mineral – oak usage.

**Structure:** Dry - medium to medium-plus alcohol - medium to medium-plus acidity - medium to medium-plus tannin.

### Pinot Noir: New Zealand - Central Otago

**Fruit quality:** Tart – ripe.

**Impact compounds:** Lighter color – possible stem inclusion – herbal/leafy – possible mineral – oak usage.

**Structure:** dry - medium to medium-plus alcohol - medium to medium-plus acidity - medium to medium-plus tannin.

### Gamay: France – Beaujolais-Villages

**Fruit quality:** Tart – ripe - candied.

**Impact compounds:** Lighter color – carbonic maceration notes - stem inclusion – earth/mineral.

**Structure:** Dry - medium alcohol - medium-plus acidity - medium-minus to medium tannin.

### Gamay: France - Beaujolais Cru

**Fruit quality:** Tart – ripe.

**Impact compounds:** Possible carbonic notes – possible stem inclusion – earth/mineral – possible oak usage (used).

**Structure:** Dry - medium to medium-plus alcohol - medium-plus acidity - medium to medium-plus tannin.

### Sangiovese: Italy - Tuscany - Chianti Classico

**Fruit quality:** Tart – ripe – dried.

**Impact compounds:** Anise/herb - considerable earth/mineral – oak usage.

**Structure:** Bone dry to dry - medium plus alcohol - medium-plus to high acidity - medium-plus tannin.

### Sangiovese: Italy - Tuscany - Brunello di Montalcino

**Fruit quality:** Tart – ripe – dried - oxidized.

**Impact compounds:** Anise/herb - considerable earth/mineral – oxidative character - oak usage (barrique or larger barrel).

**Structure:** Bone dry to dry - medium plus alcohol - medium-plus to high acidity - medium-plus to high tannin.

### Sangiovese: Italy - Tuscany - Vino Nobile di Montepulciano

**Fruit quality:** Tart – ripe – dried.

**Impact compounds:** Fruit ripeness (darker fruit from other varieties) - considerable earth/mineral - oak usage (barrique or larger barrel).

**Structure:** Bone dry to dry – medium to medium plus alcohol - medium-plus to high acidity – medium tannin.

### Nebbiolo: Italy - Piedmont - Barolo and Barbaresco

**Fruit quality:** Tart – ripe – dried - oxidized.

**Impact compounds:** Evolved color and secondary color – pronounced floral – considerable earth/mineral – oak usage.

**Structure:** Bone dry - medium-plus to high alcohol - high acidity - medium-plus to high tannin.

### Barbera: Italy - Piedmont

**Fruit quality:** Tart – ripe – dried – possible oxidation.

**Impact compounds:** Herbal notes – possible oxidation – earth/mineral – possible oak usage.

**Structure:** Dry - medium to medium-plus alcohol - medium-plus acidity - medium to medium-plus tannin.

### Corvina Blend: Italy - Veneto - Amarone

**Fruit quality:** Tart – ripe – dried – raisinated – oxidized - possible botrytis influence.

**Impact compounds:** Raisinated fruit – volatile acidity – possible botrytis – possible Brettanomyces - considerable earth/mineral – oak usage.

**Structure:** Dry to off-dry - high alcohol - medium-plus acidity - medium-plus to high tannin.

### Aglianico: Italy - Campania

**Fruit quality:** Tart – ripe – dried.

**Impact compounds:** Baked fruit quality – possible reductive/sulphury quality – pronounced earth/mineral – oak usage.

**Structure:** Dry – medium-plus to high alcohol - medium-plus acidity - medium-plus to high tannin.

### Tempranillo: Spain - Rioja Reserva and Gran Reserva

**Fruit quality:** Tart – ripe – dried - oxidized.

**Impact compounds:** Dried/oxidative character – chalk-mineral – oak usage (American oak with traditional wines).

**Structure:** Dry with medium-plus alcohol - medium-plus acidity - medium to medium-plus tannin.

### Zinfandel: U.S. - California - Dry Creek Valley

**Fruit quality:** Tart – ripe – jammy - raisinated.

**Impact compounds:** Possible uneven fruit ripeness - black/white pepper (rotundone) – lack of earth/mineral – oak usage (often American).

**Structure:** Dry - medium-plus to high alcohol - medium to medium-plus acidity - medium to medium-plus tannin.

### Syrah: France - Northern Rhône

**Fruit quality:** Tart – ripe – dried.

**Impact compounds:** Black/white pepper (rotundone) – savory meat/game qualities – possible Brettanomyces - considerable earth/mineral – oak usage.

**Structure:** Dry - medium to medium-plus alcohol - medium-plus acidity - medium to high tannin.

### Syrah: Australia - Barossa Shiraz

**Fruit quality:** Tart – ripe – dried - raisinated.

**Impact compounds:** Possible raisinated fruit - black/white pepper (rotundone) – savory meat/game qualities –– oak usage (sometimes American).

**Structure:** Dry - medium-plus to high alcohol - medium to medium-plus acidity - medium-plus tannin.

### Grenache Blend: France - Southern Rhône

**Fruit quality:** Ripe – jammy – cooked - dried.

**Impact compounds:** Mediterranean herb/garrigue - black/white pepper (rotundone) – savory meat/game qualities - considerable earth/mineral – oak usage.

**Structure:** Dry - high alcohol - medium-plus acidity - medium-plus to high tannin.

### Grenache: Australia - Barossa

**Fruit quality:** Ripe – jammy.

**Impact compounds:** Black/white pepper (rotundone) – mint/eucalyptus – oak usage.

**Structure:** Dry - high alcohol - medium to medium-plus acidity - medium-plus tannin.

### Mourvèdre: France - Provence - Bandol

**Fruit quality:** Tart - ripe.

**Impact compounds:** Black/white pepper (rotundone) - savory herb - possible reductive quality – pronounced earth/mineral - oak usage.

**Structure:** Dry - medium-plus to high alcohol - medium-plus acidity - medium-plus to high tannin.

### Monastrell (Mourvèdre): Spain - Jumilla

**Fruit quality:** Ripe – jammy.

**Impact compounds:** Raisination - black/white pepper (rotundone) - savory herb – earth/mineral – oak usage.

**Structure:** Dry - medium-plus to high alcohol - medium to medium-plus acidity - medium to medium-plus tannin.

### Pinotage - South Africa - Stellenbosch

**Fruit quality:** Tart - ripe – jammy.

**Impact compounds:** Pronounced herbal/vegetal – possible reductive/sulfur quality – possible Brettanomyces – pronounced earth/mineral – oak usage.

**Structure:** Dry - medium to medium-plus alcohol - medium to medium-plus acidity - medium to medium-plus tannin.

*Author's suggestions: Here are some recommendations on how to use the information in this chapter.*

- *There is a great deal of information above. Break it down into three-to-five wines at a time to make it manageable.*
- *Remember to use this list as a point of departure. I recommend that students use it to help create their own list.*
- *Once again, remember to have fun with the process.*

# 18

# On Tasting Notes

*Author's note: It's important for students to be able to write concise and consistent notes during tastings. This chapter breaks down tasting notes into the most important criteria. It also includes my personal tasting note template to use as a guide.*

Tasting notes. They're a blessing or a curse, depending on your viewpoint. If you're in the business, they're a necessity. For industry pros, a tasting note is a multi-layered memory device; an attempt to record impressions of a wine in the moment and usually on the fly. For collectors, a favorable tasting note paired with a high numerical score can be the make or break in any important (and usually expensive) wine purchase.

However, there's also a dark side to tasting notes, so to speak. Many consumers find the florid language used in some notes off-putting at best and completely alien at worst. In fact, critics call out certain well-known writers for exaggerated descriptors used in their tasting notes.

One of the challenges in writing a meaningful tasting note is being able to separate the technical assessment of a given wine from an emotional response. But the problem runs much deeper. Wine as an idiom has no inherent language. To compensate, we as an industry have over time shamelessly—and unconsciously—begged, borrowed, and stolen terms and nomenclature from other completely unrelated fields. The result is a messy pastiche of terminology with some parts based on cold science and others on poetry and whimsy. It's like Hello Kitty trying to play free-form jazz in a cold, unlit industrial lab.

Part of the language issue stems from the fact that anyone's reaction to a wine always involves both objective and subjective experience. Not everyone has the awareness or the training to separate the two. In an effort to create meaningful tasting notes, I'll attempt to do just that.

In Chapter 15 I cover the objective vs. subjective aspects of wine in detail. I mention that too often we hear the phrase, "wine is all subjective," which is simply not true. Certain elements in wine can be isolated, identified, and quantified through lab analysis. These criteria are objective. Other elements in the wine experience are based on a taster's unique and very personal life memories. These are subjective and will always be different for everyone.

Why is objective-subjective so important in the context of writing tasting notes? Because the florid language some consider the bane of tasting notes is directly linked to the subjective aspects of wine. However, in the context of writing tasting notes I believe the subjective aspect of wine is not only relevant — it's important. Aside from all the technical information, it's the one part of a tasting note that allows a taster's unique voice to shine through.

## A proposed tasting note template

Here's my proposed tasting note template. By no means is it written in stone. It's meant as a point of departure. The intent is to create a straightforward yet concise form that allows one to communicate the objective and subjective elements in a wine in a consistent manner.

## The basics

First, my template has a place to record the basics: what the wine looks, smells, and tastes like.

**Visual:** What color is the wine? There are different scales for wine color but practically any color can easily be understood by a reader. The clarity of the wine (or lack thereof) should also be noted.

**Nose:** Includes descriptors of the fruit, fruit quality, non-fruit, earth-mineral, and the use of wood.

**Palate:** Confirms what's already smelled and speaks to the structural aspects of the wine — acidity, alcohol, tannin, and phenolic bitterness. Can also include one's impression of the texture, balance, and finish of the wine.

## Wine profiles: Numbers with meaning

Everything above is commonly found in most tasting notes. The next segment of my proposal is definitely not—but it's desperately needed. It's a short profile that easily communicates the important information about a wine's character and physical make up in terms of intensity, sweetness, the use of oak, and more.

All credit here goes to good friend and fellow Master Sommelier, Peter Granoff. In the summer of 1994 Peter opened the cyber doors to Virtual Vineyards with his brother-in-law Robert Olson. Virtual Vineyards was not only the first online wine retail "shop," but the very first online retailer of any kind. Peter and Robert started Virtual Vineyards on a server in Olson's garage.

To avoid using numeric scores, Peter devised a system to convey the most important information about every wine that would appear in the Virtual Vineyards portfolio. His system used seven criteria to profile each wine: intensity of flavor, body, sweetness/dryness, acidity, tannin, oak, and complexity. Further, these seven criteria were represented in one-through-seven increments with one representing least/none and seven the most or maximum.

For example, with sweetness or dryness, Peter's chart lists "bone dry" at one end with dessert sweet at the other. For intensity of flavor, the chart ranges from "delicate" at number one to "intense" at number seven.

Note Peter's very deliberate decision not to use a 1-10 scale simply because it would be easy to extrapolate any number into a base 10 score—which he was trying to avoid at all costs. The results looked something like this:

Intensity of flavor - Delicate: 1  2  3  4  5  6  7  Intense

Sweetness/dryness - Bone dry: 1  2  3  4  5  6  7  Dessert

Body - Light-bodied: 1  2  3  4  5  6  7  Full-bodied

Acid - Light acidity: 1  2  3  4  5  6  7  Tart acidity

Tannin - No tannin: 1  2  3  4  5  6  7  High tannin

Oak - No oak: 1  2  3  4  5  6  7  100% new oak

Complexity - Simple: 1  2  3  4  5  6  7  Very complex

As mentioned, all the wines listed in the Virtual Vineyards portfolio were profiled with Peter's tasting chart. In addition, tasting notes were added that included descriptors for the wine, some of which could be subjective in nature. Technical information was included, if available, and a bit information about the winery. Suggested food pairings were sometimes included as well.

I joined Peter at Virtual Vineyards in 1996 and worked with him for five years until the company's tragic demise in April of 2001. It's worth noting that Virtual Vineyards/the original wine.com sold over $50 million of wine during those five years using Peter's system-and without ever using a single numerical score.

## Wrapping it up: Thoughts, impressions, and opinions

The last segment of my template is a space for personal thoughts and opinions about the wine. The remarks could range from varietal typicity, winemaking, and vintage character to simply whether the taster either likes, loves, or loathes the wine. True, this is also where things can easily get florid and messy in a heartbeat. But again, I believe it's absolutely necessary for a taster to have the opportunity to record and share their personal impressions about any given wine.

Now for the template itself. I've formatted a document that provides ample opportunities for recording what's technically in the glass, uses Peter's profile, and includes a place for opinions, musings, and more.

| Tasting Note Template by Tim Gaiser, MS | | | | | | | | | |
|---|---|---|---|---|---|---|---|---|---|
| Date: | | | | | | | | | |
| Wine: | | | | | | | | | |
| Sight: | | | | | | | | | |
| Nose: | | | | | | | | | |
| Palate: | | | | | | | | | |
| Profile | | | | | | | | | |
| Intensity of flavor | Delicate | 1 | 2 | 3 | 4 | 5 | 6 | 7 | Intense |
| Sweetness/dryness | Bone Dry | 1 | 2 | 3 | 4 | 5 | 6 | 7 | Dessert |
| Body | Light-Bodied | 1 | 2 | 3 | 4 | 5 | 6 | 7 | Full-Bodied |
| Acid | Lower Acidity | 1 | 2 | 3 | 4 | 5 | 6 | 7 | Tart/High Acidity |
| Tannin | No Tannin | 1 | 2 | 3 | 4 | 5 | 6 | 7 | High Tannin |
| Oak | No Oak | 1 | 2 | 3 | 4 | 5 | 6 | 7 | 100% New Oak |
| Complexity | Simple | 1 | 2 | 3 | 4 | 5 | 6 | 7 | Very Complex |
| Thoughts/opinions: | | | | | | | | | |

*Author's suggestion: Tasting notes will always be a genteel battleground of sorts, where individuals can quickly establish polar opposites in wine writing philosophy and then engage in a spirited—and hopefully civilized —debate. It's yet another example of the beautiful imprecision of wine. I hope that my template will help ease the conflict or at least create some constructive dialogue. Readers should feel free to use it as a point of departure and then create their own unique tasting note template.*

# 19

# A Tech Sheet Manifesto

*Author's nose: A tech or technical sheet can be a wine buyer's best friend. These one-page outlines offer important information about a wine, from vineyard to bottling, that can help with critical buying decisions. Below I've outlined what I believe to be important criteria for any tech sheet.*

At a recent conference, good friend Peter Granoff, MS, and I drew the task of taking a group through a dozen wines from the Roussillon region during a lunch. In the pregame conversation over coffee, we were going through tech sheets for each of the wines. At one point, Peter chuckled, shook his head, and said, "You're not going to believe this." He handed me the sheet for a sweet fortified wine from the Rivesaltes. I read it and had the same reaction. Here's a verbatim quote from the tech sheet printed from the winery's website:

*"Amber dress, reflections caramel. The nose on the cooked red berries, the pit (core), and the vanilla is a prelude to a molten, elegant palace, skated by the time, when gets involved in aromas of malt, peat, wax, and always cooked fruits, before one finale which lets drill the rancio."*

Immediately snippets from the "Surrealist Manifesto" by Andre Breton started ping-ponging in my head. Aside from a seriously mangled translation, the description for the wine was somewhere between appalling and nonsense. It was also useless as far as our presentation was concerned, despite the fact that the wine turned out to be delicious.

A tech sheet, if not familiar, is a single-page document about a specific wine usually written by the winery or in some cases the importer or distributor. The sheet lists pertinent technical information about the wine including how and where the fruit was grown, how the wine was made and aged, and potentially more.

Tech sheets are important. Anyone in an industry buying position, be it for a restaurant or retail, needs well-crafted tech sheets to have the right information to help make sensible purchasing decisions. Unfortunately, more often than not they fall short in providing quality information. Sometimes, as with the wine above, they border on incomprehensible.

After giving it some thought, I decided to create a template of sorts for tech sheets. I humbly submit the following. Mind you, I wrote it to be as comprehensive as possible knowing full well that the complete template would only apply to a fraction of all wines. But I wanted to create a blueprint that could be used as a starting point.

## Tech sheet template

### General information

**Complete name of the wine:** Including vintage, region, appellation, sub-region, even specific vineyard if appropriate.

**Classification:** i.e., the 1855 Classification for Bordeaux or the VDP Grosse Lage Classification in Germany.

**Cases produced:** In six or 12-bottle cases.

**Grape variety or blend:** If a blend, list percentages for each grape from highest to lowest.

## Viticulture

**Harvest dates:** Give a range if necessary.

**Ripeness levels at harvest:** In brix or other (degrees öechsle, etc.)

**Fruit condition:** Note late-harvest or botrytis-affected fruit as appropriate.

**Vineyard location:** Identify as specifically as possible.

**Vineyard elevation:** In feet or meters.

**Vineyard size:** In acres or hectares.

**Yield:** In tons per acre or hectoliters per hectare.

**Climate:** Continental, maritime, etc.

**Clonal and rootstock selections:** Clonal selections are especially important with grapes/wines like Pinot noir. But don't get carried away. A max of three clones listed does the job. Include the type of rootstock if available.

**Soil types:** Important, but keep it brief.

**Age of vines:** Listed by the year the vineyard was planted or simply the age of the vineyard. Don't bother with the always-abused "old vines" moniker unless the vineyard in question is over 50 years old.

**Trellising:** Guyot, gobelet, etc.

**Irrigation:** vs. dry farming.

**Farming practices:** Sustainable vs. organic vs. biodynamic, etc. Also list any appropriate certifications that apply to the previous.

**Harvesting:** Hand vs. machine.

## Winemaking

**Pressing:** Whole cluster, partial whole cluster, vs. destemming.

**Press type:** Basket, coquard, bladder, etc.

**Yeast type:** Native vs. cultured (keeping in mind that ultimately all yeast is "native"). List specific cultured yeast.

**Pre-and-post-fermentation maceration:** Length of time for either or both. Also, include temperature for pre-fermentation maceration (cold soak).

**Fermentation vessel:** Stainless steel, oak, or other (concrete tanks, amphora etc.)

**Fermentation techniques:** Punch-down, delestage, whole cluster, carbonic maceration, etc.

**Length of primary fermentation:** In days or weeks.

**Malolactic fermentation/conversion:** Yes/no and if yes, list the percentage of the wine that went through ML.

**Lees contact:** How long and if bâtonnage is used.

## Maturation

**Barrels:** Size (in liters or gallons), origin (country and/or forest), and times used. If the barrels are a mix of ages, list as appropriate.

**Time in wood (or tank):** In months or years.

**Fining:** Substances used (or unfined).

**Filtration:** Methods used (or unfiltered).

**Bottle age:** In months or years.

**SO2:** If added during winemaking or at bottling (or not).

**Closure type:** Natural cork, agglomerated cork, screwcap, Vinolok, plastic, etc.

**Technical Data**

**ABV (alcohol by volume):** Try to be accurate. We can tell.

**Residual sugar:** In grams per liter.

**TA (total acidity):** In grams per liter.

**pH:** Can be listed instead of TA.

## The Rest

**Growing season:** Provide 75-100 words max about the season including bud break timing, issues such as drought vs. heavy rainfall, and general temperature trends. Compare to a recent similar vintage if appropriate.

**Food and wine pairing suggestions:** Don't bother here unless you have a clue. There's more than enough, "works well with pasta, roasted lamb, and sushi," nonsense on back labels as it is. By the way, the TTB (Trade and Tax Bureau) actually calls the back label the front label and vice versa. I will say no more.

**Tasting notes:** For the sake of humanity, leave out any romantic and/or pithy suggestions about "savoring" the wine "during candle-lit walks on the beach." Seriously. Also, avoid comparing your wine to famous wines from other regions (California Chardonnay to Burgundy, for example) unless you are absolutely sure that the comparison is relevant. Finally, any tasting notes included need to be short and devoid of BS or marketing speak.

*Author's suggestions: While this may seem like a lot of information, it's actually not. When faced with choosing between five different Crozes-Hermitages or a half-dozen Russian River Valley Chardonnays, a good tech sheet can help a buyer choose one wine over the rest. Again, I'm not expecting anyone to adopt my template as is. It's intended to be a guideline. Hopefully, wineries will give tech sheets more thought and provide buyers with useful and relevant information to help make their day-to-day lives easier. Then the wineries would sell more wine. And that's always a good thing.*

# 20

# Suggested Producers for Tasting Practice

*Author's note: This chapter is a list of suggested producers for tasting practice. However, before going further, two things must be noted. First, this list has no connection to tasting exams offered by any wine certification organization. Second, this list and its contents are not affiliated with, nor endorsed by, any wine certification organization. Onward.*

One of the biggest challenges for anyone on a wine certification exam track—regardless of the organization—is knowing which wines are typical for a variety and region for tasting practice. Given that, here is a list of suggested producers of classic wines. The producers were chosen based on availability and price with the intent of keeping the average bottle retail cost below $50. With Burgundy and certain other wines, the average bottle price will, of course, be higher.

## WHITE WINES

### Chardonnay: France - Chablis 1er Cru

**Look for:** Pronounced chalky minerality, partial ML, lees contact, and possible oak usage depending on producer and classification of wine.

**Structure:** Medium to medium-plus alcohol and medium-plus to high acidity.

**Considerations:** AC vs. premier cru vs. grand cru wines and resulting cost.

- Jean-Marc Brocard
- Christian Moreau
- William Fèvre
- Louis Michel
- Patrick Piuze

## Chardonnay: France - Côte de Beaune

**Look for:** Earth-mineral-SO2 qualities, partial or full ML, lees contact, and oak usage.

**Structure:** Medium to medium-plus alcohol and medium-plus acidity.

**Considerations:** AC vs. premier cru vs. grand cru wines and resulting cost.

**Meursault:**

- Jean Boillot
- Jean-Philippe Fichet
- Guy Roulot

**Chassagne-Montrachet:**

- Bruno Colin
- Marc Morey
- Jean-Marc Pillot

**Puligny Montrachet:**

- Olivier Leflaive
- Bernard Morey et Fils

- Jean-Marc Pillot

## Chardonnay: U.S. - California and Washington State

**Look for:** Ripe-tart combination of fruit, partial or complete ML, lees contact, and partial or 100% new oak usage.

**Structure:** Medium-plus to high alcohol and medium plus acidity.

**California:**

- Gary Farrell, Russian River Valley
- Dutton-Goldfield Winery, Russian River Valley
- Mount Eden Estate, Santa Cruz Mountains
- David Ramey, Russian River Valley
- Pine Ridge "Dijon Clones," Carneros

**Washington State:**

- Abeja, Washington State
- Canoe Ridge, Horse Heaven Hills
- Columbia, Columbia Valley
- Chateau Ste. Michelle, Columbia Valley
- Woodward Canyon Estate, Walla Walla Valley

## Sauvignon Blanc: France - Loire Valley - Sancerre and Pouilly-Fumé

**Look for:** Herbal notes (pyrazines), chalky minerality, and little or no oak for Sancerre with possible oak usage for Pouilly-Fumé.

**Structure:** Medium to medium-plus alcohol and medium-plus to high acidity.

**Sancerre:**

- Henri Bourgeois
- Lucien Crochet

- Joseph Mellot
- Hippolyte Reverdy
- Vacheron

**Pouilly-Fumé:**

- Régis Minet
- Philippe Raimbault
- Michelle Redde et Fils

## Sauvignon Blanc: New Zealand - Marlborough

**Look for:** Fruit-forward, pronounced herbal-vegetal notes (pyrazines), possible minerality, and no oak.

**Structure:** Medium-to-medium-plus alcohol and medium-plus acidity.

- Brancott
- Kim Crawford
- Dog Point
- Giesen
- Greywacke

## Chenin Blanc: Loire Valley - Vouvray and Savennières

**Vouvray:**

**Look for:** Floral (terpenes), possible botrytis character (even in dry wines), chamomile-botanical-herb, chalky minerality, and used or no oak.

**Structure:** Medium-to-medium-plus alcohol, medium-plus to high acidity, and phenolic bitterness.

**Considerations:** Sec vs. demi-sec styles and the presence of residual sugar as related to style of the wine or the character of the vintage. Also, SO2 on the nose and palate is commonly found.

- Marc Brédif
- Champalou
- Philippe Foreau
- Huet
- Château Moncontour

**Savennières:**

**Look for:** Very dry, mineral-dominant, and used or no oak.

**Structure:** Medium to medium-plus alcohol, medium-plus to high acidity, and phenolic bitterness.

**Considerations:** Savennières tend to be very dry, mineral-driven, and even austere compared to Vouvray.

- Baumard, Roche aux Moines
- Domaine de la Bergerie
- Château d'Epiré
- Nicolas Joly, Coulée de Serrant
- Château Pierre-Bise

## Chenin Blanc: U.S. - California and Washington State

**Look for:** Dry to off-dry style, fruit-dominant, and little or no oak.

**Structure:** Medium to medium-plus alcohol, medium-plus acidity, and slight phenolic bitterness.

- Chappellet Vineyard, Napa Valley
- Dry Creek Vineyard, Clarksburg
- L'Ecole No. 41, Columbia Valley
- Husch Vineyards, Mendocino
- Château St. Michelle, Horse Heaven Hills

## Gewürztraminer: France - Alsace

**Look for:** Dry to off-dry style, pronounced floral (terpenes), possible botrytis influence, very ripe fruit, earth-mineral notes, and used or no oak.

**Structure:** Medium-plus to high alcohol, medium-minus to medium acidity, and phenolic bitterness.

**Considerations:** AC vs. grand cru wines.

- Lucien Albrecht
- Albert Boxler
- Hugel et Fils
- Meyer-Fonné
- Domaine Weinbach

## Muscat Blanc à Petits Grains: France - Alsace

**Look for:** Pronounced floral (terpenes), ripe fruit, earth-mineral notes, and used or no oak.

**Structure:** Medium-plus to high alcohol, medium-plus acidity, and phenolic bitterness.

**Considerations:** AC vs. grand cru wines.

- Albert Boxler
- Marcel Deiss
- Hugel et Fils
- Weinbach
- Zind-Humbrecht

## Albariño: Spain - Rías Baixas

**Look for:** Floral (terpenes), ripe-tart fruit, lees contact, stony mineral notes, and no oak.

**Structure:** Medium to medium-plus alcohol, medium-plus to high acidity, and phenolic bitterness.

- Nessa
- Raimat
- Pazo Señorans
- Valmiñor
- Vionta

## Viognier: France - Northern Rhône - Condrieu

**Look for:** Floral (terpenes), partial or full ML, lees contact, stony, mineral, and partial or considerable new oak usage.

**Structure:** Medium to medium-plus alcohol, medium-plus acidity, and phenolic bitterness.

- Yves Cuilleron
- Saint Cosme
- Guigal
- René Rostaing
- Georges Vernay

## Viognier: New World – California and Australia

**Look for:** Floral (terpenes), tart, ripe, and possible overripe fruit with partial or full ML, lees contact, and partial or considerable new oak usage.

**Structure:** Medium-plus to high alcohol, medium to medium-plus acidity, and phenolic bitterness.

- Alban, Central Coast

- Pride Mountain, Napa Valley
- Stags Leap Vintners, Napa Valley
- Yalumba "Virgilius," Barossa
- Zaca Mesa, Santa Barbara County

## Marsanne-Roussanne Blend: France - Northern Rhône

**Look for:** Ripe stone fruit, orchard fruit, and citrus with lees, butter ML notes, stony mineral, and possible nutty oxidative notes from oak-aging.

**Structure:** Dry with medium-plus to high alcohol, medium acidity, and phenolic bitterness.

**Considerations:** There are two general styles of Marsanne-Roussanne blends: one style is fermented in stainless steel and is fresher and lighter. The other style sees extended time in wood and tends to have riper fruit, more pronounced minerality, and an oxidative character. The wood-aged wines also tend to show more elevated alcohol and medium acidity.

- Chapoutier, Hermitage Blanc "Chante-Alouette"
- Coursodon, Saint-Joseph Blanc
- Faury, Saint-Joseph Blanc
- Alain Graillot, Crozes-Hermitage Blanc
- Guigal, Crozes-Hermitage Blanc

## Grüner Veltliner: Austria

**Look for:** Pepper (rotundone), herbal-vegetal notes, stony mineral, and no oak.

**Structure:** Medium to high alcohol, medium-plus to high acidity, and phenolic bitterness.

**Considerations:** Ripeness levels as applied to the Wachau classification (Steinfeder, Federspiel, and Smaragd) or reserve wines from other regions.

- Bründlmayer, Kamptal
- Schloss Gobelsburg, Kamptal
- Hiedler, Kamptal
- Emmerich Knoll, Wachau
- F.X. Pichler, Wachau
- Domäne Wachau, Wachau

## Riesling: Germany

**Look for:** Floral (terpenes), fusel-petrol (TDN), possible lees contact, slate/mineral qualities, no oak.

**Structure:** Dryness/sweetness depends on the specific wine with low to medium-plus alcohol, and medium-plus to high acidity.

**Considerations:** Dry wines - VDP Grosses Gewächs – vs. fruity wines as related to the prädikat .

**Dry wines - Grosses Gewächs:**

- Dönnhoff Hermannshöhle and Dellchen, Nahe
- Gunderloch Rothenberg, Rheinhessen
- Künstler Hölle and Kirchenstück, Rheingau
- Dr. Loosen, Treppchen, Mosel
- Wittmann Morstein, Rheinhessen

**Fruity wines:** Kabinett, Spätlese, and Auslese levels.

- Von Buhl, Forster Ungeheuer, Pfalz
- Dönnhoff, Niederhäuser Hermannshöhle, Nahe
- Gunderloch, Nackenheimer Rothenberg, Rheinhessen
- Reinhold Haart, Piesporter Goldtröpfchen, Mosel
- J.J. Prüm, Wehlener Sonnenuhr, Mosel
- Selbach-Oster, Zeltinger Sonnenuhr, Mosel
- Wegeler, Bernkasteler Doctor, Mosel
- Robert Weil, Kiedricher Gräfenberg, Rheingau

## Riesling: France - Alsace

**Look for:** Floral (terpenes), fusel-petrol (TDN), possible botrytis character, possible lees contact, earth-mineral qualities, and no oak.

**Structure:** Dry with medium to medium-plus alcohol, and medium-plus to high acidity.

**Considerations:** AC vs. grand cru wines.

- Trimbach
- Albert Boxler
- Kuentz-Bas
- Weinbach
- Zind-Humbrecht

## Riesling: Austria

**Look for:** Floral (terpenes), possible fusel-petrol (TDN), possible lees contact, earth mineral qualities, and no oak.

**Structure:** Dry with medium to medium-plus alcohol, and medium-plus to high acidity.

**Considerations:** Ripeness levels as applied to the Wachau classification (Steinfeder, Federspiel, and Smaragd).

- Alzinger
- Bründlmayer
- Hirsch
- Emmerich Knoll
- Nigl

## Riesling: Australia

**Look for:** Floral (terpenes), fusel-petrol (TDN), possible lees contact, pronounced mineral notes, and no oak.

**Structure:** Dry with medium to medium-plus alcohol, and medium-plus to high acidity.

- Frankland Estate, Great Southern
- Jeffrey Grosset, "Polish Hill," Clare Valley
- Henschke "Julius," Eden Valley
- Leeuwin Estate Artist Series, Margaret River
- Pewsey Vale "The Contours," Eden Valley

## Pinot Gris: France - Alsace

**Look for:** Floral (terpenes), possible botrytis character, mushroom-earth-mineral notes, used or no oak, and dry to off-dry in style.

**Structure:** Medium-plus to high alcohol, medium to medium-plus acidity, and phenolic bitterness.

**Considerations:** AC vs. grand cru wines.

- Marcel Deiss
- Hugel et Fils
- Domaine Schlumberger
- Weinbach
- Zind-Humbrecht

## Pinot Grigio: Italy - Alto Adige

**Look for:** Delicate floral (terpenes), lees contact, stony mineral, and no oak.

**Structure:** Medium alcohol, medium-plus acidity, and slight phenolic bitterness.

- Alois Laegeder
- St. Michael-Eppan
- Terlano
- Tiefenbrunner
- Cantina Tramin

## Pinot Gris: U.S. - Oregon

**Look for:** White floral (terpenes) ripe fruit, lees contact, and no oak.

**Structure:** Medium-plus alcohol, medium to medium-plus acidity, and phenolic bitterness.

- Ponzi
- A to Z
- Adelsheim
- Cristom

## Assyrtiko: Greece - Santorini

**Look for:** White floral, ripe fruit, pronounced volcanic minerality, and little or no oak.

**Structure:** Medium plus to high alcohol, medium-plus to high acidity, and phenolic bitterness.

- Argyros
- Boutari
- Gai'a
- Hatzidakis
- Domaine Sigalas

# RED WINES

## Gamay: France – Beaujolais-Villages and Beaujolais Cru

**Look for:** Candied, confected red fruit from carbonic maceration, green stemmy quality from stem inclusion, green herb, stony-earth, and little or no oak. Little—or no—carbonic character in Cru wines with much more depth and complexity.

**Structure:** Medium alcohol, medium-plus acidity, and medium-minus to medium tannin.

**Considerations:** Villages vs. cru wines.

**Beaujolais-Villages:**

- Georges Duboeuf
- Henry Fessy
- Robert Drouhin
- Louis Jadot
- Trénel Fils

**Beaujolais Cru:**

- Damien Coquelet
- Jean Foillard
- Jean-Claude Lapalu
- Marcel Lapierre
- Château Thivin

## Pinot Noir: France – Burgundy – Côte de Nuits

**Look for:** Red fruit, rose-floral, tea-herb, possible green stem quality (stem inclusion), soil-mineral-game, and oak usage.

**Structure:** Medium to medium-plus alcohol, medium-plus acidity, and medium to medium-plus tannin.

**Considerations:** AC vs. premier cru vs. grand cru wines in regards to oak usage and price. No producers for Clos Vougeot are included because of high average cost.

**Gevrey-Chambertin:**

- Domaine Lucien Boillot
- Domaine Dujac
- Domaine Fourrier
- Domaine Armand Rousseau

**Morey St. Denis:**

- Domaine des Lambrays
- Domaine Perrot-Minot
- Maison Frédéric Magnien
- Domaine Ponsot

**Chambolle-Musigny:**

- Joseph Drouhin
- Robert Groffier Père et Fils
- Domaine Perrot-Mino
- Domaine Roumier

**Vosne-Romanée:**

- Domaine Robert Arnoux
- Domaine Hudelot-Noëllat
- Domaine Comte Liger-Belair
- Bouchard Père et Fils

**Nuits-Saint-Georges:**

- Robert Chevillon
- Domaine Jean Grivot

- Domaine Méo-Camuzet
- Domaine Jacques Frédéric Mugnier

### Pinot Noir: France – Burgundy – Côte de Beaune

**Look for:** Red fruit, rose-floral, tea-herb, possible green stem quality (stem inclusion), soil-mineral-game, and oak usage.

**Structure:** Medium to medium-plus alcohol, medium-plus acidity, medium to medium-plus tannin.

**Considerations:** AC vs. premier cru wines in regards to oak usage and price.

**Volnay:**

- Marquis d'Angerville
- Henri Boillot
- Michel Lafarge
- Dominique Laurent
- de Montille

**Pommard:**

- Comte Armand
- Jean-Marc Boillot
- Domaine de Courcel
- Jean Garaudet

**Beaune:**

- Bouchard Père & Fils
- Champy
- Joseph Drouhin
- Louis Jadot
- Domaine Albert Morot

**Savigny-lès-Beaune:**

- Boillot
- Jean-Claude Boisset
- Jaffelin
- Albert Morot
- Henri de Villamont

## Pinot Noir: U.S. - California

**Look for:** Fruit-dominant (primarily red), floral-herbal notes, possible earth-mineral, and oak usage.

**Structure:** Medium to medium-plus alcohol, medium-plus acidity, and medium to medium-plus tannin.

- Domaine Carneros, Carneros
- Gary Farrell, Russian River Valley
- Flowers, Sonoma Coast
- Rochioli, Russian River Valley
- Sanford, Santa Barbara County

## Pinot Noir: U.S. - Oregon

**Look for:** Tart and ripe red fruit, floral, green and savory herb, possible earth, and oak usage.

**Structure:** Medium to medium-plus alcohol, medium-plus acidity, and medium to medium-plus tannin.

- Adelsheim
- Domaine Drouhin
- Eyrie Vineyards
- Domaine Serene
- Ken Wright

## Pinot Noir: New Zealand

**Look for:** Tart red fruit, rose-floral, pronounced herbal/vegetal, mineral-earth, and oak usage.

**Structure:** Medium to medium-plus alcohol, medium-plus acidity, and medium to medium-plus tannin.

- Ata Rangi, Martinborough
- Burn Cottage, Central Otago
- Felton Road, Central Otago
- Neudorf, Central Otago
- Palliser Estate, Martinborough

## Cabernet Sauvignon Blend: France - Left Bank Bordeaux

**Look for:** Ripe and tart black fruit, violet-floral, green herb (pyrazines), graphite-earth-mineral, and oak usage.

**Structure:** Medium-plus to high alcohol, medium-plus acidity, and medium to medium-plus tannin.

**Considerations:** Vintage still matters a good deal in Bordeaux; riper vintages are richer and higher in alcohol.

- Domaine de Chevalier, Pessac-Léognan
- Château Phélan Ségur, Saint- Estèphe
- Château Meyney, St. Estèphe
- Château Smith Haut Lafitte Le Petit Haut Lafitte, Pessac-Léognan
- Château Sociando-Mallet, Haut Médoc

### Cabernet Sauvignon: U.S. - California

**Look for:** Ripe/jammy black fruit, green herb (pyrazines), and pronounced oak usage.

**Structure:** High alcohol, medium to medium-plus acidity, and medium-plus to high tannin.

**Considerations:** County appellation wines are usually the best values.

- Beringer, Knights Valley
- Dry Creek Vineyard, Sonoma
- Honig, Napa
- Laurel Glen Counterpoint, Sonoma
- Obsidian Ridge, Red Hills, Lake County

### Cabernet Sauvignon: Australia - Coonawarra and Margaret River

**Look for:** Ripe black and tart red fruit, pronounced green herbal-vegetal notes (pyrazines), possible earth-mineral notes, and oak usage.

**Structure:** Medium-plus alcohol, medium to medium-plus acidity, and medium-plus tannin.

- Cape Mentelle, Margaret River
- Leeuwin Estate Artist Series, Margaret River
- Majella, Coonawarra
- Petaluma, Coonawarra
- Wynn's, Coonawarra

### Cabernet Sauvignon: Chile

**Look for:** Ripe and tart black fruit, violet-floral, elevated herbal notes (pyrazines), slight earth-mineral notes, and oak usage.

**Structure:** Medium to medium-plus alcohol, medium-plus acidity, and medium-plus tannin.

- Cousiño-Macul, Maipo Valley
- Lapostolle, Maipo Valley
- Montes Alpha, Colchagua
- Santa Carolina, Maipo Valley
- Santa Rita, Maipo Valley

## Merlot Blend: France - Right Bank Bordeaux

**Look for:** Ripe black fruit, violet-floral, herbal-vegetal notes (pyrazines), earth-mineral notes, and oak usage.

**Structure:** Medium-plus alcohol, medium-plus acidity, and medium to medium-plus tannin.

- Puy-Blanquet, St.-Emilion Grand Cru
- Château Fleur Cardinale, St.-Emilion Grand Cru
- Château La Gravette de Certan, Pomerol
- Château Laroze, St.-Emilion Grand Cru
- Château Nenin, Pomerol

## Merlot: U.S. - California and Washington State

**Look for:** Ripe black and red fruit, violet-floral, herbal notes (pyrazines), possible earth notes, and oak usage.

**Structure:** Medium-plus to high alcohol, medium to medium-plus acidity, and medium-plus tannin and more if Cabernet is added.

**California:**

- St. Francis, Sonoma
- Frog's Leap, Napa Valley
- Matanzas Creek, Sonoma
- Newton, Napa Valley
- Pride Mountain, Napa Valley

**Washington State:**

- Columbia Winery, Columbia Valley
- L'Ecole No. 41, Columbia Valley
- Ch. Ste. Michelle, Columbia Valley
- Seven Hills Vineyard, Walla Walla Valley
- Woodward Canyon, Columbia Valley

## Carménère: Chile

**Look for:** Ripe and tart black fruit, violet-floral, pronounced herbal-vegetal-peppery notes (pyrazines), possible earth-mineral notes, and oak usage.

**Structure:** Medium to medium-plus alcohol, medium-plus acidity, and medium-plus tannin.

- Concha y Toro, Maipo Valley
- Errazuriz, Aconcagua
- Montes Alpha, Colchagua Valley
- Santa Carolina, Maipo Valley
- Santa Rita, Maipo Valley

## Cabernet Franc: France - Loire Valley - Chinon and Bourgueil

**Look for:** Combination of ripe-tart dark and red fruit, violet floral, pronounced green herbal-vegetal notes (pyrazines), chalky-earth, possible Brettanomyces, and oak usage.

**Structure:** Medium to medium-plus alcohol, medium-plus acidity, and medium to medium-plus tannin.

### Chinon:

- Bernard Baudry
- Domaine Breton
- Château de Coulaine
- Couly-Dutheil
- Domaine Charles Joguet

- Domaine de Noiré

**Bourgueil:**

- Domaine Audebert et Fils
- Domaine Yannick Amirault
- Catherine et Pierre Breton

## Malbec: Argentina - Mendoza

**Look for:** Combination of ripe blue, black, and tart red fruit with violet floral, herbal notes (slight pyrazines), slight earth qualities, and oak usage.

**Structure:** Medium to high alcohol, medium to medium-plus acidity, and medium-plus tannin.

- Achaval-Ferrer
- Altos las Hormigas
- Catena
- Doña Paula
- Zuccardi

## Syrah: France - Northern Rhône

**Look for:** Combination of ripe and tart dark and red fruit with pepper (rotundone), savory herb, leather, possible Brettanomyces, earth-mineral, and oak usage (usually large cooperage).

**Structure:** Medium to medium-plus alcohol, medium-plus acidity, and medium-plus tannin.

**Crozes-Hermitage:**

- Albert Belle
- Delas Frères
- Ferraton

- Alain Graillot
- Guigal

**St.-Joseph:**

- Chapoutier
- Domaine Coursodon
- Delas Frères
- Philippe Faury
- Ferraton

**Côte Rôtie:**

- Guigal
- Jamet
- Ogier
- René Rostaing
- Vidal-Fleury

## Syrah: Australia - Barossa Shiraz

**Look for:** Combination of ripe-jammy dark, tart red, and raisinated fruit with pepper (rotundone), savory herb, leather, mint-eucalyptus, little or no earth-mineral, and oak usage.

**Structure:** Medium-plus to high alcohol, medium to medium-plus acidity, and medium to medium-plus tannin.

**Considerations:** Traditional wines are often aged in American oak.

- Elderton
- Langmeil
- Peter Lehmann
- Penfolds
- Yalumba

## Grenache Blend: France - Southern Rhône

**Look for:** Combination of tart, ripe and even baked dark and red fruit with pepper (rotundone), savory herb (garrigue), sanguine notes (roasted meat, blood, iodine), pronounced earth-mineral, and oak usage (large cooperage).

**Structure:** High alcohol, medium-plus acidity, and medium-plus to high tannin.

**Châteauneuf-du-Pape:**

- Château de Beaucastel
- Clos des Papes
- Château La Nerthe
- Domaine du Pégaü
- Domaine du Vieux Télégraphe

**Gigondas:**

- Delas Frères
- Domaine du Grand Montmirail
- Domaine Les Pallières
- Ferraton Père et Fils
- Château de Saint-Cosme

## Grenache: Australia - Barossa

**Look for:** Ripe and jammy red fruit with pepper (rotundone) mint-eucalyptus, little or no earth-mineral, and oak usage.

**Structure:** Medium-plus to high alcohol, medium-plus acidity, and medium to medium-plus tannin.

- D'Arenberg "The Custodian," McLaren Vale
- Langmeil, Barossa
- Charles Melton, Barossa

- Yalumba Old Bush Vine, Barossa
- Yangarra, Barossa

### Mourvèdre: France - Bandol

**Look for:** Ripe dark and tart red fruit with pepper (rotundone), savory herbal qualities, sanguine notes (iron, blood, game, etc.), pronounced earth-mineral notes, and oak usage.

**Structure:** Medium-plus to high alcohol, medium-plus acidity, and medium-plus to high tannin.

- Domaine Bunan
- Domaine du Gros Noré
- Domaine Ott
- Château de Pibarnon
- Domaine Tempier

### Monastrell (Mourvèdre): Spain - Jumilla

**Look for:** Ripe and jammy dark and raisinated fruit with pronounced savory herb, earth-soil-mineral notes, and oak usage.

**Structure:** Medium-plus to high alcohol, medium to medium-plus acidity, and medium-plus to high tannin.

- Bodegas Bleda
- Castillo de Jumilla
- Chopo
- Bodegas Juan Gil
- Sierra Norte

### Nebbiolo: Italy - Piedmont - Barolo and Barbaresco

**Look for:** Ripe and dried red and dark fruit with rose-floral, dried herb, mushroom-earth-tar, and oak usage–both large cooperage or barrique are used.

**Structure:** Medium-plus to high alcohol, medium-plus to high acidity, and high tannin.

**Considerations:** Degree of oak influence to use of barriques vs. larger barrels.

**Barolo:**

- Elio Altare
- Aldo Conterno
- Silvio Grasso
- Bartolo Mascarello
- Paolo Scavino

**Barbaresco:**

- Produttori del Barbaresco
- Bruno Giacosa
- Marchesi di Grésy
- Sottimano
- La Spinetta

## Sangiovese: Italy - Tuscany - Chianti Classico

**Look for:** Ripe and tart red fruit with darker fruits in riper vintages or those containing Cabernet family grapes; also tomato-green herb, anise, sandalwood, chalk-mineral-earth, and oak usage with large cooperage and barrique both used.

**Structure:** Medium to medium-plus alcohol, medium-plus to high acidity, and medium-plus tannin.

**Considerations:** Degree of oak influence to use of barriques vs. larger barrels.

- Castello di Ama
- Badia a Coltibuono
- Fèlsina

- Fontodi
- Castello di Volpaia

### Sangiovese: Italy - Tuscany - Brunello di Montalcino

**Look for:** Ripe and tart dark and red fruit with dried herb, sandalwood, chalk-mineral-earth, and oak usage – both large cooperage or barrique are used.

**Structure:** Medium-plus alcohol, medium-plus to high acidity, and medium-plus to high tannin.

**Considerations:** Degree of oak influence to use of barriques vs. larger barrels.

- Altesino
- Argiano
- Il Poggione
- Ciacci Piccolomini
- Silvio Nardi

### Sangiovese: Italy - Tuscany – Vino Nobile di Montepulciano

**Look for:** Ripe and tart dark and red fruit with anise, tomato leaf, green herb, sandalwood, earth, and wood.

**Structure:** Dry with medium to medium plus alcohol - medium-plus to high acidity – medium-plus tannin.

**Considerations:** Degree of oak influence to use of barriques vs. larger barrels.

- Avignonesi
- Boscarelli
- Carpineto
- Dei
- Poliziano

## Tempranillo: Spain - Rioja Reserva and Gran Reserva

**Look for:** Dried dark, red, and raisinated fruit with dried floral-potpourri, dried herb, dust-soil-terra cotta, considerable oak American oak usage, and oxidative character.

**Structure:** Medium to medium-plus alcohol, medium-plus acidity, and medium to medium-plus tannin.

**Considerations:** Traditional wines are often aged in American oak. Gran Reserva wines are oakier and more oxidative in character than Reserva wines.

- Artadi
- CVNE
- Marqués de Cáceres
- Marqués de Murrieta
- La Rioja Alta

## Zinfandel: U.S - California - Dry Creek Valley

**Look for:** Combination of dark, red, and raisinated fruit with pepper (rotundone), herb, possible mint and eucalyptus, possible peach-yogurt notes, and oak spice.

**Structure:** Medium-plus to high alcohol, medium to medium-plus acidity, and medium to high tannin.

- Dry Creek Vineyard "Heritage Clone"
- Rafanelli
- Ridge "Lytton Springs"
- Seghesio
- Unti Vineyards

*Author's suggestion: This producer list is meant to serve as a suggested guideline for tasting practice. Students should use it as a point of departure and create their own lists as appropriate.*

# PART III

# The Inner Game of Tasting

## Introduction

In the first two parts of the book I've covered a great deal of information regarding the basics of tasting as well as advanced concepts. Part III is a departure from the previous material in that it's based on strategies I've used myself and have taught to students over the past 20-plus years. The strategies concern improving focus and concentration for general tasting purposes and exams. They've also proven useful for improving smell and taste memory, structural assessment, and grape variety/wine identification. The strategies borrow ideas from various fields including sports psychology, behavioral psychology, and energy psychology.

Before going further a few disclaimers are needed. As stated previously, I'm a strategist. My continuing goal as an educator is to find ways to help students and consumers alike use their unique natural abilities to become better and more proficient tasters. To accomplish this I've looked at a broad range of different fields to find new ideas that will make learning the tasting process easier. Given that, consider the following:

- Practically all the strategies are based on visualization. If you've not previously worked with visualization, the strategies may be initially challenging for you.
- It's quite possible that some of the strategies may not work for you. That could actually be beneficial and I'll explain why below.
- Even though humans share the same nervous system and five senses, everyone is wired differently. No one strategy will work for everyone.
- A major assumption I use is that over 90% of the human race is visual-dominant internally—we think in pictures and movies. Given that, an important key to olfactory and taste memory is that both are visually-based internally—like many other things we experience.
- Most of us—but not all—create internal images for smell and taste memories. Many times these images are at the unconscious level in that we're not aware of them. However, awareness of the visual-smell/taste memory connection and using it can be an important tool for improving one's overall tasting ability.

This is important. To repeat, some, most, or even all of the strategies in this section of the book may not work for you. If that's the case, consider this. Practically all the strategies here have to do with recognition and memory. If a particular strategy doesn't work after you've tried it a few times, stop for a moment. Odds are your brain is wired differently and the strategy may not work for you. However, pay close attention to the feedback you're getting at this point because your brain will probably show you what does work.

Finally, I strongly suggest that you work with one of the chapters/strategies at a time until you become familiar with it. Too many new ideas at the same time will only serve to confuse. One more thing, have fun with the process. I wouldn't be surprised if you discover new things about how your thinking cap works, so to speak. And that's a very good thing indeed.

Message in the Bottle

## Part III Chapter Guide

*Chapter 21: Clearing the mechanism*
A basic strategy for focus and concentration.

*Chapter 22: How to use overlapping to find your zone*
Using layers of a memory to establish a deeply focused state of concentration that can be used for tasting and beyond.

*Chapter 23: Front loading and the basic set*
Using internal visual and auditory to improve recognition and memory of the most common aromas and flavors found in wine.

*Chapter 24: Using submodalities in tasting*
Using submodalities to improve recognition, sensitivity, and memory for aromas and flavors.

*Chapter 25: Using an internal visual cue to help calibrate structure*
Creating and using an internal visual cue to accurately and consistently calibrate structural elements in the wine.

*Chapter 26: Installing olfactory memories*
Using submodalities to install new olfactory memories.

*Chapter 27: Label check*
Using labels of best examples to represent memories of classic wines.

*Chapter 28: Associative rehearsal: Tasting practice without wine*
How various aspects of tasting can be practiced internally—without actually tasting.

*Chapter 29: Dealing with a dominant aroma in the glass*
How to use internal imaging to manage a dominant aroma.

*Chapter 30: Using a Coravin for tasting practice*
Recommended exercises for tasting practice using a Coravin.

*Chapter 31: Eating the elephant*
Advice for the beginning taster.

*Chapter 32: Tasting exam prep strategies*
A list of useful strategies for exam prep and beyond.

## 21

# Clearing the Mechanism

*Author's note: This is the first of two strategies to help improve focus and concentration when tasting, especially in an exam setting. Some may find "Clearing the Mechanism" simple to do, others may experience it as challenging. The intent is to quickly drop into a deep, focused state of concentration despite nerves and stress.*

Anxiety during an exam can cause your thoughts and nervous system to speed up and even start racing, making it difficult to focus on the task at hand. Being able to control this is therefore one of the most important aspects of exam preparation. The exercise below is about taking back control of your internal state during an exam.

### The 30 Second Challenge

First, find a quiet place where you won't be interrupted. Next, choose one of your favorite memories. Pick an experience that was really enjoyable. Once you have that great memory, do the following:

*Think about it in detail for 30 seconds.*

That's right. That's all there is to it. Hold the memory for 30 seconds. Time yourself with your phone. Go for it.

Welcome back. How did you do? You may not have made it for the entire 30 seconds before another thought crept in. I didn't make it the first several times I tried it. If you did get to 30 seconds, congratulations. However, if you didn't get there, reset your clock and try again.

How did it go? If you still didn't get to 30 seconds before other things started creeping into your brain there's a trick to it. Try the following:

Go back to your memory and really get into it.

Now freeze the memory like a still photograph and be aware of EXACTLY where your eyes are looking while experiencing the memory. If your eyes were closed, open them and pinpoint where you're looking.

Note the exact eye position by pointing precisely to the spot where you're looking while thinking about the memory. Really get the exact location—this is important.

Now clear your head of the memory by looking around the room you're in and thinking about anything else—what you had for breakfast, for example.

Then go back to the exact eye position/location for the memory and when you get there bring up the memory as completely as you can. Do it quickly.

Once you're in the memory, soften the focus of your eyes, focus on your breathing, and "play" the memory in as much detail as possible.

AVOID holding your eyes in a hard stare. It will probably put you in a deep trance and might result in your head hurting. Soft focus, please.

Et voila! You'll find you can really stay with the memory for a long time—even beyond 30 seconds—by finding the eye position for it, holding your eyes in a soft gaze, and also focusing on your breathing.

## Practice

The goal is to get where you can hold a memory/thought for at least 30 seconds. Then increase it to 45 and even 60 seconds. This is where your

## Message in the Bottle

eye position, quality of your gaze, and focus on breathing will really come into play.

Now let's expand your repertoire to different kinds of memories. As before, choose one of your favorite memories that have to do with the following:

**Confidence:** Pick a time when you were really confident and felt unstoppable.

**Focus:** A time when you noticed everything in high-definition clarity—even peripherally.

**Calm and peace:** Find that memory of when you were really centered, calm, and quiet inside.

**Determination:** A time when the going was tough but you got something done and felt really good about accomplishing it. Note that when you focus on the two physical spots just below your eyes, the feeling of determination gets even stronger.

**Important:** Remember to find the exact eye position for each one. Work with each one of these using the same formula of eye position, soft eye gaze, and mindful breathing. Again, the goal is to get to where you can hold any of the memories for at least 30 seconds, if not longer.

### "Clearing the Mechanism"

Once you can hold a memory for 30 or more seconds easily the next step is being able to quickly clear your head when you need to. For lack of a better term, I'm calling it "Clearing the Mechanism," as in being able to clear your mind and really focus on the fly. Go back to your calm and peaceful memory. Practice a bit more until you can get there in 1-3 seconds whenever you want.

### Using "Clearing the Mechanism"

Here's how to use the strategy during tasting exam practice or an exam.

**When you first sit down to start tasting practice or for an actual exam:** Take a few deep breaths and use the eye position for inner calm and focus. Your nervous system may be amped up, but using a specific eye position, soft focus, and mindful breathing for 30 seconds or so will really make a difference.

**Reset after each wine:** "Clear the Mechanism." Start each wine fresh and intensely focused REGARDLESS of what just happened with the previous wine.

**In the middle of a wine:** Reset after each section in terms of the sight, nose, and palate by closing your eyes, taking a deep breath, then opening your eyes and refocusing. I think it's especially valuable to reset before assessing the structure. In particular, rushing the structural calls on a wine can be disastrous.

**Before the conclusion:** Reset your brain by dropping inside and taking 5-10 seconds to review all the major makers. Be sure to connect the dots to the important things you've seen, smelled, and tasted.

*Author's suggestion: I hope you can see the value of this simple strategy. I think that we often get into set patterns of thinking without being aware of it. Clearing the Mechanism is a useful tool and, if anything, beneficial for dealing with just that.*

## 22

# How to Use Overlapping to Find Your Zone

*Author's note: This is the second of two exercises for improving focus, concentration, and establishing one's "zone" when it comes to tasting. This particular exercise, called "Overlapping" involves sequentially layering different senses that are facets of a single memory. In doing so, one's focus becomes deeper and the awareness of all parts of the memory is increased. Both are needed when tasting for an exam or for judging wine quality on the job.*

Throughout the course of a day, we constantly change our focus and state of awareness, from holding a conversation to driving, watching TV, or taking part in physical activity such as jogging. We also process information from the outside world with our preferred sensory system or modality, which is visual for practically all of us. In short, most of us represent our experience of the world internally with pictures and movies.

Tasting is one of the many things we do that requires a special kind of focus or a zone. The ability to shut the world out is a vital key to becoming a proficient taster. But how can we work on our focus or zone? One way might be through an exercise called "Overlapping." "Overlapping" involves using a memory—primarily visual—while paying close attention to all the other sensory information associated with the memory. The result is a deeply focused, one might even say altered, state of awareness. "Overlapping" is very effective and simple to do. Here are the instructions:

First, find a quiet place to sit where you won't be interrupted. Next, have a seat and get comfortable. Now go inside and think of a time when you took an enjoyable walk. Bring up the memory as vividly as you can. As you're walking, see the path in front of you in detail as you easily move along.

Now add another sensory modality. Feel your arms moving back and forth and your legs striding with each step.

After you've added a second sensory modality, think of a third. In this case, you might hear the sound of your feet hitting the ground with each stride.

Next, go back and add detail to each modality (sense). Make the scene in front of you as clear and bright as possible. Feel the breeze on your face as you're walking as well as the ambient temperature of the air around you. Then hear the sounds of traffic around you or birds chirping in nearby trees.

Now pause the memory and notice the quality and depth of your state of awareness at this point. Odds are it's a pretty deep state of focus which is exactly the kind needed for tasting, or any other activity requiring exacting detail. Also—and this is key—when you pause, notice exactly where you're looking as you go through your memory. If your eyes are closed, where are they looking once you open them? Note the exact place as it will be useful. You might even point to it so you know exactly where it is.

### "Overlapping" using a wine memory

Now try "Overlapping" using the memory of a wine you've tasted. Let me suggest using a botrytis dessert wine like Sauternes because it's so detailed—and delicious. Using the model above, go through every aspect of the wine in sequence.

First, see the color of the wine as vividly as you can. A Sauternes would be a deep yellow in color.

Now add some primary aromatics to the memory such as in the form of honey and ripe peach and apricot fruit from botrytis influence.

Next, feel the luscious texture of the wine. Pay close attention to the balance of sweetness and tart acidity and how it tastes and feels on your palate.

Now add more sensory data and deepen your state of awareness, your zone. Go back to the visual and add the secondary colors which could be glints of green and gold. Also, see how the wine moves in the glass with richness and density from residual sugar.

Next smell more components in the wine focusing on non-fruit, earth, and oak. Bring up the ginger from botrytis, the mushroom-earth elements, and all the spice notes from oak-aging.

Then feel the warmth from the alcohol on your palate and note the precise temperature of the wine.

Stop once again and notice the depth and quality of your focus or zone. If your eyes are closed, open them and pay close attention to the exact spot where you're looking. Also, be aware of the soft quality of your eyes.

### Practice "Overlapping" to discover your zone of concentration

From here the goal is to get into your zone quickly when you actually taste wine. A few repetitions of the exercises above should do the trick. The final step is to practice getting into your zone with a wine glass in hand. Try the following sequence:

First, move your eyes to the spot where you focused during the exercise. Then let your eyes go into a soft focus and then pick up an empty wine glass. Hold for a few seconds.

Then set the glass down and focus on something else in the room. Repeat by moving your eyes to the spot, going into a soft focus, and picking up the glass.

Practice this sequence at least ten times making sure that you break up your zone each time by looking at other things in the room or thinking about something totally unrelated to tasting—like what you had for breakfast that morning.

For me the sequence begins with picking up a glass with my right hand, eyes going down in a soft focus slightly to the left about 15 inches away (the length of my arm), and saying internally, "What's there?" The combination of eyes down left, soft focus, and the internal phrase acts as a consistent starting place for my tasting sequence. Consistency here is the most important word.

Practice "Overlapping." It's easy to do and you'll quickly discover your starting place and be able to get into your zone quickly. And you'll be glad you did.

*Author's suggestion: After practicing "Overlapping" be sure to completely come back to present time—as in current reality—before driving or doing anything that requires your complete focus. Remember, safety first.*

23

# "Front-Loading" and the "Basic Set"

*Author's note: Most people enter the wine world with the expectation that learning how to taste is somehow different than everything else they've ever learned, which is visually based. What's missing is the awareness of the key internal visual component to smell and taste memory. Specifically, that there's an internal image connected to practically all smell and taste memories. This chapter is about using that olfactory-image connection to improve recognition of key components in wine.*

Practically all the professional tasters and students I've worked with over the years use internal images in some form or another to represent what they smell and taste in the wine. These range from two-dimensional internal still images all the way to multisensory internal panoramic life-size movies. At this point, I'll go as far to say that if you can't create an internal image for something you're smelling or tasting in a glass of wine, odds are you probably won't be able to recognize it. One of the challenges for beginning tasters then becomes clear. How to bring awareness to the connection between internal images and olfactory/taste memories. It's important to note that I'm not talking about actual physical smell and taste, I'm talking about a function of memory. In that case, it's possible to improve one's memory for aromatics and flavors commonly found in wine–but without actually having a glass of wine in hand.

In the past few years I've worked with a technique I call "Front-Loading" combined with a subset of the most common wine aromas and flavors that I've dubbed the "Basic Set." Front-Loading is, in effect, working backwards, in a sense, to improve one's memory of the most common aromas and flavors--but without smelling and tasting wine. I've found that using both strategies in tandem can improve one's overall tasting ability, in some cases considerably.

Here are suggested components for the "Basic Set," the most common aromas and flavors found in most wines. Keep in mind that this list is not set in stone, but merely a guideline to serve as a vehicle for learning. The list can always be altered as needed.

**"The Basic Set": Common Wine Aromas and Flavors**

- Green Apple
- Yellow/Golden Delicious Apple
- Pear
- Lemon
- Lime
- Orange
- Banana
- Peach
- Apricot
- Black Cherry
- Blackberry
- Red Cherry
- Strawberry
- Cranberry
- Raisin/prune
- Roses
- Violet
- Mint/Eucalyptus
- Green bell pepper
- Rosemary

- Black/white pepper
- Vanilla
- Cinnamon
- Clove
- Toast
- Coffee
- Chocolate
- Mushroom – forest floor
- Chalk

## "Front-Loading" using the "Basic Set"

Before working with the entire "Basic Set," we'll do an exercise with a smaller subset of the list. The goal is to quickly bring up one of your olfactory memories by simply seeing and hearing the word of the aroma/flavor in question. With that, consider the four aromas/flavors below and then do the following:

- Lemon
- Green apple
- Vanilla
- Mushroom/earth

1. Say the names of each aroma internally or out loud.
2. After hearing the word, bring up the image/memory of the aromatic as quickly and vividly as you can.
3. Make your memory of the fruit, spice, or other element as complete and intense as possible down to the aromas, flavors, and texture.
4. Practice the list several times. With each repetition, see if you can get to the memory faster and more with more intensity.

## Using the entire Basic Set

Now it's time to use the strategy above with the entire "Basic Set." Take your time going through the list. I suggest focusing on three to five aromas/flavors at a time. Some will be easy while others may need repetition and practice. There may also be some on the list for which you don't yet have memories. If that's the case, you may need to purchase the components in question and do some work on smelling and creating memories for them (see Chapter 26). Soon you'll be able to move them over into the rotation. Regardless, remember to have fun with the strategies.

*Author's suggestions: Here are some parting thoughts on using the Basic Set:*

- *Repetition is key. After going through the initial exercise, work with the images/words until your memories become automatic. It won't take long to get through several repetitions.*
- *Remember the goal is to be able to bring up vivid smell, taste, and tactile memories for any of the aromas/flavors on command.*
- *Don't limit your work to the "Basic Set." Expand your repertoire to include as many other aromas/flavors as you can.*
- *In time, start to put different aromas together in groups or sequences to form markers for classic wines.*

# 24

# Using Submodalities in Tasting

*Author's note: Consider for a moment that our connection to the physical universe is our five senses: seeing, hearing, feeling, smelling, and tasting. These are called "modalities" after "moda," the Greek term for our senses. Internally, we also use our five senses, our inner modalities, to organize our experience. These inner modalities also have structural qualities or "submodalities."*

*Internal visual—the pictures and movies that we generate in our mind's eye—have dozens of these structural submodalities including size, proximity, dimensionality, and more. We constantly use submodalities in our thinking to code our experiences and also to create memories for future use. Knowledge and use of submodalities can be a profoundly useful strategy for wine tasting — and for everything else. The following is an introduction to submodalities including two basic exercises.*

When most experienced tasters put their nose into a glass of wine, they recognize multiple aromas in rapid succession, sometimes a half dozen or more in the first few seconds. What's not necessarily known is the fact that practically all of us generate images for each of the aromas we smell. Otherwise, how would we know if what we're smelling in a glass of Cabernet Sauvignon is ripe black cherries or a catcher's mitt?

The interesting thing about these images we create for aromas and flavors is that they have structural aspects in terms of how we perceive them, including location, proximity, dimensionality, and more. These structural qualities are called submodalities after the term "moda" which translates as "sense" in Greek. With visual alone, there are over 60 submodalities. That means the image we create of black cherries in that glass of Cabernet has a position in our mind's eye (what I call the internal IMAX theater) as well as proximity, is in 2D or 3D, and many more aspects.

What's fascinating is how changing one of a handful of the most important visual submodalities of an aroma can actually change our experience of it — and the wine as well. Submodalities for internal auditory and kinesthetic exist as well. However, we'll only deal with visual submodalities in this chapter. Here's a partial list of some of the most common visual submodalities:

- Black and white or color
- Proximity: near or far
- Location
- Brightness
- Size of image
- Three dimensional or flat image
- Associated/dissociated
- Focused or unfocused
- Framed or unframed
- Movie or still image
- If a movie, fast/normal/slow

## Submodality exercise No. 1

For the first exercise we'll use a simple memory of a common aroma/flavor found in wine like lemon. To begin, bring up a vivid memory of smelling a freshly sliced lemon. Next, map the submodalities of your "lemon" memory. Be sure to *write down* your answers so you can reference them later. Here are questions to consider:

**Still image vs. movie:** Is the internal representation of your memory of lemon a still image or a movie?

**Size:** Is there a specific size to the image of your memory in your mind's eye? How large or small is it?

**Proximity:** Is the image of the lemon out in front of you at a distance? Or is it closer to you?

**Dimensionality:** Is the image of the lemon flat or is it in 3D?

**Color vs. black and white:** Odds are the image of the lemon is in color. But it's important to note if it's not.

**Brightness:** Is the image/movie of the lemon bright and colorful or more like a dull image?

## Changing submodalities

Now that you have the structure behind your memory of lemon–and you've written it down, it's time to play with the submodalities and discover which ones are important for you.

**Important:** There is only one rule for working with submodalities. Only change ONE thing at a time. If you change more than one thing, you'll completely muddle the experience.

After you make each change, remember to RESET your image/movie to the original before going to the next.

Also, as you make each change, pay close attention to how the change affects the intensity and quality of your experience, and feelings toward your memory of lemon. Does a particular change make your memory of lemon more intense–or less intense?

Again, remember to only change ONE thing at a time and reset it before going to the next.

**Still image or movie:** If your memory is a still image, change it to a movie with movement. For instance, the movie could be you reaching out to pick up a lemon. However, if your memory of lemon is a movie, freeze-frame it to a still image. How does either change affect your response/feelings toward the memory? Does it make it more intense? Less intense? Reset.

**Size:** Shrink the image/movie of lemon to the size of a postage stamp. How does that affect the memory? How does that change in the intensity of your memory? Now reset it and make the image/movie gigantic—50 feet tall. How does that change the memory? Reset again.

**Proximity:** Move the image/movie away from you–at least 20 feet. After resetting, move it closer, right up against your face. How does either change affect your response to the memory? More intense? Less intense? Reset.

**Dimensionality:** If your memory is 2D, make it 3D with depth, and vice-versa. How does either change affect your response to the memory? More intense? Less intense? Reset.

**Color vs. black and white:** Make the image/movie black and white. After resetting, make the colors striking and beautiful. How does either change affect your response to the memory? More intense? Less intense? Reset again.

**Brightness:** First, make colors of the image dull. Reset. Then make them really bright. How does either change affect your response to the memory? More intense? Less intense? Reset for the final time.

Which of the preceding changes altered your experience the most? For some, changing the distance, proximity, brightness, or dimensionality (2D vs. 3D) completely changes the intensity of the feelings connected to the memory. Did you find your important submodalities? Odds are it was pretty easy to do. Now for more fun.

## Submodality exercise No. 2

In the first exercise we took an image of a smell memory and played with changing major visual submodalities. In doing so we were able to get an idea of how changing submodalities can impact experiencing a memory.

In this second exercise we'll take two memories of different foods and map the differences between their respective submodalities.

The first thing you'll need to do is pick your favorite food—something that makes you swoon at the very thought of it. That's easy for me—good dark chocolate. Bring up a great memory of your favorite food, be it chocolate or whatever.

Next choose your least favorite food, something you will absolutely NOT eat under any circumstances. If for any reason you don't have one, choose something that you really would rather not eat. For me, this is easy once again. My least favorite food is calf's liver. I can't stand it and absolutely won't eat it. There's a long story here having to do with an unfortunate childhood experience. I will say no more.

Now that you have your two foods in mind, go back to your favorite. As you think about it, where is the image of your favorite food located in your internal field? Is it a life-size memory? In color? How bright are the colors? Is it in 2D or 3D? Really be thorough in investigating the structure of your memory. I strongly suggest writing down all the answers to the previous questions.

Next, think about your least favorite food and do the same. Note the location of the image, size, distance, color, and brightness. Again, write down all the details.

Now compare how you represent the two different foods internally. Are the images in different locations? Are they different sizes? Is one image closer than the other? Is one brighter than the other? For the record, I did a quick inventory for both my choices. Dark chocolate was a large image (five feet square), front and center, in 3D, and about 4-5 feet away. The image was in bright colors and had lots of detail. In contrast, the calf's liver image was down on the floor to my left and almost out of sight. It was a small dark image and very dull in terms of brightness. The colors were all faded grays and browns. It looked almost like a blurred daguerreotype photograph from the 19$^{th}$ century.

I think you get the picture... literally. The only other part of this exercise is to try the following: for a moment try moving the unliked food over to the favorite food location and make all the structural components the same. Notice if you feel any different about the unliked food after doing so. Then put it back where it was. Let sleeping dogs lie–and your least favorite foods remain as so.

## Tasting and submodalities

How can we use submodalities in tasting wine? I thought you'd never ask. The answer is, in a multitude of ways. However, in this chapter, we'll focus on improving olfactory memory. In Chapter 23 I wrote about working on one's memory of the most common aromas in wine using what I called the "Basic Set." If you did any work with the images you probably improved your memory, maybe even considerably. Using submodalities, here are some further exercises to try.

**Images, aromas, and submodalities:** Bring up an image of a lemon internally (or another aromatic from the list). Use the suggested submodality changes above in terms of altering the size of the image, its location, the brightness, 2D vs. 3D, etc. Note how the changes increase or decrease the intensity of your memory of what a lemon smells and tastes like. Remember to reset your image after every change.

**Expand your repertoire:** Now isolate what different parts of the lemon smell and taste like in terms of the pith, the rind, and the oil. Again, use images to increase or decrease the intensity of your memory of lemon and all its constituent parts.

**Refine and calibrate:** Once you've discovered your most influential submodalities (be they size, proximity, brightness or whatever), use them to improve your sensitivity to the given aromatic. For example, consciously decrease the intensity of your memory of lemon until you can barely detect it. To do so, take your image of lemon and either gradually make it smaller until the memory fades or push the image away until you can no longer detect lemon. Find the limits of your sensitivity and then work on them. By doing so you'll be able to detect trace amounts of lemon—or any other aroma.

**Quality of fruits:** Take your image/memory of lemon and change it from freshly sliced lemon to dried lemon to preserved lemon. Morph your images and adjust your smell memory accordingly.

*Author's suggestion: Submodalities are perhaps the most profound thing I've ever learned. They are the fabric and structure of our internal experience of the world. Knowing about submodalities and how to change them gives us an important strategy to improve our memory for smell and taste —and show us one of the many ways our mind works.*

# 25

# Using An Internal Visual Cue to Help Calibrate Structure

*Author's note: In Chapter 4 I introduced the concept of structure in wine; the levels of acidity, alcohol, phenolic bitterness, and tannin. I also suggested how these different elements are often sensed on the palate and offered some quick strategies on how to practice tasting for them. In this chapter I'll take structure one step further by providing a strategy to help anyone quickly become more accurate and consistent when assessing it. This strategy (like many others you will find in this book) is based on visualization. Once you create your own personal visual representation, assessing structure will become routine.*

Any experienced taster should be able to quickly, accurately, and consistently judge structural levels in a glass of wine. But this is no easy task. In fact, it's a challenge for many people. Why? Because it can be difficult to quantify a physical sensation (as in sour or bitter) much less to be sensitive to it in the first place. How then can one become proficient at assessing the degree of structural elements? Perhaps the answer has to do with the mechanisms of how we think.

As mentioned before, scientists believe that most of the human race (as in over 90%) is visual-dominant internally. That means most of us think in pictures and movies. If that's the case, then practically all of us represent a great deal of the internal tasting experience visually. Assessing structure is no exception to the internal visual rule. In fact, it's the key to being consistent with it. To that point, in conversations and interviews with colleagues and students over the last decade-plus, I've found that with very few exceptions, all of us use internal visual scales or dials to help calibrate structural levels in wine.

Personally, I use an internal scale that resembles an old slide rule that's positioned several feet out in front of me. Yes, I know what you're thinking. That's more than a bit strange. But stay with me. The scale is out in front of me just below eye-level. It's about four feet long by one foot wide with marks for low, medium-minus, medium, medium-plus, and high that correspond to similar marks on the deductive tasting scale. A red button of sorts is positioned on medium in the middle of the scale. When I taste for structure (be it acidity, alcohol, or whatever), I watch the button as it moves until it stops at the appropriate mark on the scale that matches what I'm tasting/feeling in the wine.

For example, if I'm tasting a wine to assess the level of acidity, I watch the button on the scale move to the appropriate mark. Then I internally point to the mark and say (internally again), "it's medium-plus acid," or whatever the level happens to be. If I'm not quite sure about the accuracy, I can bring the scale closer to me, and smaller increments on the scale appear as it gets closer.

Do you use internal visuals to assess structural levels when you taste? You may already do so, but not be aware of it. Regardless, if you don't, you should. Using an internal visual cue or scale takes the mystery out of assessing structure and makes it a relatively easy task. Installing an internal scale or dial in your internal field is also easier than you may think. To do so, try the following:

1. First, take a look at the scale below used for assessing structural elements taken from the deductive tasting grid: Low – Medium-Minus – Medium – Medium-Plus – High
2. Next place a red *dot* or *button* squarely in the middle of the word "Medium." Next, slide the button sideways to the left to "low." Reset the button on "medium." Now slide the button

to the right on "high." And reset the button on "medium" again. Got it?
3. Now it's time to create your own personal scale, dial, or whatever design works best for you. It goes without saying that if the above scale/design doesn't work for you, create a different kind of dial or a scale. Remember, it's your internal IMAX theater. You can design whatever works best for you. Remember that it's also best to keep the design of your scale or dial simple. Once you've settled on a design, put markers on it for all the levels: low, medium-minus, medium, medium-plus, and high. Then put a brightly-colored button of sorts on the medium marker that can move over all the levels as needed.

## Calibrating your scale with extremes

Now that you have your internal scale, taste wines in pairs for extremes: lower vs. higher alcohol, acid, tannin, and phenolic bitterness. As you taste the wines, match your internal scale to the level of acidity (or other structural element) that you're tasting. You can also confirm structure levels by using internal auditory. For example, when tasting for alcohol with your scale, you can also say (inside voice, please), *the alcohol is high* or whatever the appropriate level. Here are some suggested pairs of wines to taste that will show extremes in structure.

Acidity: Alsace Gewürztraminer vs. Clare Valley Riesling

Alcohol: Mosel Kabinett Riesling vs. Central Coast Viognier

Phenolic bitterness: Chablis AC vs. Alsace Gewürztraminer

Tannin: Beaujolais-Villages vs. Barolo

Once you've calibrated the extremes for structure (Low and High), you can quickly branch out to find "Medium" and then "Medium-Minus" and "Medium-Plus." With some practice, tasting for structure using internal visual will become easy and something you do automatically. And that's a very good thing.

A final note: I've taught beginning students to taste for structure using an internal scale for many years. It takes only a few minutes to introduce the concept and then students quickly get the hang of it with a bit of practice. In no time, they easily calibrate structure and they're consistent with it.

*Author's suggestion: Initially, try my suggestion for a simple scale as described above. If it doesn't work, try a dial or some other kind of measuring image. Your brain will let you know when you come up with something that works. Above all, keep it simple. The purpose of the scale/dial is nothing more than confirming what you're already feeling on your palate—an internal visual connection to something that is kinesthetic.*

## 26

# Installing Olfactory Memories

*Author's note: This is another strategy involving visualization and olfactory memory that I've used a good deal over the years. I've taught it to students ranging from novices to experienced professionals. As the name implies, the strategy initially involves discovering what one already does with internal visuals in order to easily remember what something smells or tastes like. Then one uses the structure of an "easy" memory as a template to install new memories.*

The memory of a number of key aromatics is needed to recognize classic grapes and wines. Some are more problematic than others. The tough ones can become "blind spots" for student tasters and lead to habitual confusion between similar—but in reality very different—wines. Can't find black pepper in a red wine? Then Barossa Shiraz and Mendoza Malbec will forever seem like the same wine. Can't find bell pepper/pyrazines? Then identifying Sancerre and Chinon will always be a nightmare.

The phenomenon of these olfactory "blind spots" is really curious to me. How is it that someone can recognize any number of different aromas and yet be seemingly immune to a specific one? Mind you that in some cases these aromas, like pyrazines, are light years from being subtle. I've also read various sources about how certain individuals may be genetically disposed to have these olfactory blind spots.

In an upcoming chapter of the book called "For Love of a Rose" (Chapter 35), I describe one of my favorite olfactory memories of being in an heirloom rose garden at the Weingut Wittman estate in the Rheinhessen, and the role strong positive feelings play in a profound smell memory. Also, how one's affinity for the object of the memory only serves to intensify the experience as well as strengthen the memory for future recall. My theory is that the stronger the feeling associated with the memory, the easier, more accurate, and faster we're able to recall it.

With these so-called blind spots, let me suggest the following: We can use our most profound smell memories to help improve our overall olfactory memory. Further, we can use an "easy" olfactory memory to help install one of these blind spot aromas. The answer lies in discovering the *template* or *sequence* of how we construct our profound smell memories so it can be used to install new smell memories, even the tough "blind spot" ones that evade us. We'll also use strong feelings to make the entire process a deeper experience.

### Discovering your "easy" olfactory memory template

There are two parts to discovering the template of one of your profound olfactory memories.

**Content:** As in the subject of the memory itself, like a childhood memory of freshly baked bread or the best espresso you've ever had. We'll use my rose garden memory for content.

**Structure:** Is arguably more important than the actual content of the memory. In the case of the rose garden, I mentioned the structural elements of internal images including size, brightness, and proximity. These are key to the intensity and longevity of the memory. They are called submodalities (see Chapter 23). There are over 60 possible submodalities for internal visual alone, but we'll focus on a handful of the most important ones.

To demonstrate how to deconstruct the template of an important smell memory we'll use my experience in the rose garden. To keep score, I'll create a checklist that includes a group of the most important visual submodalities.

**Still image vs. movie:** The rose garden memory is a movie—which is more powerful than a simple still image.

**Size:** It's life-sized and all around me—panoramic.

**Associated/dissociated:** Fancy talk for either seeing the memory out of your eyes as if you're actually there (associated) or seeing yourself from a distance in the memory (dissociated). Whenever I drop back into the rose garden memory, I'm there in a flash looking at everything out of my own eyes Answer: associated.

**Proximity:** The rose garden memory literally envelops me. I'm standing in the middle of it. This versus a memory where the focus of activity or whatever is a distance out in front of you.

**Dimensionality:** Is the memory 2D and flat, or is it in 3D and has depth? My rose garden memory is definitely three-dimensional.

**Color vs. black and white:** Easy answer—the memory is vivid, almost more than lifelike color.

**Brightness:** My memory is really bright in terms of color and light—again almost more than lifelike.

**Sounds:** In the memory, I can hear the sounds of my colleagues conversing in the background and the buzzing of bees (quite a few of them!) around me.

**Internal feelings:** In the memory, every time I stop to smell a rose, I close my eyes and experience an internal feeling of reaching out to something. But then a vital part of the memory occurs: a feeling of happiness and connection. The longer I think about it (memory), the stronger it gets.

**Internal dialogue:** I distinctly remember saying, "Wow!" internally when smelling a given rose.

## Your turn

Now it's time to discover your own template using my rose garden memory as an example. Choose one of your favorite smell memories. It can be from childhood, home, or travel. Once you have a memory in mind, ask yourself the following about it:

Is it a still image or movie?

**Size:** How big is the memory?

**Associated vs. dissociated:** Are you looking out of your eyes at the "scene" in your memory or watching yourself do something?

**Proximity:** How close is the action in your memory to you?

**Dimensionality:** Is your memory 2D or 3D?

**Color or black and white:** Which one?

**Brightness:** Dull, bright, or HD bright?

**Sounds:** Note any sounds in the memory.

**Internal feelings:** How does the memory make you feel? *Remember, the feelings part of your memory are important.*

**Internal dialogue:** Are you saying something to yourself in the memory?

Go through your memory several times using the list above. Really get an idea of how your memory works in terms of its structure, even the sequence of action if there is one.

## WRITE EVERYTHING DOWN

This is important as you need a script or sequence of how one of your profound smell memories work. Once you've got it, it's time to play.

## Drag and drop

Now that you have the structure behind a formative smell memory it's time to use it to great benefit. Next we'll use the structure as a kind of template to install other memories.

First, take an aroma that gives you a problem in terms of consistent recognition. For some, white pepper or green bell pepper can be a nightmare. Make sure you have the object of the desired memory—be it white pepper or bell pepper or whatever–actually *in your hand* as you go through this strategy. You'll be smelling it repeatedly to help install the memory.

Now smell the bell pepper, white pepper, or whatever. Then close your eyes and generate an image of it—a large colorful picture. Do this several times until the aroma stays with you and an image pops up immediately when you close your eyes.

Make it the same! Next take the image of white pepper or green bell pepper and drop it into the template of your previous favorite memory. Using the submodality list you wrote down, do the following trying to match your previous template as closely as possible:

**Still image or movie:** Make it the same—and a movie with movement if you can.

**Size:** Make the image/movie the same size.

**Associated vs. dissociated:** Make it the same.

**Proximity:** Make the new memory the same distance from you as in your favorite memory.

**Dimensionality:** Make it three dimensional.

**Color vs. black and white:** Make the colors of the new image striking and beautiful.

**Brightness:** Make it the same brightness as in your favorite memory.

**Sounds:** Put sound into the new memory if it's not already there.

**Internal feelings:** Use the feelings from the previous favorite memory. Remember, the feelings in memory are important.

**Internal dialogue:** If you're saying something to yourself in your favorite memory, say the same thing in this new memory—or something similar to make it appropriate for the context.

## Higher, louder, faster*

Now it's time to make the memory more intense and easier to recall. To do so, make your internal image/movie larger, more colorful, much brighter, the sounds louder, and double the intensity of the smell. That goes for any feelings you have in the memory. Amp those way up too.

**Repetition:** Spend two or more sessions with the "new" aromatic. If you really use the template of your previous memory fully, the new aromatic will quickly pop and be easy to recognize in the future.

**Test:** After a session, test your memory of the aromatic. Bring up the image and see if the smell memory pops. If it doesn't, no worries. Spend more time with it using the process above.

**Piece it together:** Once you've installed the new memory, practice putting it into context of your memory of the appropriate grape or wine. Mentally "drop" pyrazines into Sancerre along with the usual tart citrus fruits, pronounced minerality, and high acidity. Same for white pepper in Grüner Veltliner (or Northern Rhône Syrah).

Practice! Because it's a noble thing we do.

À votre santé!

*For all my trumpet playing friends out there. They know exactly what it means.

*Author's suggestion: As with any new memory strategy, make it EASY in the beginning. Choose a favorite smell memory that you can quickly bring up on command. Then sit down and write out all the structure of it in detail. Again, the submodalities are more important than the object of the memory itself. Your list of these submodalities will help create a template to put new memories in—and make them just as easily accessible.*

*A final thought: I've said it before and I'll say it again: if a strategy is not working, odds are you're trying too hard or forcing it to work. Back off, back up, and start over with another memory that's simpler and easier. Remember, easy and simple are usually best when starting to learn something new.*

# 27

# Label Check

*Author's note: Time is a funny thing. It can pass in the blink of an eye or it can seem like an eternity. For a student taking a tasting exam, it can be a bit of both when they're faced with having to recognize and describe certain critical elements in a given wine—or avoid hallucinating said criteria if they don't actually exist.*

*For example, the student has to be able to recognize if the wine has oak or not, or whether the used oak they're perceiving in white wine is actually phenolic bitterness. Another critical yes/no moment is if a wine displays aromas and flavors of earth/mineral—or the lack thereof.*

*There are others, but oak/phenolic bitterness and earth/mineral are almost gut-check moments because any decision made in regards to them will either take the student home to the right grape/wine in their conclusion, or land them in an unrelated—and completely wrong—universe. These yes/no decisions are made in an instant. What can help the student in these moments of truth, so to speak? Is there a strategy that can help them make an instant—and correct—decision? Read on.*

## A single picture...

It's said that a picture is worth a thousand words. I would go further by saying a single image can trigger a complex memory that's not just visual—it can involve multiple senses. If that's the case, can one consciously use images to build strong non-visual sensory associations? The answer is yes and we'll explore that below. But first, let's consider the common challenges facing students preparing for tasting exams. I've mentioned two of them above but here is a more complete list.

## Major Challenges

**Old World vs. New World style:** Is the wine fruit or earth-driven? Does the presence of earth and/or mineral elements dominate the wine or is the wine from the New World and driven by fruit, winemaking, and oak?

**Used oak vs. phenolic bitterness in white wine:** Does the slightly bitter and astringent finish signify oak aging in a white wine or is it phenolic bitterness from skin contact? If oak is the answer, then other markers such as spice, toast, vanilla, smoke, etc., will usually accompany the bitter sensation. If not, skin contact is the likely answer.

**Cool vs. warm climate:** Does the wine show restrained alcohol, high acidity, and tart/under-ripe fruit from a cooler climate? Or does the wine produced from fruit grown in a warm/hot climate in terms of ripe, even jammy fruit, high alcohol, and restrained acidity—which is then usually adjusted through acidulation.

## Calibrating structural elements

**Acidity:** How much? Is the wine flabby or more like a liquid laser beam?

**Alcohol:** How much? Does the wine show a lot of heat on the nose and palate or offer the barest trace of warmth?

**Tannin:** How much? Extremes in tannin are easy to find: Nouveau Beaujolais will usually offer lower tannin while a young vintage of Barolo can be ferociously tannic.

## Impact compounds

Recognizing key markers that are critical to identifying a classic wine.

**Pyrazines:** The green bell pepper, vegetal, herbal notes in Sauvignon Blanc and Cabernet Sauvignon Family wines.

**Terpenes:** The floral and sweet citrus aromas and flavors found in semi-aromatic grapes such as Chenin Blanc and fully aromatic grapes like Gewürztraminer.

**Rotundone:** The peppery qualities found in Grüner Veltliner and Syrah.

**TDN:** The gasoline/petrol notes found on the nose and palate of Riesling.

## Pass the easy button, please...

Maybe I'm lazy here but I want easy solutions to all the above. Pictures —the right pictures—could be the easiest possible solution. By pictures I'm thinking of the labels of certain wines that offer extreme examples of the criteria listed above. Labels that, if briefly brought up internally to one's mind's eye during one of the "moments of truth" above, can trigger instant and intense memories of the important aromatics/flavors. I call these "label checks." Granted, this is anything but hard science, but I'm operating on several presuppositions here:

First, as previously mentioned, over 90% of the human race is visual-dominant internally. Most of us tend to think in pictures and movies.

Second, calibrating using extremes is not only the easiest way to learn anything, but to also remember what you've just learned. For example, if you can see black and white on opposite ends of a spectrum, it's easy to almost instantly find a shade of gray in the middle.

Third, in keeping with the "one picture equals a thousand word" idea, a single image can trigger a complex sensory memory for us. That's important for us in the wine world.

Fourth, if anything else, when using an extreme example or polar opposite, it's easy to get to a simple yes/no answer in an instant. For our purposes, that's also important.

There's a method to the madness here. To begin, we'll use extreme examples for all the criteria listed above in the form of specific labels for classic wines to get an immediate yes/no answer. Then we'll use the same strategy to calibrate sensory memory in terms of the level of structural elements, as well as important impact compounds such as pyrazines and terpenes. Now for the instructions to the strategy.

## Instructions

Choose one of the elements/challenges mentioned above. For example, let's use oak in white wine.

Choose the label of a wine that represents an extreme example of new oak in white wine—in this case a California Chardonnay.

Once you choose a label, bring it to mind.

Make the label enormous in your internal mind's eye out in front of you: five-by-seven feet will do nicely.

Now make the label as bright as you can.

As you look at the huge, bright label in your mind's eye, really get a sense of the wine in terms of new oak with aromas of strong vanilla, toast, and spice, and what all that smells and tastes like.

Now amp up your impression of the oak in the wine while looking at the label. Make it as strong as you can.

**Repetition:** Practice several times or until you can bring up the label in mind and immediately get a strong impression of oak.

# Message in the Bottle

## Application

Now it's time to test the strategy. In your next tasting practice as you go through the grid with a white wine, when you get to the point of assessing oak, bring up the Chardonnay label, huge and bright in your mind's eye, and ask yourself, "Yes or no?" The answer will be immediate in the form of a strong *yes* or *no* or even *in between* in the case of used oak. But the important thing is that you have an internal reference that can help you detect oak in the moment– and to be able to do so quickly. With that, here are suggested labels of wines that show extremes that can be used to address a challenge in similar fashion.

The labels I've chosen below are suggestions to work with. By all means choose labels of wines you know best and that will create the strongest and most immediate memories and associations. Remember that the golden rule is to always choose the label of a wine that shows something to the extreme. Also, choose colorful labels that are easy to remember.

## Major challenges

**Old World vs. New World style:** Ramey Cellars Russian River Valley Chardonnay vs. Domaine des Baumard Savennières.

I've chosen David Ramey's Russian River Valley Chardonnay for several of the challenges because it's a great example of a New World white wine in terms of a combination of ripe and tart fruit, relative lack of earth/mineral, lees contact, ML, and oak. It's also a personal favorite. The Baumard Savennières by comparison is very dry with intense minerality and high acidity. Thus it's a perfect wine/label for the earth/mineral check for Old World style.

**Cooler vs. warmer climate:** Domaine Christian Moreau Chablis 1er Cru vs. Ramey Cellars Russian River Valley Chardonnay.

**Two labels:** A steely, chalky, high-acid Chablis vs. a ripe and buttery California Chardonnay with new oak.

**Phenolic bitterness vs. oak:** Domaine Weinbach Gewürztraminer vs. Ramey Cellars Russian River Valley Chardonnay.

This is definitely one of the big challenges facing tasters, so choose wines/labels that are extreme. We'll go with Ramey Chardonnay for oak and use the opulent Domaine Weinbach Gewürztraminer for phenolic bitterness. Get these two down and you'll never mistake phenolic bitterness for oak again.

**Oak influence:** Ramey Cellars Russian River Valley Chardonnay vs. Cloudy Bay Sauvignon Blanc.

The Ramey Chardonnay excels here again because of the use of new oak. The Cloudy Bay by contrast offers a perfect example of a stainless steel-fermented white without oak aging.

## Calibrating structural elements

In keeping with the idea of using labels of wines that show extremes, I want to reiterate that once you can quickly calibrate *high* vs. *low* in terms of acidity, alcohol, phenolic bitterness, or tannin, it will be just as easy to find *medium* much less *medium-minus* or *medium-plus*.

**Alcohol:** J.J. Prüm Wehlener Sonnenuhr Riesling Spätlese vs. Biale Black Chicken Zinfandel.

**For calibrating alcohol level we'll use two extremes:** The intense, luscious Biale Black Chicken Zinfandel which often weighs in at over 15% ABV vs. a delicate Spätlese Riesling from J.J. Prüm in the Mosel that usually ranges between 8 and 9%.

**Tannin:** Jadot Beaujolais-Villages vs. Parusso Barolo "Bussia."

An excellent juxtaposition of two reds—one with less medium tannin and the other with high tannin.

**Acidity:** Domaine Weinbach Gewürztraminer vs. Domaine des Baumard Savennières.

On its own, the Weinbach is a gorgeous example of Alsace Gewürztraminer—exotically floral, perfumed, and spicy. But acidic the wine is not, and using our label strategy, the Baumard by comparison has much higher acidity.

## Impact compounds

Beyond the above challenges and calibrating structural elements, we can use the label strategy to help recognize important impact compounds that are key markers for identifying certain classic grapes and wines.

**Pyrazines:** Brancott Estate Reserve Sauvignon Blanc.

Pyrazines are a vital marker for tasters to know and recognize and New Zealand Sauvignon Blancs are known for their pyrazinic character.

**Terpenes:** Bodega Colomé Torrontés.

We could easily choose the Weinbach for the floral/sweet citrus notes of terpenes but we need some variety at this point and the Torrontés fits the bill perfectly. It also shows considerable phenolic bitterness as well.

**Rotundone:** Alain Graillot Crozes-Hermitage.

Although the peppery-savory quality of rotundone is found in most Syrahs, I'm choosing the Alain Graillot because it's a personal favorite. It also commonly offers sanguine notes such as game, meat, and dried blood.

**TDN:** Pewsey Vale Contours Riesling.

TDN is often associated with the Rieslings from Clare and Eden Valleys. There are more than a few great Australian Rieslings I could choose from, but The Pewsey Vale Contours is again a personal favorite.

Lots of petrol notes here with the bonus of high acidity and unusually pronounced minerality for a New World wine.

*Author's suggestion: Play with the label check strategy. Once you get the hang of it, labels can be used for any number of instant yes/no recognition moments needed during the tasting process. One more thing: once you get the instant recognition part of the label strategy down, take it a step further using submodalities which are discussed in an earlier chapter.*

*Specifically, practice making the label images smaller and larger in your mind's eye. As you make them larger, increase the intensity of the oak/phenolic bitterness/mineral/alcohol or whatever. As you make the images smaller, decrease the intensity of your memory for said element. Reset the image/memory every time for consistency. You can build heightened sensitivity to the aforementioned elements just by doing this alone.*

28

# Associative Rehearsal, or Tasting Practice Without Wine

*Author's note: A great deal of the tasting experience can—and should—be practiced without a glass of wine in hand. That's because looking at, smelling, and tasting wine has a lot to do with perception, recognition, and memory. If that's the case, one can work backward, so to speak, by doing memory work on everything from wine colors and what they mean, aromatics and flavors, and combinations of all the previous ones which equal classic grapes and wines. With that, read on.*

As I've mentioned, my original training was in classical music. No surprise I'm a big fan of the composer Felix Mendelssohn. His music is brilliant and utterly enjoyable. As I write this, I'm listening to his fourth symphony called "Italian" played by the Cleveland Orchestra conducted by George Szell. It's filled with gorgeous tunes you could easily hum after a couple of hearings.

Mendelssohn also wrote a series of piano pieces called "Lieder ohne Worte," or *Songs without Words,* between 1829 and 1845. The eight volumes, each containing six songs, were written at a time when the piano was just becoming popular in European middle-class households. Hence the demand for and popularity of well-crafted works that could be played by amateurs and professionals alike. His intent, like so many other composers of his time, was to write a series of lyrical pieces for the piano, songs for the piano that didn't require lyrics much less singing.

How do Mendelssohn and his songs without words connect to tasting? To have any success, every wine student on an exam track must practice tasting individually and as part of a tasting group. Both are valuable experiences and irreplaceable. However, any tasting exam is all about memory—primarily olfactory and palate memory. Improving your memory doesn't require having a glass of wine in hand.

After years of teaching and coaching innumerable students, I've come to believe that associative rehearsal of tasting—as in practicing tasting without a glass of wine physically in hand—can be just as valuable as actual tasting. Why? Simply because once a student gets beyond the novice level, odds are they've tasted a lot of wine and have a considerable database of memories of previous wines.

I suggest students preparing for an exam regularly—even daily—take time to mentally mock up a flight of classic wines in an exam-type setting (again, all of this in terms of visualization) and then talk through the wines out loud using whatever tasting grid they're using, just as they would during an actual exam. During this rehearsal time the student needs to remember and experience each wine as completely and intensely as possible: seeing the wine clearly in their mind's eye, smelling it completely, tasting it fully, and noting the flavors and structural elements accurately. Finally, they should nail the conclusion of the wine while feeling utterly confident. All this is easy to do and just takes a bit of time, practice, and privacy.

Practicing tasting using associative rehearsal accomplishes several things:

It connects you to previous memories of various specific aromas and flavors and also to your memories of specific classic wines in a sensory package of sight, smell, and taste.

It builds recognition and memory for wines in terms using the auditory channel—your speaking voice. In doing so, it improves the number of ways that you can *get* to the identity of a wine via more than one sense.

In this case, practicing "talking about wine" becomes yet another key for memory.

Practicing talking through wines out loud using a grid also helps to build your inner exam comfort zone in terms of being confident when you have to speak aloud in front of examiners if you're taking an oral exam.

## Other aspects of associative tasting practice

What other aspects of wine can be practiced without having a glass of wine physically in hand? Plenty. Here are a few worth considering.

**Color:** Practice seeing the important major colors in wine in your mind's eye: straw, yellow, and gold for whites; purple, ruby, and garnet for reds. Make the colors intense, and bright, and really get the difference between them. Once you've got the colors down—and that shouldn't take much time—begin to make them closer in appearance until you can spot subtle differences and combine two different colors to best describe a wine (yellow-gold or ruby-garnet, etc.)

**Common aromas:** Practice your memory of the common aromas in wine. There are around thirty of them (see chapter 22 on the Basic Set). Develop a good working memory for any fruit in the five major fruit groups for white wines and the four fruit groups for red wine. Do the same with the major non-fruit elements including flowers, spices, herbs, and more.

**Impact compounds:** It's important to have a good working memory for impact compounds such as pyrazines, lees contact, stem inclusion, use of oak, terpenes, and more (see Chapter 11 for the complete list). I could argue that the ability to remember and recognize these compounds, and connecting them to classic grapes and wines, is a gauge of one's level of tasting experience and expertise.

**Fruit quality:** Take your memory of a common aroma such as black cherry. Once you have your memory of black cherry in mind (i.e. your image), begin to change its condition. First make it young, tart, under ripe, and barely edible. Reset it. Now make it riper until it's over ripe, then stewed, then dried. Reset it again. With some practice you can do this to practically any component in wine, from flowers (fresh to dry to pressed) to oak (new to used) and beyond.

**Wine age:** Once you can change the condition of a fruit aroma/flavor doing the same thing with a complete wine. Start by taking something straight forward like a Napa Valley Cabernet Sauvignon: First make it youthful—as in just bottled—with intense, youthful fruit, and astringent tannins. Then gradually morph the wine's age until it's old, oxidized, and barely drinkable. Then reset it.

**Wine faults:** Practice your memory for the major wine faults including TCA, H2S, mercaptan, Brett, VA, and others. In doing so you'll also develop more sensitivity to them as well. Also be able to place your memories in the context of wines that traditionally display one or more of these so-called faults but aren't considered flawed as a result (Brett in Northern Rhône Syrah, etc.).

**Structure:** Internally bring up another wine that's easy to remember. New Zealand Sauvignon Blanc is a good example. Taking the structural elements one at a time—the levels of acid, alcohol, phenolic bitterness, and tannin (if a red wine)—gradually change the level from higher to lower or vice versa. With acid, start with the level intensely high (feel the acidity on your tongue, gums, and salivary glands) gradually lower the level down to medium-plus then medium then medium-minus and finally flabby. Then take the level up gradually again back to "high." You might be curious to see how the quality of the fruit changes from tart to over ripe at the same time. Do the same with the alcohol, phenolic bitterness, tannin, and even the length of the finish.

**Grape varieties:** Practice your memory of the best examples of the classic wines you've ever tasted. With enough repetition, the major grapes/wines will become so distinct that it will become difficult to confuse them. Personally, the major grapes occupy different "locations" in my mind's eye. In keeping with the previous chapter, using labels of best examples can help considerably.

**Conclusions:** Practice taking the major markers found in a classic wine and making the "right" conclusion." Do it forwards and backwards. By backwards I mean starting with declaring a grape, origin, and vintage and then explaining to yourself why and how you got to the conclusion. Then explain why it can't be other grapes that are often confused with the grape/wine in your conclusion. Example? Nailing the conclusion for a Châteauneuf du Pape and explaining internally—or out loud—why it can't be Tempranillo/Rioja Gran Reserva or Sangiovese/Chianti Classico. Impact compounds and differences in structural levels will be key.

*Author's suggestion: I can't recommend tasting practice using associative rehearsal strongly enough. So much of a tasting exam is about having confidence with one's own internal experience, sensitivity, calibration, and above all, memory. There's no better way to improve them.*

# 29

# Dealing With a Dominant Aroma In the Glass

*Author's note: Sometimes a single aroma/flavor will be so dominant in a wine that it's difficult to identify anything else in the glass. The following is a strategy using internal visuals which will help.*

Once I received an email from a student who had recently taken a class asking what to do about an apparent dilemma. It seems that when smelling the Barossa Shiraz that had been used in one of the flights, he couldn't get past the intense mint and eucalyptus aromas to be able to pick out anything else. He's not alone with this challenge.

It's a common problem for students—even professionals. When something in a wine dominates to such an extent it becomes difficult to find anything else. Or a taster is so hyper-sensitive to one aroma in the wine that she or he can't pick out anything else. What to do? Here is my strategy for dealing with a dominant aroma in the glass.

## The setup

First, let's warm up your brain in regards to smell and internal imaging. Go inside now and think about one of your favorite smell memories.

Make it simple like the smell of just-baked bread, coffee roasting, or slicing a ripe peach.

Once you've got your memory, be aware of your visual representation of it. The form will be either a still image or a movie if it's a powerful memory. It's important for you to make a visual connection to your memory. You're going to need it.

Now consider the following common aromas in wine: lemon, green apple, cinnamon, and vanilla. Once again, note the images you use to bring up memories of these aromatics. Got it? Good. Now it's time for the strategy.

## The strategy

If you're having trouble with a dominant aroma in a wine like the mint/eucalyptus in the Shiraz mentioned above, try the following. We'll be using submodalities as described in Chapter 24.

Important: remember that whenever working with submodalities it's imperative to only change ONE thing at a time. After, reset the image to the way it originally was. Otherwise, everything will quickly become a muddled mess. With that, it's time to explore.

First, smell the wine. While you're doing so, create a big, bright image of the dominant aroma you smell in the wine just like the exercise above.

Next, make sure the image of the dominant aroma and bring it front and center in your internal field as you smell the wine. I'm going to use the mint/eucalyptus as an example.

Now it's time to play with some simple submodalities (structural qualities of the image):

**Movie vs. still image:** If your representation of mint/eucalyptus is a movie, freeze it and make it a still image. Now smell the wine again and see if you can pick out other aromatics.

*Reset the image of mint/eucalyptus to whatever was previously.*

**Color vs. black and white:** If the image of the mint/eucalyptus is in color (and it probably is), make it black and white. Smell the wine again. Odds are the intensity of the mint/eucalyptus will have decreased significantly and you can pick out other aromas that weren't as noticeable as before.

*Reset the image of mint/eucalyptus again.*

**Dimensionality:** If the image of mint/eucalyptus is in 3D (again, it probably is), make it flat like a photograph. Smell the wine again and see if you can note other aromas.

*Reset the image of mint/eucalyptus again.*

**Size:** Take the image of mint/eucalyptus and shrink it. Make it as small as a postage stamp. Again, your perception of the wine will probably change as a result.

*Reset the image of mint/eucalyptus again.*

**Proximity:** Take the image of mint/eucalyptus and push it a great distance away making the image tiny. Again, your perception of the wine will probably change as a result.

*Reset the image of mint/eucalyptus again.*

**Position:** Finally, take the image of mint/eucalyptus and move it way off to one side or behind you. Smell the wine again and note the difference.

*Reset the image of mint/eucalyptus again.*

*Author's suggestions: There are lots of possibilities here. Odds are that one —or even several—will work and even be effective and easy to do. Remember that you can always put the image of the dominant aroma back the way it originally was—or you can alter it however you want. It's your show. Finally, if you stop and think about it for a moment, there are any number of possibilities here, not only for building sensitivity to any aroma, but for installing smell memories as well. Regardless, explore and have fun with it.*

# 30

# Using a Coravin For Tasting Practice

*Author's note: Though not inexpensive, a Coravin is by far the most useful wine accessory there is for tasting practice. Using a Coravin will allow you to buy high quality examples of classic wines and to taste them repeatedly over a period of time, thereby saving thousands of dollars on wine purchases. Here are some suggestions for using a Coravin during your tasting practice.*

Taste wines in pairs: Our brains learn easily with binary. Practice tasting wines in twos and do the following.

Calibrate structure using extremes: One of the easiest ways to learn consistent calibration of structural elements is by comparative tasting that uses extremes. Using a Coravin, here are suggested pairs of wines that show extremes in structure. Taste for one structural element at a time. Remember—only two wines at a time.

- Alcohol - low vs. high: Mosel Kabinett Riesling vs. high alcohol Napa Valley Chardonnay or Central Coast Viognier
- Acidity - lower vs. high: Alsace Gewürztraminer vs. Clare Valley Riesling

- Phenolic bitterness - lower vs. high: Chablis AC vs. Alsace Gewürztraminer
- Tannin - lower vs. high: Beaujolais-Villages vs. Barolo

Practice With the Evil Dwarves: Semi-aromatic white wines and lighter pigmented red wines can be a nightmare for the student. I call them the "Evil Dwarves" because when poured next to each other, they can all look almost exactly the same and offer similar fruit character (see Chapter 12). However, the impact compounds and structure levels for each of the wines is unique. To conquer the Evil Dwarves, use the Coravin to taste (and drink) them in pairs next to each other repetitively on a daily basis for as long as it takes to get clarity on them and avoid any confusion (see Chapter 12). Here is the list of Evil Dwarves for both white and red grapes:

- White wines: Albariño, Grüner Veltliner, Loire Chenin Blanc, Alsace Pinot Gris, Northern Italian Pinot Grigio, and dry Riesling from Alsace or Germany.
- Red wines: Pinot Noir, Gamay, Sangiovese, Tempranillo, Nebbiolo, and Grenache.
- Important marker recognition: There are several factors that any student—and professional—needs to be able to recognize the presence—or lack of—in wine. Use the Coravin to taste wine in pairs to help with the following important decisions that have to be made during the tasting process.
- Oak vs. no oak in white wines: Chablis vs. heavily oaked California Chardonnay.
- Earth/mineral vs. no earth/mineral in both white wines: same wines as above.
- Used oak vs. phenolic bitterness in white wines: Vouvray Sec vs. Alsace Gewürztraminer.

Finally, if two wines keep confusing you, try tasting them separately against an easier control wine. New Zealand Sauvignon Blanc is a good example of a control white wine. Then compare and contrast how the problem wine is different from the control wine. Finally, practice tasting them again next to each other. It should be easier.

*Author's suggestions: If only I had had a Coravin when I was studying for the exams. Not to be redundant, but I'll repeat that tasting wines in pairs is the easiest way to build memory and create the necessary connections for recognition. Otherwise, be patient and give yourself time to learn. Persistence will ultimately pay off.*

## 31

# Eating the Elephant: Advice for Beginning Tasters

*Author's note: Becoming a professional taster is a process that requires a duration of time and lots of tasting practice with wine in hand—and not. I've emphasized the fact that there are no shortcuts. That's the bad news. The good news is that this is wine we're dealing with and not widgets. Wine, as in one of the greatest gifts from nature mankind has ever discovered. This chapter provides some suggestions and guidelines to help break down the tasting process into manageable bits for the beginning taster.*

Regardless of the specific curriculum, learning how to taste may seem overwhelming to the beginner or novice student. There are so many terms to learn plus the challenge of becoming proficient with smell and taste memory. It brings to mind the old proverb about eating an elephant—as in, one bite at a time. With tasting, this ancient quip applies in the form of incremental learning and practice. Keeping the elephant in mind, here are some tips to help learning the tasting process manageable.

**Memorize the grid:** Regardless of the specific tasting grid, the very first thing you must do is memorize it. Break the grid down into groups of three terms and memorize their definitions. Be able to explain the terms and the grid to someone who's not in the wine industry. I again have to mention the physicist Richard Feynman, who once said that if you can't explain something to an eight-year-old, you really don't know it. Nothing could be truer.

**Learn common wine terms:** Find a good glossary of wine terms and begin to chip away at it daily, again in three-to-five-word increments. In the beginning, focus on terms that have to do with tasting. Again, be able to explain the terms to someone who's not in the industry. Otherwise, you don't really know them and you certainly won't remember what they mean during an exam.

**Improve your memory for basic aromatics and flavors:** Work on your memory for all the aromas/flavors listed in the "Basic Set" (Chapter 22) for a few minutes every day—without wine. Tasting will become much easier if you do.

**Structure practice:** Practice tasting focusing on structure—the levels of acidity, alcohol, phenolic bitterness, and tannin in any given wine. In particular, practice isolating the elements on your palate. Separate what each tastes and feels like as in the bitter taste and astringent feeling of tannin (see Chapter 4 on assessing structure).

**Connect the dots:** When you taste for structure, start to connect the fruit quality of the wine and the structure to the kind of climate where the grapes were grown. For example, a wine with higher alcohol and less natural acidity that shows really ripe fruit is almost always from a warmer growing region. Likewise, a wine with restrained alcohol and higher natural acidity with tarter fruit is usually from a cooler growing region (see Chapter 8 on Cause and Effect and Chapter 5 Using a Decision Matrix).

**Write your own grape variety/varietal wine descriptions:** There are many lists of descriptions available including the ones in Chapters 6 and 7. However, you need to create a personal list with your own markers for each grape and what makes them easy to identify—for you. Start with the easy wines/descriptions and write one or two a day, or any time you taste an appropriate wine. Read them regularly—out loud if you can. It's yet another way to use multi-sensory memory to identify a classic wine when the time comes.

**Get a Coravin:** As mentioned in the previous chapter, the one wine accessory that's almost a must-own for tasting practice is a Coravin. It's not inexpensive, but using a Coravin on a regular basis will allow you to purchase high quality examples of classic wines and taste them multiple times, saving you untold thousands of dollars in the long run.

**Practice tasting wine in pairs:** Taste wines in pairs using the Coravin. Always compare a more challenging wine with a wine that's easy to recognize. For example, a dry Chenin Blanc from the Loire vs. a New Zealand Sauvignon Blanc. Focus on impact compounds—the most important aromas and flavors—and the differences in structure. These two aspects are the most important in varietal recognition.

*Author's suggestion: One bite at a time. Keep a journal of the work you're doing each day and the wines you're tasting/working with. Be patient with your improvement. You'll be surprised at how much progress you can achieve even in a short period of time with consistent work and a plan. Otherwise, learning how to taste requires the use of multiple senses simultaneously or in rapid sequence. It's not exactly easy—but more than worth the effort. Remember to enjoy the learning. That's important too.*

# 32

# Tasting Exam Preparation Strategies

*Author's note: In a recent conversation with a student, I was asked how I would prepare for the Master Sommelier tasting exam if I had to take it again. What strategies would I use to prepare? And what strategies would I use to practice focus and confidence for exam day? I promised the student I would put together a list of strategies I would employ in preparation for the exam. The following is that list. Please note that some of the ideas and strategies are presented in other parts of the book—but others are new. Consider the following a detailed checklist.*

The MS tasting exam is the most remarkably difficult test I've ever taken–and passed. While two music degrees and seven years of college down the drain may have given me an edge with the theory exam and my restaurant career with the service exam, nothing prepared me for becoming a professional taster much less passing the exam.

If I had to do it all over again, I would train for the exam just as a professional golfer practices for a major tournament. Mind you, I've never played golf and have no intention of adding a source of immense frustration to my life at this point. However, golf is a perfect analogy to professional tasting and the exam because the game is made up of multiple aspects that have to be practiced individually to achieve overall competence and consistency.

Likewise, in preparing for the exam I would break down the tasting process into smaller chunks and work on each separately. I would focus on the concentration and confidence aspects separately from tasting. Finally, I would practice as many parts of the tasting process internally—without actually tasting—as possible.

Here is a program of sorts for preparing for a tasting exam. As everyone is wired differently, some strategies will be useful for certain students but not others. I certainly don't expect anyone to adopt the entire program. Rather, read through the list and pick and choose strategies that will help the most.

## The obvious

- Get into a good tasting group and work with it regularly.
- Taste good examples of the wines. Don't waste time tasting bottles that are outside the profiles for classics.
- Get occasional coaching from a professional in your market. There may not be someone living near you, much less someone that has the time to coach. In that case, Zoom or Skype are useful options.

## General strategies

**Get a Coravin:** A Coravin can also be used in any number of ways to prepare for the exam (see Chapter 31). More on that below.

**Memorize the grid:** Regardless of the tasting grid you'll be using for the exam, you simply must know it cold to the extent of always knowing what's next in the tasting sequence. To really commit the grid to long term memory, be able to explain it to a proverbial eight-year-old—or at least someone who's not in the wine industry. If you can't easily explain it to someone who's not in wine then you really don't know it (see Chapter 3).

**Cause and Effect:** Memorize Cause and Effect behind each criterion on your tasting grid. Be able to break down varietal, environmental, and winemaking causes as they apply to every line on the grid. As with basic memorization of the grid, be able to explain the concept of Cause and Effect to someone who's not in the business (see Chapter 8).

**Memorize common aromas and flavors:** Work on your memory of the aromas and flavors found in the Basic Set (see Chapter 23). Although you can buy one of the pricey aroma kits, it's just as effective to work with the real aroma sources found in most grocery stores—and far less expensive.

Write out personal descriptions for classic wines. Include common aromas and flavors for each and focus on important impact compounds (see below) and structure levels. To start, use the descriptions in Chapters 6 and 7. However, it's important for you to use these descriptions as a starting point and then create your own, more personal, list.

## Internal imaging, sensory experience, and memory

Use imaging to improve olfactory and palate memory. As mentioned previously, the tasting experience—like practically everything else we do—is visual internally. Work with internal images of your life memories of the common aromas/flavors above. You'll find that you already *own* most of them (see Chapter 23).

**Submodalities:** Improve your olfactory memory and sensitivity by using internal imaging and submodalities (see Chapter 24). Consciously manipulate submodalities to improve your sensitivity to specific memories.

**Fruit and fruit quality:** Work on memory of common fruits and non-fruits in regards to their age and quality. Internally compare memories/images of fresh fruit vs. dried fruit vs. stewed fruit. Do the same for various flowers, spices, and herbs. No surprise that imaging is key here (see Chapter 13). Example: Picture a rose and then gradually morph the image of it aging as your memory of what it smells like changes accordingly (even what it feels like to the touch). Be able to work from one extreme to the other—old to young and young to old. Also connect fruit quality to uneven ripening grapes (i.e. Zinfandel) as well as grapes/wines that show oxidation even when young (i.e. Nebbiolo).

**Impact compounds:** Other than accurately assessing structure, knowing the major impact compounds (terpenes, carbonic maceration, lees contact, etc.) and being able to detect them even in trace amounts is one of the most important ingredients for success with the grid and ultimately the exam. One also needs to connect these impact compounds to their causes in terms of appropriate wines (see Chapter 11).

**Structural assessment:** Use an internal visual cue to be precise with structure. Install a simple scale or dial (or whatever works best for you), that provides a visual confirmation of the levels of acidity, alcohol, phenolic bitterness, and tannin, as well as the length of finish being tasted/sensed in any given wine (see Chapters 4 and 25).

## Conclusions

Study theory! There's a great deal of theory involved in tasting, specifically when making a conclusion. Knowing various wine quality laws for Bordeaux, Burgundy, Germany, and other regions is key to being able to make a logical conclusion.

**Use a Decision Matrix to help with conclusions:** Write out wine "maps" or short grids for each classic wine that only show important impact compounds, fruit quality, and structure levels. Practice mentally rehearsing the information to come up with the "right" conclusion. Compare and contrast how similar wines are different (see Chapter 5).

## Associative rehearsal

As previously mentioned, a good deal of the tasting process can be mentally rehearsed/practiced without actually tasting. Here are some recommendations.

**The obvious:** Practice imaging/memory of common aromas and flavors daily. You can go through a list of several dozen in a few short minutes.

As you go through your list, make the images large, bright, close in proximity, and in three dimensions. Here is where you can also play with fruit quality/age with most of the aromas.

**Label check:** Install visual "label checks" for oak vs. no oak, earth vs. no earth (Old World vs. New World), and phenolic bitterness vs. used oak. Use large, bright images of labels of wines that are extreme examples of oak vs. no oak, earth vs. no earth, etc., to help make quick but informed decisions (see Chapter 28).

**Practice rehearsing complete wines:** Talk through an imaginary flight of wines aloud using the grid on a daily basis. Internally, see, smell, taste, and ID wines in the flight as intensely as possible using your memories of the best examples of classic wines. I advise mentally rehearsing wines five times as much as actually tasting (see Chapter 32).

## Strategies for focus and confidence

One of the major differences between how I prepared for the exam back in the day and how I would prepare now would be what I call "game day skills," or strategies for focus and confidence. I'm convinced that the ability to bring laser focus to the exam and deal with the nerves and stress could be as much as 35% (or more) of one's potential to pass regardless of the level of preparation.

Confidence is not something that comes easily for most. It can be very contextual in that being confident during tasting practice may not necessarily carry over to an exam. With that, here are several strategies for quickly going into a deeply focused state, dealing with nerves/fear, and installing and improving one's level of confidence for tasting—and beyond.

**Eye positions and consistency:** Finding one's starting eye position when smelling (and tasting) wine is absolutely critical to consistency and success. Using the golf analogy again, it's like lining up a golf shot in that one has to have a routine or there will be no consistency in the results. Also, realize that consistency of a starting eye position is an important key for establishing a focused state of concentration, or one's "zone" (see Chapter 21).

**Finding your zone:** Use the two strategies I call "Clearing the Mechanism" (see Chapter 21) and "Overlapping" (see Chapter 22) to find your zone. Be able to trigger your zone instantly using an eye position. Practice going into a deep, focused state of concentration. Be able to get there quickly and stay there.

Once you fine-tune it, practice your "zone" by getting into it and listening to a song or other piece of music that's at least three minutes long (if not longer), being completely absorbed into the music listening to it as completely as possible.

**One more note on the zone:** A mistake students often make is "projecting" things smelled and tasted in the wine, which inevitably leads to getting the conclusion completely wrong. Using your zone consistently will allow you to, for lack of a better way of putting it, be present to the wines vs. projecting things in them. It also allows the necessary curiosity and feeling of discovering what's actually in the glass to take place vs. making things up.

*Author's suggestions: Even though it was years ago, I clearly remember the ups and downs of getting ready for the exams. Some days everything clicked and the tasting process was easy. Other days nothing seemed to work and it was like I was incapable of getting anything out of a glass of wine. On days like that, it's important to have a good group to support you—and to remember that no one learns without getting it wrong. On those less-than-stellar days, it's also important to keep the grid front and center as an all-important checklist and to be as thorough and disciplined with it as possible.*

*Once again, there are no shortcuts to becoming a professional taster, much less passing an important exam. Both rely on a duration of time, a plan, the right strategies, and consistent work. All lead to incremental improvements that will ultimately mean success.*

# PART IV

# Thoughts On Wine

### Introduction

After three-plus decades in the industry, it's safe to assume I have more than a few opinions about everything having to do with wine. The following essays comprise some of them, from the overall importance of context in wine to the difference between great wines and great wine experiences to navigating the murky waters of natural wine in regards to wine hygiene and quality. I hope you enjoy them.

### Part IV Chapter Guide

*Chapter 33: C is for context*
The importance of context in the wine experience and its many manifestations.

*Chapter 34: For love of a rose*
The importance of how smell memories make us feel.

*Chapter 35: Food and wine pairing in less than 500 words*
The basic tenets of food and wine pairing explained.

*Chapter 36: It's only natural*
Thoughts on natural wine and judging wine quality.

*Chapter 37: The Tao of tasting*
Thoughts on how wine tasting has changed my thinking.

*Chapter 38: The dining ritual*
The value of sharing a meal regularly with family and friends.

*Chapter 39: Four great wine experiences*
Great wines vs. great wine experiences.

*Chapter 40: Taking flight*
Tasting, multi-sensory memory, and synesthesia.

## 33

# C Is for Context

In June of 2014 I was at the historic Fairmont Peace Hotel in Shanghai. It was the second of three times that year I would be in China for a project training sommeliers and hotel F&B directors on California fine wines. That night at the Fairmont I was hosting a dinner for a group of CEOs from multinational corporations. The menu was a multi-course affair melding Western and Chinese elements including such delicacies as sea cucumber—a dish whose flavors and texture almost defy wine pairing.

The wine I chose for the evening's entrée was the 1995 Ridge Montebello, a remarkably complex wine from one of California's great terroirs and from an outstanding vintage. As I opened, checked, and tasted the bottles of Montebello, I noted that the wine had more than a bit of Brettanomyces. In fact, on a Brett scale of 1 to 10, it was easily a solid four.

If not familiar, Brettanomyces is a non-spore forming yeast often referred to as "Brett." It's soil-borne but often gets into winery environments where it can potentially wreak havoc. The dark side of Brett is a range of off-aromas and flavors including sweat, barnyard, fecal, and medicinal. Think of small, unkempt rodents sporting multiple Band Aids.

However, such is not always the case. With the '95 Montebello to be served that night, the Brett surfaced in the form of savory-leathery-earthly complexities that lent richness to the texture of the wine and length to the finish. No argument, the wine was simply delicious and sure to please. I doubted anyone would have a problem with it, much less consider it flawed.

Our dinner was not the only gala affair taking place at the hotel that evening. The late Paul Pontellier of Château Margaux was hosting a dinner for local collectors in the penthouse suite. Paul came down to see me shortly before our dinner started. It would be my only time meeting him as he died unexpectedly less than two years later. I'm still saddened by his passing as I write this. Paul was utterly charming, warm, and gracious. He inquired about our project and generously offered me a glass of 1995 Château Margaux.

Paul stayed briefly and then had to return upstairs. I then put my nose in the glass of Margaux only to be greeted by—you guessed it—Brettanomyces. I quickly picked up my glass of the Montebello and went back and forth between the two wines repeatedly. The Margaux had even more Brett than the Ridge.

After a few seconds, I put both glasses down and experienced what I call an "alone at the edge of the universe moment," where one is faced with a paradox—something that flies in the face of previous experience that must somehow be reconciled. After a few moments, I wondered if Brettanomyces was an important part of the equation for any great, age-worthy red wine. My answer at the moment was I don't know. I still don't know.

Brettanomyces could be the Pandora's Box of wine. Everyone's threshold, much less tolerance for Brett is unique and completely personal. Some, including very famous wine critics, have a high tolerance, even preference, for red wines with high levels of Brett. Others, even entire winemaking cultures, have a zero-tolerance for it.

To that point, I was chairing a panel at a wine competition several years ago. One of the other panelists was a winemaker from Australia. On the morning of day two, my panel drew 30 Northern Rhône Syrahs, all retailing over $35. In other words, expensive wines from top appellations. As we started tasting through the first flight Brettanomyces quickly became a common denominator. The Australian winemaker responded by awarding all the wines "no medal."

When their results for the second flight were the same, I called a time out and asked the other two panelists to take a quick break. I then asked the winemaker what was up with refusing to award any of the wines a medal. They responded by saying Brett—even trace amounts—was considered a flaw in their training. I then had a quick reality check discussion about context, Brett, and Northern Rhône Syrah. The winemaker then grudgingly agreed to reconsider their scores—and awarded all the wines a bronze medal. It was a small victory for context.

Brettanomyces shows just how important context is to wine. Further, how it rarely pays to adopt an absolute position in wine. Both of the stellar 1995's from the Shanghai dinner displayed high levels of Brett that would be unacceptable in many other wines. Find the same amount of Brett in an uber expensive Napa Valley Cabernet or top flight Shiraz and the critics would howl and an immediate inquisition regarding the hygiene of the guilty winery would be demanded.

Find Brett in a white wine or sparkling wine and the universe might be rent asunder, as they used to say in the middle ages. But for some reason —and here we're pointing directly back to context—high levels of Brett in certain old-school European red wines is not only acceptable, it's actually expected and a historically-established part of the wine's character.

My early memories of tasting classified growth Bordeaux from the '50's and '60's always included at least trace amounts of leather, barnyard, and pronounced soil notes which could easily have been cultured out as Brett or its cousin Dekkera. That all seemed to change with vintages in the early '90's when improvements in the vineyard produced higher quality fruit. That, combined with better technology in the winery, resulted in cleaner and more concentrated wines. Gone are the days when every chateau seemed to have its own distinctive micro-biome that was reflected in the bottle. There are, of course, always exceptions. That, too, is context.

## C is for Context

Context is the eight-zillion pound elephant in the cellar. It's arguably the most important part of any wine experience, an equation that also includes the taster and the wine. With any wine experience, change the glassware, the temperature of the wine, even the temperature of the room where the wine is being tasted, and the experience of the person tasting the wine will be altered, sometimes radically.

Context works in any number of ways and not all of them are detrimental. One of the greatest wine experiences I've ever had was at Trattoria Zà Zà, a student/tourist hangout in Florence. It was the first time my wife Carla and I ever went to Europe together. That night we drank a young vibrant Chianti drawn from a huge cask behind the bar served in clunky glasses. It was—and still is—one of the most delicious Chiantis I've ever tasted. And all because of that particular evening, my fabulous company, and the fact that we were in Florence. Face it, if you're in Florence with a glass of wine in hand and you're not happy, you may be the one with issues.

Context reminds us that mood and company are valuable parts of any great wine experience.

Context reminds us that tasting even the greatest vintages while experiencing frustration, boredom, or anxiety can render the pedigree of the wine moot and the experience less than memorable—or tragically memorable in some cases.

Context reminds us to be mindful of adopting absolutes in the wine world because the universe will always be willing to immediately show us exceptions to the rule. Count on it.

Context also reminds us to be wary of sources using numerical scores given the three variables in any tasting experience mentioned above. How accurate could any number possibly be?

Finally, context reminds us that sharing wine and a meal with friends and family is perhaps the most satisfying thing we can do. I can't think of anything better.

# 34

## For Love of a Rose

In August of 2007 I was in Germany attending the Grosse Lage tasting in Wiesbaden with a group of writers and other industry professionals from the UK and the US. If not familiar, the Grosses Gewächs wines from the Grosse Lage classification are the pinnacle of Germany's top quality dry wines from its best vineyard sites. These wines can only be produced by members of the VDP, or Verband Deutscher Prädikatsweingüter, Germany's growers' association. The VDP is arguably the greatest organization of its kind on the planet. Of the thousands of entities making wine in Germany, its membership averages just 200.

After the two-day VDP tasting, our group was treated to a day-plus of winery tours and tastings. It was the last day of the tour and the group was at the final stop at Weingut Wittmann in the Rheinhessen, not far from Mainz. Philipp Wittmann makes superb dry Rieslings, especially his Grosses Gewächs wine from the Morstein vineyard. It's racy, intense, and laser-focused with shameless minerality and shocking acidity. I'd known the Wittmann wines for a long time and was looking forward to meeting him.

Philipp took us through the vineyard and then into the winery to taste the new vintage just bottled. Each wine was like experiencing a small dose of delicious electric shock. After the tour, everyone headed outside to a lunch of sandwiches and Riesling. After eating, I wandered off to check out the grounds. The first thing I spotted was a group of diminutive garden gnomes perched high on a pole and covered in cobwebs just outside the cellar door.

A few steps further and I stumbled across what had to be the most enormous and beautiful rose garden I'd ever seen. It was easily over an acre of the most gorgeous roses of every color and kind. To be honest, I should note that I was assaulted by a tsunami of rose floral scent long before I turned the corner and actually spotted the garden. I spent the next half hour going through the garden taking photographs and yes, smelling the roses.

I have lots of favorite smells/aromas but there is one far above all else—a rose. Not just any rose--and definitely not the roses you buy at Trader Joe's or Safeway because you completely spaced out your girlfriend or wife's birthday… or worse yet, anniversary. Nyet. A true heirloom rose. To me, the smell of an heirloom rose is perfection. It's the zillions-to-one against all odds when somehow some way countless molecules assemble themselves into a sublimely beautiful form that smells even more sublimelier. So much for good English.

The aromatics of an heirloom rose to me aren't simply "floral" as with other kinds of flowers. They have a visual arc or a curve almost like a musical chord with brighter, higher aromatics, fruitier middle notes, and earthy low tones. Internally for me, there's also a color gradation to the curve going from lighter hues at the top gradually down to deeper hues at the bottom. The color range changes depending on the actual rose. I experience pepper and certain other aromas the same way.

## Hardware: How do we physically smell?

As you can easily tell by now, I find the aroma of an heirloom rose to be transcendent. No surprise then that my time in the Wittmann rose garden instantly became a formative olfactory memory. But how is it we're able to physically smell anything at all? What's the apparatus for detecting all things olfactory?

Thinking back to that beautiful rose garden at Wittmann, when I smelled one of the roses the odor molecules traveled up my nasal cavity to behind the bridge of my nose where they were absorbed by very unique receptor cells. These cells have microscopic hairs called cilia. There are some five million of these olfactory cells that constantly fire up impulses to the brain's olfactory center.

These olfactory regions in the upper nasal cavity are moist, yellow regions of fatty substances found at the upper reaches of each nostril. When the olfactory bulb detects an aroma, it sends a signal to the cerebral cortex, a message directly into the limbic system which is one of the most ancient parts of the brain. Unlike the other four senses, there is no filtering our response to an aroma and thus the reason why our smell memories can be so incredibly vivid and powerful.

## Software: The anatomy of a smell memory

This is all well and good, but how do we recognize an aroma? For that matter, how do we remember what something smells like? What's surprising is that the answer is visual. Like practically everything else we learn, we use internal images and movies to remember what things smell (and taste) like.

The aromas I recognize in a glass of wine are represented by internal visual images based on my life memories of the various compounds I perceive in the glass. These could be various fruits, spices, earth tones, or whatever. Also important is the fact that these internal images I generate to represent the aromas in a given wine also have structural qualities called submodalities including size, brightness, proximity, and dimensionality.

## The feeling factor

Are internal images and movies alone enough to create a profound smell memory? Probably not. Like a favorite movie, song, or person, strong feelings are also involved in that you have to care about the movie, song, or person (or not!). You probably like—even love—said movie, etc., and so can instantly recognize it in an instant much less bring up a complete memory of it just as quickly.

When I think back to that rose garden or any of my favorite smell memories my experience is not just visual. It's a rich tapestry that always involves multiple senses. Perhaps a profound smell memory is the confluence of strong neuro-association, a moment when sight, smell, auditory, and kinesthetic combine to crystallize a moment. If I step back into my rose garden memory I can almost instantly feel the heat and humidity of early afternoon on my skin and the sun on my face. I can hear the drone of my colleagues conversing in the distance as well as the sound of bees buzzing around me. As I lean forward to smell a given rose I remember closing my eyes to focus on the aromatics.

At that moment there's also an internal feeling of reaching forward or out to something. Finally—and arguably as important as any of the components of my memory—there's also the most amazing feeling when I actually smell the rose, something for me that's akin to being in the presence of a beautiful painting, seeing a gorgeous sunset, or hearing a great piece of music. Without going completely Marin County on you, it's like being in the presence of beauty and source, however you define it. For me, any such experience is always accompanied by a feeling of gratitude if only for just having a chance to be here and play the game.

What I take away from the rose garden memory is not only how incredible the roses smelled on that day at that time—but how the experience made me feel. That's probably why I can bring up a complete IMAX memory of that rose garden in microseconds and why I can also detect "rose" in the top note of any wine almost as quickly.

In the end, I would venture to say that my love of roses and how they smell is a barometer of how important olfactory is to me not only as a professional, but personally as well. I also have a strong desire to remember how things smell, which is why olfactory memories are so important in the first place. How our most powerful wine memories make us feel may be one of the most profound things we experience as professionals. I wouldn't have it any other way.

## 35

# Food and Wine Pairing in Less Than 500 Words

Not long ago I had lunch with a colleague. At some point during our conversation, he bemoaned the complexity of food and wine pairing and how difficult it was to get the right match, much less explain the concepts. I countered saying it was a lot easier than he thought and offered to prove it. He challenged me to do just that. I upped the ante by saying I could do it in less than five hundred words. You are now the benefactor—or the victim—of that challenge. Read on.

*Disclaimer: The following is in no way intended to be the ne plus ultra—the last word—on food and wine pairing. Like many other things in life, the basics are straightforward but the potential to go down a rabbit hole, drop into an abyss, or be sucked into a vortex, is always possible. All nonsense aside, I have to humbly submit that good friend Evan Goldstein's two books on food and wine pairing, "Perfect Pairings"[1] and "Daring Pairings,"[2] are nigh untouchable. If you don't own them, you should. Now to business.*

# Message in the Bottle

## Food and wine pairing in less than 500 words

### Elements in wine

**Acidity:** The single most flexible element in wine for pairing with food. Higher acid wines are more versatile.

**Tannin and oak:** The least flexible elements—both dictate a narrow range of dishes that pair well.

**Alcohol:** Higher alcohol in a wine requires more intensity in the dish. Lower alcohol wines are more versatile.

**Sweetness:** White wines with residual sugar are chameleons—they work with a wide range of dishes, with the exception of red meat.

**Dessert:** The wine must *always* be sweeter than the dessert or both taste lousy.

### Elements in food

**Salt:** Takes the edge off acidity but exacerbates tannin in red wines.

**Butter/animal fat:** Takes the edge off tannin but needs acidity for contrast.

**Fish oil:** Needs dry, high acid white wines or bubbles. Avoid tannin in red wine.

**Sugar:** Makes dry wines taste more austere; needs wines with residual sugar.

**Spicy heat:** Needs residual sugar—avoid tannin!

**Umami-earthy-savory elements:** Need higher acidity, less tannin, and possible earthiness in aged red wines.

## A few apparent truisms

Matching the intensity of the wine to the dish is usually key.

If the dish is too spicy/intense it will dominate the wine.

Likewise, if the wine is too powerful/tannic it will overwhelm the dish.

With any dish, the sauce, condiments, or method of preparation can dictate the choice of wine.

For example, take chicken. It can be boiled, sautéed, roasted, or grilled. The intensity of the preparation will usually dictate the kind of wine paired—unless the sauce or sides on the plate are more intensely flavored.

## Complement vs. contrast

To complement or contrast—that is the question.

Trying to find similarity/same flavors between the wine and the dish is usually pointless.

Finding contrast between the wine and the dish—a high acid wine with a rich sauce—is usually the way to go.

## The almost golden rules

**The most versatile wines:** Unoaked high acid whites with moderate alcohol or medium-bodied red wines with moderate tannins and less oak.

**The least versatile wines:** High alcohol, oaked whites and high alcohol reds with high tannin and new oak.

**Versatile white wines:** Riesling, Sauvignon Blanc, Albariño, lighter Grüner Veltliner, Pinot Bianco, Pinot Grigio, and unoaked Chardonnay.

**Versatile red wines:** Pinot Noir, Gamay, Sangiovese, Barbera, Tempranillo, and lighter Grenache blends.

**Bubbles:** Dry sparkling wines and Champagnes are brilliant with a wide range of dishes.

**Rosé:** Dry rosés from any number of different grapes and places are among the most versatile wines of all.

**Context:** Despite everything I've just written, some will end up drinking whatever they like to drink, which might be the oakiest Chardonnays and Cabernets on the face of the earth—regardless of what's on the plate. *C'est la vie.*

**Advice:** When handed the list at a restaurant for a party of 10 ordering everything possible, go for unoaked Sauvignon Blanc for white and Pinot Noir for red. The two will cover practically everything.

## 36

## It's Only Natural

"Wine is complicated. Almost impossibly so."

Jamie Goode

Recently I was in Brooklyn for a meeting. Dinner the first night with four MS colleagues was at a small neighborhood joint. The menu was shellfish and seafood-based and the wine list was small but eclectic—no surprise given that we were in Brooklyn. Dinner was delicious and the conversation ranged from sports to books to movies to politics to—you guessed it—wine.

For the last bottle of the evening, someone in the group decided to order the most expensive wine on the list, an Etna Rosso that was a natural wine. If not familiar, natural wine is loosely defined as wine made with minimal intervention and without added sulfur. Mind you, all wine-making, by its very definition, is interventional.

In short order, the bottle was brought to the table and opened. In the glass the wine was cloudy and fizzy. On the nose it showed a tsunami of fingernail polish remover from EA (ethyl acetate)—the highest level in any wine I've ever tasted. On the palate, the wine was fizzy, funky, and tasted like a cross between kombucha and homemade cider still fermenting. No doubt the wine was still going through malo-lactic fermentation. The EA was another problem entirely.

A spirited discussion immediately ensued, or erupted, to be more precise. Mind you, the five of us sitting at the table collectively had well over a century of experience in the industry. In short order, many global-level questions were quickly fired out:

*Does wine quality actually matter?*

*Should quality always be a top priority in buying wine for a restaurant list?*

*Does the winemaking process—or lack thereof—trump place/terroir and/or quality?*

*Does appellation matter in the context of natural wine?*

*How does natural wine fit into the context of a wine list and program?*

*How should natural wine be explained and sold tableside to diners unfamiliar with the category?*

*Does natural wine need standards and a certification like organic wine and biodynamics?*

*Ultimately, is this an age-demographic issue?*

*Should we, as wine professionals, even care?*

The initial point I made to my colleagues after we tasted the wine was this: our generation and those before us focused on studying and mastering classic grapes and wines as part of our training with the goal of being able to judge quality measured against historically established benchmarks. That's what our jobs as buyers required us to do. The generations that have followed haven't necessarily used the same model.

They didn't always pursue formal training or certifications with the focus on the classics. Instead they focused on what potentially could and would be the most novel and different style of wine possible in the moment — and that definitely includes natural wine. And wine quality — and knowledge of it — seems to have become a secondary goal.

One of my colleagues offered the thought that sommeliers have a unique window into the wine universe. It's a view of immediacy where buying decisions are informed by previous experience that helps to create a wine list/program based on quality, typicity, and balance. And the wines chosen for the list should be able to sell without the buyer on the floor to explain them. Further, our years of experience provide us the knowledge to make consistent buying decisions that will please our guests tonight... and not months or even years in the future. That point alone separates us from everyone else in the industry.

Another remark during the discussion was that there are any number of great wines made "naturally," with little so-called intervention and minimal use of sulfur. However, these wines are made by skilled winemakers who have formal training and considerable experience. With few exceptions, they choose not to call their wines "natural" and for obvious reasons. Finally, someone else in the group equated the more vocal proponents of natural wine camp to be not unlike the anti-vaccination movement.

## Context and wine faults

In the way-back machine when I was studying for the exams, I paid $250 to smell and taste bad wine for an entire day. Such is the life of a budding wine acolyte. Wait, there's more. I had closed down the restaurant on a Friday night around 1:00 AM with a good friend/fellow sommelier. A few hours later, we both got up at the crack of dawn and met. Strong coffee and something fried and topped with sugar were quickly procured and then we drove to UC Davis, about 90 minutes away from San Francisco.

There, under the instruction of a Davis professor who was a wine chemist, we were tutored for an entire day on the perils of common wine faults. The professor's delivery was about as scintillating as drywall.

The class notes came in the form of a thick binder filled with diagrams of chemical compounds that for all the world looked like Sanskrit to me. Mind you, my science career ended with ninth grade biology.

Throughout the day, we were subjected to glasses of wine doctored with varying levels of faults, some at high levels. Regardless of the tedium and confusion, the class worked. TCA, Brett, VA, and other faults were indelibly burned into my brain and nervous system. For better or worse, they can probably never be removed. Beyond the olfactory trauma, the instructor hammered home the idea that even trace elements of faults can render wine quality questionable, if not compromised. That maxim, too, stuck for a long time.

Looking back, I now know that the topic of wine faults is not so easy. It never is. As with everything else in wine, context has a major role to play in wine faults. I'm not alone here. In his book, *Flawless: Understanding Wine Faults,*[1] author Jamie Goode offers a different view on Brett, excessive VA, and more. He writes that context, place, and the specific wine all are parts of the wine hygiene equation. With some wines, higher levels of Brett and VA are not only commonplace but historically acceptable. He does draw the line at TCA, which he universally considers a flaw. Here are two of my favorite quotes from the book's introduction:

*"I want to introduce a concept that I think is really helpful for understanding wine faults, and for grasping the notion that some flavor chemicals can be both faulty and positive, depending on the concentration and context."*

*"I will argue that the most attractive, compelling wines are those that have elements of their character that, if they were in a different context or present at higher levels, might be considered faulty. When is volatile acidity too high? When is greenness good and when is it too bad? When are tannins too grippy and firm? When are earthy, spicy characters off-putting? When is savoriness or gaminess too prominent? When is new oak too obtrusive? When does a wine pass from mature to senescent?"*

Goode's book then goes on to break down all the common wine faults in detail, including lady bug taint and eucalyptus taint that I hadn't previously considered as such. But his questions above stayed with me long after I had finished the book. In many cases, how much is too much? And how is it that we as a group at the table *instantly* knew the Etna Rosso had unacceptable levels of EA and was in fact completely flawed? After all, there are more than a few classic wines (Amarone and Barolo to name two) where high levels of VA are not only found, they're both historically commonplace and even expected. The same goes for Brettanomyces.

Perhaps the answer to this fault vs. flawed dilemma lies in the mercurial concept of wine balance. That if a "fault" dominates the aroma-flavor profile of a given wine rendering it mono-dimensional, the wine should be considered flawed. To point, a touch of VA — volatile acidity — gives any wine an aromatic lift on the nose. But any wine that reeks like fingernail polish is flawed and frankly shouldn't be served in a restaurant. Likewise, the presence of Brett in a wine can lend complexity to the nose and a savory-earthy quality to the palate. But too much Brett and the wine becomes a rodents-covered-in-Band-Aids experience. Beyond that, the same rule could also apply to the use of new oak, over ripe fruit, high alcohol, and more.

I think Goode's book should be required reading for any student on an exam track, and most professionals too. Be forewarned that there is more than a fair amount of chemistry in the text.

## Back to Brooklyn

As we tasted the volatile, fizzy, and very pricey Etna Rosso, what came up unanimously was that the natural wine category desperately needs standards and a certification like organics and biodynamics. The industry — and the public for that matter — needs to be able to clearly understand what the term "natural" actually means in regards to wine in the bottle. To this point, in 2020 the *Vin Méthode Nature* designation was passed for natural wines produced in France. It's recognized by the country's National Institute for Origins and Quality (INAO) and seems promising. But there's still a long way to go.

Where does that leave us? In the end, I can only address the questions our group posed with my own answers. Here goes.

*Q: Does wine quality actually matter?*

A: Yes, it absolutely does. Otherwise there are no metrics for consistency, much less standards, for what constitutes great, good, indifferent, and bad wine. Judging wine quality can only come about through a process of education about classic grapes and wines. And that process presupposes a duration of time and experience.

*Q: Should quality always be a top priority in buying a wine for a restaurant list?*

A: Once again, absolutely. The traditional role of a buyer has always been to serve as a filter of sorts, with the goal of being able to offer guests/clients wines that are clean, well-made, and typical of the appellation; wines that ultimately can be recommended and sold without hesitation. This is not pie-in-the-sky whimsy I'm talking about. It's business. And any business cannot survive, much less thrive, without long-term repeat customers. Selling lousy or completely flawed wine is not exactly a win-win for a restaurant, much less anyone else.

*Q: Should winemaking process — or lack thereof — trump terroir and/or quality?*

A: In my opinion, the answer is an emphatic NO. Any sense of place/terroir can easily be blurred, much less obliterated by bad winemaking. Fizzy, unstable wine is universal. It knows no specific style, place, or grape. That is not to say that there is an entire category of commercially produced — sometimes mass-produced — wine that is totally devoid of a sense of place. In that case, it's all about overprocessing and lowest common denominator for the sake of price point.

*Q: Does appellation matter in the context of natural wine?*

A: I think it potentially can if the tradition and long-term practice in a particular place point to a wine style that can be called natural.

*Q: How does natural wine fit into the context of a wine list and program?*

A: I think natural wine can potentially be part of any wine program with the caveat that the buyer/sommelier and staff must be trained on the wines and how to sell them. Further, everyone involved also understands that natural wine is a style of wine and not the end-all or be-all of the entire wine universe.

*Q: How should natural wine be explained and sold tableside to diners unfamiliar with the category?*

A: I think natural wine should be sold at the table as a specific style of wine with an explanation about the intent of the winemaker, lack of preservatives used during winemaking, non-filtration, etc. Mind you, all this has to be explained in a way where a diner/consumer can easily understand what they're getting in the glass. That's not exactly easy. Finally, any mention that natural wine is the only "true" style of wine should be avoided at all costs. This is utter nonsense.

*Q: Do natural wines need standards and certification like organic wine and biodynamics?*

A: All roads lead to the answer "yes" (see above).

*Q: Ultimately, is this an age-demographic issue?*

A: I think this is often a knee-jerk reaction/response by those in the natural wine camp when they get pushback for seriously variable wine quality — as in a $150 red wine that is fizzy and has off-the-scale EA. It's not exactly, "you kids get off my lawn," but it does point to the ability — or lack thereof — to judge wine quality based on experience.

*Q: Should we as wine professionals even care?*

A: Yes! We absolutely should and must care. Otherwise, we should get out of the business and go do something else entirely.

## Coda

Sometimes I think that the wine universe is like a never-ending moveable feast that constantly changes and evolves. Some wines offer delight while others simply confound. But the possibility of surprise will always exist and often in unexpected places. With that, I won't hesitate to taste natural wines in the future. I'll also look forward to further development in regards to standards and a certification for natural wine with great anticipation.

## 37

# The Tao of Tasting

Any career in wine ultimately comes down to tasting. It's the work we do as well as the most enjoyable aspect of our industry. In fact, I would go as far as to say that tasting is the heart and soul of what we do as wine professionals. After 30-plus years and tasting tens of thousands of wines, I will submit that tasting has given me a wealth of knowledge. It's also given me many other things you might not expect: insight into how I perceive the world around me, awareness of people, food, culture, and context among others.

I would argue that beyond a certain point, some of the benefits of becoming a professional taster have little to do with wine. Instead, they have to do with changing how we perceive the world. Some changes are subtle, others can be profound.

How has my tasting evolved since passing the MS exam over 30 years ago? What has tasting taught me about myself that I wouldn't have learned otherwise? And what have I learned through tasting that has nothing to do with wine? Are there things beyond places and grapes in a glass?

Perhaps the most profound thing tasting has taught me is how I think. It has shown me the sequence in which I process sensory information.

## Message in the Bottle

In 2009 I worked with Tim Hallbom on a tasting project. During two sessions that were filmed, Tim tracked my eye movements and language patterns while I tasted through and described a dozen or so wines. Together we were able to deconstruct my internal tasting strategy. The result is that now I am vividly aware of how I perceive and organize sensory information from a glass of wine. Further, that smell and taste memory for me are visual experiences internally.

Without Tim's help this wouldn't have been possible. Trying to be aware of how you do something while you're doing it is like asking someone to be in two places at once. It's like the Firesign Theater quote, "How can you be in two places at once when you're really nowhere at all?"

To be aware of how you think is a gift. It maps over to all parts of your life. I use the strategies I learned in those two sessions every day in a multitude of ways.

Tasting then can teach us how we think. It reveals in layers of smell and taste how we perceive and experience the world. In an age where mindfulness has become a precious commodity, tasting also teaches us how to still the mind and shut the world out. Through practice we're able to build ferocious yet gentle levels of concentration. The intense focus of smelling and tasting wine is multi-layered.

We alternate between going into the glass to "see" what's there and then back again inside our head to process the information. This alternation between outside and inside happens so quickly that we're usually not aware of it. At some point, with enough experience and repetition, we find ourselves between the two places, holding them both at the same time in our awareness. I can only describe it as a tasting trance. There are eye positions that correspond to all three places as well as a soft, slightly unfocused quality to one's gaze.

Tasting teaches us how to calibrate sensory impressions precisely, in the form of structural levels as in the levels of alcohol, acid, phenolic bitterness, and tannin in a wine. Surprisingly, we do so also using internal visual cues.

Tasting shows us how to keep a multitude of sensory information in our field of awareness, and how to be aware of all this information either in rapid sequence or simultaneously. To do so we create a complex internal wine "map" that allows us to keep all the information in the glass organized in an orderly fashion so that it doesn't go away, so we can easily retrieve it for the sake of comparison, or simply to review and/or remember it.

Teaching tasting to consumers or professionals shows us how to communicate about a complex process and to chunk it down so it can be easily understood.

## Blind tasting

I played the trumpet from the time I was in fourth grade until the end of 1988 when I played my last rehearsal as an extra with the San Francisco Opera Orchestra. For me, blind tasting is similar to playing the trumpet, which is arguably the most frustrating instrument there is to play. Why is the trumpet so frustrating? Simply because the vibrating medium that produces sound is part of your body. Which means that your playing, regardless of skill level, will vary from day to day depending on how good you physically feel. Or not.

One can be an outstanding trumpet player, but completely suck on any given day. I've seen big name trumpet players take a dive. It's not pretty. I've also been there myself, having utterly tragic days where I shouldn't have taken the horn out of the case.

Blind tasting is exactly the same. It's humbling. Our "instrument" is our physical body and therefore variable at times and even fallible. Blind tasting practice is a day-to-day process, trusting your body and your senses but knowing that on certain days you will be under par. It's about accepting mistakes, learning from them as quickly as possible, and then moving on. It's also about raising the bar every time you taste so that on a given day at a given time you have more than enough to be successful in an exam–or at your job. That was my approach to taking trumpet auditions and it was my approach to taking the tasting exams as well.

No surprise that trumpet auditions and tasting exams both taught me to focus under pressure. If anything, having taken auditions as a student and a professional were an advantage for me when I took the exams. Both taught me how to give my nervous system a choice between flight, fight, or freeze. The auditions, for the record, were far more stressful.

Is one ever a great taster? I'm not sure. For me, having a belief of being a "great taster" is simply not useful. Adopt that belief and the universe will be all too happy to quickly show you someone who's better than you are. Count on it. My belief about my tasting is that I'm exceptionally good at analyzing and assessing wine. For me, that's a much more useful belief. It's also more open ended and definitely win-win. Ultimately, perhaps one isn't a good or a great taster. Perhaps one is always in process—or on a journey—to become a better, more proficient taster.

## Beyond the work

Beyond the focus and repetition required to become a professional taster there are a multitude of things tasting teaches us if we allow it. First, that wine is the great connector; it connects us to people, cultures, history, and different geographical points on the globe. The ritual of sharing wine with friends or family is thousands of years old. With wine we're able to connect with other people in a meaningful way not often found otherwise.

Through wine we're also able to experience a unique appreciation—even gratitude—for a product of the earth and the seasons. And certain wines allow us to experience a connection to places that have produced wine for centuries—even millennia. In a certain context these ancient wine places might be considered sacred spaces.

## Coda

Scientists tell me that my sense of smell will start to diminish now because I'm getting older. Their assumption doesn't take neuroplasticity into account or the mechanics of memory. My memory for aromatics and wines has never been better. But how will my tasting change in the future? A better question might be, how will tasting change me in the future. If anything, tasting—especially the olfactory part—will become more synesthetic for me as time goes on. I fully expect the feeling part of reacting to aromatics in a glass of wine to become more profound. My tasting trance, if anything, will become easier to access and deeper.

I'm looking forward to it.

# 38

# The Dining Ritual

One of my core beliefs about wine is that it's the great connector — it connects us to each other in ways that no other thing, substance, or small household appliance does. For thousands of years, since the time primitive man first started decanting wine for aeration purposes, we humans have shared meals with members of our clan. Nothing could be truer in my life than that connection with family.

I grew up in a household with six kids in the 1960s. Dinner time could only be described as barely controlled chaos. With four boys swimming in a morass of testosterone, it was not uncommon to have a dinner roll ka-tonked off the side of your head when you requested bread from the other end of the table. Asking for butter (which was actually margarine, of course), was likewise completely risky business.

In short, dinner was a Darwinian affair requiring cunning and dexterity. Any and everything was passed around the table only once. If you didn't get enough of something on the first shot, you weren't getting more. A gallon of milk barely made it around the table. The oldest three of us quickly figured out that the only way to get more was to pour your glass full, drink half of it, then refill before passing it on, causing an immediate firestorm of protest from my younger brothers and sister. It was also imperative that you quickly identified and skewered the biggest-ass pork chop/ham slice/slice of meatloaf on the platter when it came your way because it was your one and only shot at sustenance for the evening.

When my schoolmates joined us for dinner, they were always a bit shaken by the carnal frenzy that defined our family meals. They soon learned to adapt or went home hungry. It's also worth noting that my then-future brother-in-law did not return to our house for over six months after his first Easter dinner at the Gaiser table. Enough said.

Eventually, with the patience of a saint and the aid of blunt instruments, my mom managed to instill some semblance of table manners in the six of us. That in itself is a minor miracle. Beyond that, she also managed in a very sly way to instill the dining ritual in us as a family, and not because she and my dad were raised in the European tradition of fine dining with candlelit extravaganzas and lengthy erudite conversations. That was as remote as the Dog Star.

Instead, it was the mere act of gathering the entire herd once a day so we could sit down and have dinner. We knew that even if all hell had broken loose during the previous 12 hours — and it often did — we had the certainty of knowing that we as a family would share a meal, for better or worse.

Years later after Carla and I married, moved to San Francisco, and were both bartending, the dining ritual continued. On our rare nights off together, we either went out or stayed in and cooked dinner for one another. Explorations into the Byzantine menus of the now sadly long-gone *Gourmet* magazine often ensued with the kitchen getting completely trashed and us limping to the dinner table like wounded livestock after vigorous and sometimes pyrotechnic experiments in the kitchen.

The dining ritual continued unabated after our lives went from "man on man" to "zone" in terms of having kids. Looking back on those years, I've come to believe that one of the greatest things Carla and I have given our kids is the many years of the dining ritual. When it was dinnertime, life came to a screeching halt. Once dinner was plated and hit the dinner table, everyone gathered regardless of whatever else on the planet was going on.

My daughter Maria, now out of grad school and working, has told me many times that the thing she misses most about home life is sharing dinner, especially the hours of hanging out at the table after dinner was over, finishing a bottle of wine and chatting about everything under the sun.

Does the dining ritual guarantee a happy family or a long relationship and/or marriage? No guarantees, but it's a primo opportunity to spend time with your partner and family. And that's not a bad thing. It's worked for Carla and me for over 40 years. It might just work for you. Sharing a meal and a bottle of wine is not only sustenance — it's a much-needed balm for the soul. I hope everyone reading this missive is able to do just that and on a regular basis.

# 39

## Four Great Wine Experiences

Good friend and fellow MS, Evan Goldstein once explained to me the difference between a great wine and a great wine experience. The former, he said, is just as implied: a prohibitively expensive, great, and/or legendary bottle tasted at a trade event or via the cellar of a generous collector. A great wine experience, he went on to say, was something completely different. Where context, as in the people, place, and time, is just as important, if not more so, than the wine itself. In fact, in some cases, the actual wine may not even matter.

Recently I've given some thought to Evan's definitions of great wines and great wine experiences. In regards to the former, I've been incredibly fortunate to have tasted more than my share of great, even legendary wines over the years: 1971 Egon Müller Scharzhofberg TBA, 1961 Krug Collection, 1945 Château Latour, 1985 Romanée Conti, 1961 Château Cheval Blanc, 1982 Vega Sicilia Unico, 1974 Heitz Martha's Vineyard, and 1941 Beaulieu Vineyard Burgundy all come to mind (the last, perhaps the greatest California Pinot Noir I've ever tasted).

Memories of all these wines are frozen like crystalline moments in time for me. Beyond that, there have been great wine experiences over the years as well. As Evan mentioned, with each experience there's a profound emotional connection not just to the wine, but more so to everything else in the memory as far as the people, the occasion, and the place. These experiences and memories are part of the joy of being a wine professional. Here are four of my favorite great wine experiences.

## Baby Maria and 1979 Pol Roger Brut Rosé

March 1990: my daughter Maria's baptism at St. Dominic's Church in Pacific Heights in San Francisco. The wine I chose for the reception was the 1979 Pol Roger Rosé. It showed beautifully that day. I clearly remember holding Maria in one arm with a glass of the delicious rosé in the other. I also remember feeling a muddle of emotions; part proud new dad, part freaked out new dad, and the amazing love you feel for your first child — especially a daughter.

Some months later I was invited to a Pol Roger trade dinner in the city. As luck would have it, Carla and I were seated next to Christian Pol Roger. At some point during the meal, I told him that we had chosen the '79 Rosé for Maria's christening. He smiled, put his hand on my shoulder, and said, "May your daughter have a long and happy life."

## Trattoria Zà Zà and the perfect no-name chianti

October 1987: Carla and I were in Europe together for the first time. We started our trek in Paris and then rented a car and drove to Blois. We spent several days in the Loire before heading to Burgundy. From there, we took the train to Nice, Pisa, and finally Florence.

Florence didn't disappoint. It was the most remarkable place I'd ever experienced. After spending an afternoon in the Uffizi Gallery (!) and shopping in the square, we wandered about looking for a place for dinner. Not far from the cathedral we stumbled on a joint called Trattoria Zà Zà, crammed to the rafters with local students. Once inside, we managed to find a table. The noise was near stadium level.

The menu was limited to just pasta, pizza, and lighter fare — and the wine selection was even more limited. We opted for a liter of the house red, a young Chianti. I watched as the woman serving us drew it directly into a carafe from a huge cask behind the bar. She immediately delivered it to our table with two clunky glasses that would have been handy in a bar fight. The first sip was unforgettable — the essence of Sangiovese and autumn in Tuscany.

It was the most delicious red wine I had ever tasted up to that point in time. Looking back, it still *is* the most delicious Chianti I have ever tasted. How good? Carla and I managed to work our way through the better part of two liters of it with dinner. Enough said.

## Paris Sigalas and his remarkable Assyrtiko

September 2006: Nothing can replace tasting a wine at its place of origin. The combination of place and wine often makes for a great wine experience. Such was the case during the legendary MS tour of Greece. Ten days of seeing every part of the country that has anything to do with wine, spending an average four-plus hours a day in a van driven by a young Greek lad who wore the same synthetic disco shirt the entire trip, thereby re-defining the concept of terroir.

The highlight of highlights was visiting the island of Santorini, surely one of the most beautiful spots on the planet. On the drier leeward side of the island Paris Sigalas and his crew tirelessly cared for old Assyrtiko vines that are pruned close to the ground into round basket-like shapes called ampellari. I have vivid memories of our group standing in the late afternoon sun with Sigalas and his winemaker. Paris repeatedly mentioned the terroir, pointing at the ground which was covered with a proliferation of volcanic rocks of every kind including chunks of whitish pumice that were so light in the hand they were almost weightless.

We headed back to the winery to taste verticals of oaked and unoaked Assyrtiko. The experience was revelatory. Sigalas's Assyrtiko is one of a kind due to its great depth and richness with the alcohol level often up to 14.5% balanced by ferociously high natural acidity. But the hallmark of all Sigalas wines is the minerality, which is completely off the charts. There probably isn't a better example of volcanic minerality in a wine made anywhere.

## Message in the Bottle

To this day, Sigalas' Santorini remains one of my very favorite white wines. Whenever I taste it, I'm instantly transported back that late afternoon standing in Sigalas's vineyard bathed with golden Mediterranean sunlight looking at the arid, windswept vines in their odd basket shapes. The feeling is remarkable.

### The doctor is in

May 2002: my third trip to the Mosel. It was early evening and the fourth and last winery stop for the day. By now, residual sugar and insanely high acidity from tasting dozens of young Rieslings had managed to fry the palate of everyone in the group, including mine. Since early morning, we'd been tasting wines from the superb 2001 vintage just bottled. But the best of the day was saved for last.

Our final appointment was at Weingut Wegeler in Bernkastel with winemaker Norbert Breit as our host. After meeting us at the winery off a narrow cobblestone street in Bernkastel, we drove up the steep and winding road hundreds of feet above the river to the very top of the legendary Doctor vineyard. Breit pulled a newly minted bottle of 2001 Wegeler Doctor Spätlese from his leather bag, opened it, and poured. From there, he really didn't need to say anything else.

Wines from the Doctor vineyard are considered the best in the Mosel and easily the top ten in all of Germany. They are known for their concentration, opulence, and precision. The 2001 didn't disappoint. It's one of the greatest young German Rieslings I've ever tasted. Standing on shifting dark slate, I looked down the perilously steep slope with the tiny village below and the river snaking away in the golden late afternoon sunlight. I reached down to pick up a chunk of dark slate and took another sip of utterly delicious Riesling. It was the nectar of the gods.

### Coda

Sometimes I'm asked if one can script a great wine experience, or if it can somehow be predicted. My answer is that I doubt it because part of the recipe seems to be serendipity and being open and receptive to a confluence of elements that make up the experience. However, chasing an elusive great wine experience is always more than worth the effort. In reading this chapter, memories of both great wines and great experiences probably came up for you. I hope many more of both are in your future.

# 40

## Taking Flight

Deborah Ory began dance lessons at age seven. Years later she injured herself in ballet class, and while convalescing, she picked up her father's camera and started photographing rehearsals. Deborah's injury prevented her from continuing a dance career. The camera took its place. She would go on to work as a photo editor for *House & Garden* and *Mirabella*, as well as do editorial work for *Self*, *Health*, *Martha Stewart Living*, and *Real Simple*.

Ory later married Ken Browar, a renowned fashion and beauty photographer whose work has appeared in *Vogue*, *Elle*, *Marie Claire*, and other European fashion magazines. He, too, had a passion for dance that started when he lived in Paris and photographed dancers for the Paris Opera Ballet.

The combination of Ory and Browar's love of dance with their photography careers was the genesis of the NYC Dance Project. In the last several years the couple has photographed principal dancers from the top ballet and dance companies in New York and beyond in their Greenpoint, Brooklyn home studio where they live with two teenage daughters — also ballet students.

The photographs from the project are stunning. Each shot is meticulously planned including lighting, movement, and even the apparel worn by the dancers. The fruit of Ory and Brower's labor is their first book, *The Art of Movement*,[1] published in the fall of 2016. It quickly won an International Photography Award for best book. The couple released a second book, *The Style of Movement*,[2] in 2018, capturing more remarkable images of top dancers but this time in designer clothes.

What is striking about the images is the remarkable athleticism of the dancers, something rarely appreciated about ballet. Further, how incredibly hard the dancers work at their craft for long years. Finally, how fleeting their careers are due to age and the high incidence of injury. In quotes included in the book's text, several of the dancers express their gratitude for the project saying how thankful they are that there is a photographic record of their talent for all eternity. Most of the time there is no record of their careers after the fact.

Perhaps the most intriguing insight from the various dancer's quotes is how only through hard work and great repetition is it possible for one to be free onstage and to be able to create in the moment. Fana Tesfagioris from the Alvin Ailey Dance Theater calls it "like flying."

*"Doing a show and knowing that I just left everything on the stage, like my guts are on the stage, is literally euphoria. It's the best feeling ever. When I am able to be totally in the moment and free on stage, that's pretty rewarding!"* ~ Isabella Boylston, Principal, American Ballet Theater[3]

*"I wish more people knew what it felt like to actually dance. I'm not referring to the difficulty of learning a technique or a combination. I mean the part that comes after everything clicks. When your most focused mind, your most moldable body, and your truest spirit all intertwine at the highest level. That point will look different for everyone, of course, but I wish everyone could attempt to reach it at least once. It can literally feel like flying."*[4] ~ Fana Tesfagioris, Alvin Ailey Dance Theater

What has dance got to do with wine tasting? Both require years of experience and work to truly appreciate and understand the nuances of the craft. And they're not something you can pick up at a weekend workshop. Both also have rewards that touch the soul, spirit, heart, and mind in ways that can't be bought. You have to invest time, attention, and passion in them to find and claim the rewards both can offer. Most importantly, the experiences involved in achieving mastery in both can't be taken away. Once acquired, they remain core memories and experiences for a lifetime.

## Tasting and taking flight

One of the events I do every year is the Santa Fe Wine and Chile Fiesta, one of the best smaller wine and food festivals in the country. One year I was fortunate to draw the assignment of tasting through a flight of 2005 Burgundies with friend and colleague Mary Margaret McCamic, MW. The 2005 vintage, a warm one for Burgundy, was initially praised by the press. After more than a decade, it was a good time to revisit it.

First up were three whites from Chassagne, Puligny, and Corton Charlemagne. With the exception of the Puligny-Montrachet 1er Cru Les Folatières from Paul Pernot, which showed oxidation probably due to storage issues, the other two wines — the Vincent Girardin Chassagne-Montrachet Les 1er Cru Blanchots Dessus and the Camille Giroud Corton-Charlemagne — showed beautifully.

The five reds that made up the rest of the flight were 1er Crus from Volnay. All were superb showing the soft voluptuous core of fruit, intense earthiness, and firm tannins the appellation is known for. However, the third wine, the Henri Boillot Volnay 1er Cru Les Frémiets, gave me pause. When I first put my nose in the glass, a cascade of dried rose petals, dried red fruits, black tea, autumn leaves, and wood spice appeared in seconds.

Immediately I internally "saw" shades of red, orange, and gold — autumn colors — and the first movement of Mozart's Piano Concerto No. 23 in A, which to me has always *sounded* like fall, started playing internally. All this sensory information quickly morphed into a memory over three decades old of being at Château Chenonceau in the Loire in late October and walking down a long tree-lined lane awash in brilliant autumn afternoon colors.

How does smelling a wine become color, music, and abstract memory? For those who are true synesthetes, crosstalk between the senses is involuntary, habitual, and not always pleasant. I am anything but a synesthete, but there are times when I experience wine as colors, shapes, and even sounds in the form of music.

These experiences are infrequent and anything but predictable. I think they occur for a very simple reason: I've tasted thousands of wines over the last 30-plus years, using a very structured framework — the deductive tasting grid — to perceive and experience wine.

Like the dancers quoted above, many years of work with tasting has sharpened my perceptions and hardwired sensory information into my long-term memory to the extent that olfactory and taste impressions can at times quickly, even instantly, be associated in very abstract ways to other senses and life memories. In a way, working in a narrow and disciplined way for such a long time has freed me to be able to do just that.

These associations may come down to the part of the wine tasting experience that is subjective (see Chapter 15). I personally believe that less than 25% of the tasting experience will always be intensely personal and therefore subjective. To this point, my perception of the various fruits and certain non-fruit elements in any wine will always be based on my life memories — which are again personal and subjective. The rest of the tasting experience, from a wine's color to various impact aromas to the structural elements is objective as practically all can be either widely agreed upon or isolated in a lab setting.

Perhaps it's this 25% of the wine experience that creates the potential and opportunity for crosstalk and "flight." With enough experience and repetition, impressions from a given wine might create internal responses that take the form of colors, sounds, feelings, and memories.

Should you expect to find colors, music, and more in a glass of wine? I can't answer that. I'm just letting you know it happens, and that anything is possible. Everyone may have the same nervous system, but we're all wired differently. Does one need to taste thousands of wines to be able to experience sensory cross talk? I'm not convinced of that either. But I do believe that one has to at least be open to the possibility of this kind of experience actually happening in the first place.

A useful strategy might involve asking questions internally when tasting. After all, that's what we do constantly, but not necessarily consciously. It's called thinking. The questions might include:

*"If this wine were a color, what would (could) it be?*

*"If this wine had a shape to it, what would (could) it be?"*

*"If this wine was like a song or piece of music, what would (could) it be?*

No guarantees here, but it's definitely worth exploring because it can make one think and associate in ways not previously experienced. And that's worth the price of admission.

Much like dance, the ritual of tasting wine goes back thousands of years. The act of putting our nose into a glass of wine connects us to civilizations long past and symbolizes one of nature's greatest gifts to man. I will never tire of smelling and tasting wine. With each glass comes the potential to make new connections and the possibility of taking flight.

# Acknowledgments

This book is a byproduct of teaching tasting to thousands of students and consumers over the last 30-plus years. My heartfelt thanks to them for their inspiration to create a text with the needed skills and strategies to become a professional taster.

Thanks to the entire team at Networlding.com, especially my publisher, Melissa G. Wilson, who guided me through the Byzantine process of publishing a book for the first time. Also, my copy editors Becky Blanton and Cheryl Booth who made the manuscript so much better with their deft touch and great ideas. Thanks to Amy Albert, Wayne Belding, Evan Goldstein, Peter Granoff and Madeline Triffon for proofing the manuscript. Thanks also to Chip Scanlan for his advice on writing and getting published.

Thanks to Kelly McCarthy for all the photography. Thanks also to Miladinka Milic of milagraphicartist.com for the cover design, and to Damian Jackson for the text formatting.

Thanks to Ramey Wine Cellars and Domaine des Baumard for the use of their wine labels.

Special thanks to those in my original MS tasting/study group including Peter Granoff, Steve Morey, and the late Michael Bonacorsi. I never would have passed the tasting exam without your help and support.

Thanks also to Master Sommeliers Nunzio Alioto, Brian Julyan, Evan Goldstein, and Madeline Triffon for their mentorship during my studies for the exams and beyond. I treasure your wisdom and continued friendship and camaraderie.

Thanks to Tim Hallbom and Taryn Voget for letting me be part of their Everyday Genius project. Our findings during those sessions led to many of the strategies included in Part III of the book.

Over a decade ago I conducted in-depth interviews with colleagues as part of a long term tasting project. The best practices I gleaned from these top industry pros became the basis for many of the ideas in the book. In particular, I would like to thank Gillian Balance, Geralyn Brostrom, Matt Citriglia, Doug Frost, Peter Granoff, Evan Goldstein, Gilian Handelman, Sur Lucero, Peter Marks, Karen MacNeil, Roland Micu, Christopher Miller, Alan Murray, Emily Pikral, Thomas Price, Sabato Sagaria, Madeline Triffon, and Emily Wines. Your brilliance and insights have been invaluable.

My heartiest thanks to the entire Master Sommelier community, both in the U.S. and the U.K. Here in the U.S. I'd like to especially thank the following individuals with whom I've had the great pleasure of teaching and examining over the last 30 years, and who also patiently listened to me endlessly drone on about my tasting project and a potential book. In particular, Darius Allyn, Serafin Alvarado, Gillian Balance, Christopher Bates, Jesse Becker, Wayne Belding, Randall Bertao, Robert Bigelow, Shayn Bjornholm, John Blazon, Devon Broglie, Thomas Burke, Brahm Callahan, Scott Carney, Ian Cauble, Gilles de Chambure, Matt Citriglia, Craig Collins, William Costello, Brian Cronin, Brett Davis, Laura de Pasquale, Cameron Douglas, Desmond Echavarrie, Ron Edwards, Rebecca Fineman, Jay Fletcher, Doug Frost, Keith Goldston, Yoon Ha, Scott Harper, Greg Harrington, Jason Heller, Eric Hemer, Jennifer Heuther, Jay James, Michael Jordan, Max Kast, Dennis Kelly, Mariya Kovacheva, Steve Morey, Alan Murray, Andrew McNamara, Andy Meyers, Kathy Morgan, Alexander LaPratt, Sur Lucero, Michael Meagher, George Milliotes, Sally Mohr, Melissa Monosoff, Peter Neptune, Larry O'Brien, Virginia Philip, Emily Pikral, Steven Poe, Thomas Price, John Ragan, Paul Roberts, Jim Rollston, Sabato Sagaria, Joe Spellman, Larry Stone, Guy Stout, John Szabo, James Tidwell, Scott Tyree, Laura Williamson, and Emily Wines.

More information about the Court of Master Sommeliers, Americas can be found at: https://www.mastersommeliers.org/

Thanks also to the following colleagues from the Court of Master Sommeliers Worldwide: Bryan Dawes, Gearoid Devaney, Brian Julyan, Otto Hinderer, Frank Kämmer, Hendrik Thoma, Dimitri Mesnard, Laura Rhys, Ronan Sayburn, Matt Wilkin, Nigel Wilkinson, and the late Gerard Basset.

Many thanks to others in the industry who have been a part of my wine journey: Doug Biederbeck, Michael Bugella, John Cunin, Mark Davidson, Dawn Dooley, Fernando de Luna, the late Randy Goodman, Eapen George, Margie Jones, Ron Merlino, Dan Noreen, Molly Stevens, Paul Wagner, and Rudi Wiest. And a very special thank you to Amy Albert, who gave the book its title.

A huge thank you to Steve Goldberg, who over 35 years ago convinced me I could have a career in wine. I will never be able to repay the favor.

Finally, endless thanks and love to my family; to my wife Carla, with whom I've shared a bottle of wine over dinner for more than 40 years and who also read early drafts for many of the chapters in the book. To my daughter Maria, a better writer than me, and who did the final round of editing on the manuscript. Finally, to my son Patrick, who always helps me keep it real.

## About the Author

Tim Gaiser is an internationally renowned wine expert and lecturer. He is one of less than 300 individuals worldwide to ever attain the elite Master Sommelier title. He is the former Director of Education and Education chair for the Court of Master Sommeliers, Americas, and an instructor for the Napa Valley Wine Academy.

Over his 30-plus year career, Tim has taught thousands of students in wines and spirits classes at every level as well as developing wine education programs for restaurants, winery schools and wine distributors. He has experience in all phases of the wine industry: online, wholesale, retail, winery, and restaurants.

Tim has written for a number of publications including Fine Cooking Magazine and the Somm Journal and also writes for numerous wine and spirits clients. He has served as the author and lead judge for the Best Young Sommelier Competition and the Top Somm Competition.

Prior to developing his wine expertise, Tim received an M.A. in Classical Music. He played classical trumpet as a freelance professional and as an extra with the San Francisco Opera Orchestra. He currently lives with his family in New Mexico.

www.timgaiser.com
www.timgaiser.com/blog